Masters of Peace

Series editor
W. Dietrich, Igls-Vill, Austria

Masters of Peace is a book series edited by the University of Innsbruck's UNESCO Chair for Peace Studies. It has been founded to honour outstanding works of young academics in the field of Peace and Conflict Studies. It is reserved for selected Master theses of the Innsbruck School and published twice a year. The Innsbruck School follows the principles of Transrational Peace Philosophy. It defines peace as a plural and regards all aspects of human nature relevant for the understanding of peace and conflict. Its applied method is Elicitive Conflict Transformation, a pragmatic approach to conflict rooted in Humanistic Psychology that entrusts the responsibility for finding alternative options of behaviour, communication and encounter to the conflict parties. Facilitators provide a safe frame, tools and methods for this quest without imposing their own solutions on the parties.

Edited by
Wolfgang Dietrich
UNESCO Chair for Peace Studies
University of Innsbruck/Austria

Editorial Board
Josefina Echavarría
Daniela Ingruber
Franz Jenewein
Norbert Koppensteiner
Fabian Mayr
Andreas Oberprantacher
Johney Xavier
Austria

More information about this series at http://www.springer.com/series/13769

Liridona Veliu

#Balkanization: A Critical Study of Otherness through Twitter

With a foreword by Dr Pascual Pérez-Paredes

Springer

Liridona Veliu
UNESCO Chair and MA Program
for Peace Studies
University of Innsbruck
Innsbruck, Austria

ISSN 2364-463X ISSN 2364-4648 (electronic)
Masters of Peace
ISBN 978-3-658-23823-0 ISBN 978-3-658-23824-7 (eBook)
https://doi.org/10.1007/978-3-658-23824-7

Library of Congress Control Number: 2018957570

© Springer Fachmedien Wiesbaden GmbH, part of Springer Nature 2018
This work is subject to copyright. All rights are reserved by the Publisher, whether the whole or part of the material is concerned, specifically the rights of translation, reprinting, reuse of illustrations, recitation, broadcasting, reproduction on microfilms or in any other physical way, and transmission or information storage and retrieval, electronic adaptation, computer software, or by similar or dissimilar methodology now known or hereafter developed.
The use of general descriptive names, registered names, trademarks, service marks, etc. in this publication does not imply, even in the absence of a specific statement, that such names are exempt from the relevant protective laws and regulations and therefore free for general use.
The publisher, the authors and the editors are safe to assume that the advice and information in this book are believed to be true and accurate at the date of publication. Neither the publisher nor the authors or the editors give a warranty, express or implied, with respect to the material contained herein or for any errors or omissions that may have been made. The publisher remains neutral with regard to jurisdictional claims in published maps and institutional affiliations.

This Springer imprint is published by the registered company Springer Fachmedien Wiesbaden GmbH part of Springer Nature
The registered company address is: Abraham-Lincoln-Str. 46, 65189 Wiesbaden, Germany

Prindërve të mi,
Farije dhe Ismail Veliu,
për dashurinë e tyre
të pafund.

* * *

To my parents,
Farije and Ismail Veliu,
for their infinite
love.

Acknowledgments

This thesis would not have been possible without the advice and support of colleagues, friends, and family.

I am especially indebted to my supervisor, Josefina, for the perfect balance of continuous guidance and constructive criticism, as well as encouragement of academic freedom not only for this project, but also for the many other instances during my personal and professional growth; for teaching by example.

I would like to thank the Faculty Board members of the MA Program for Peace Studies, especially Wolfgang, Norbert, and Daniela for being always there and for believing in me. I truly cherish their presence in my life.

I am grateful to all of those who professionally supported my research with no account of compensation: Martin Cassai, Maura Conway, Trime Halili, Leonora Saliju, Besnik Rizmani, Pepijn Westen, Verena Wulf, Christine Andreeva, Meltem Öktü, Harikrishnan Sasikumar, and Yessita Herrera. I thank them for their generosity. As a friend and colleague, I could not feel luckier and prouder.

To my friends Alma, Sweta, Miraj, Denise, and Vidushi, for the many words of encouragement and constant reassurance, listening, inspiration, and care; for the "… you are nearly there, Liri"; to Husni for adding colors to my thesis, I am unconditionally thankful.

Finally, I would like to thank my parents and my brothers, Liridon and Musa, the pillars of who I am today, whose love is with me in whatever I pursue, and whose understanding is limitless to the compromised time I spend with them.

To you all, I owe this thesis. Thank you wholeheartedly.

Liridona Veliu
August 27, 2018
Dublin

Foreword

The Oxford English Dictionary (OED) defines balkanization as the action or fact of balkanizing or dividing a region into separate political or territorial units, and traces back its use to E. H. Bradford Amer 1914 College of Surgeons Fellowship address where he said: "How long the present Balkanization of Europe is to continue, no one can tell, but it is certain that the Mexicanization of North America will stop at the Rio Grande" ("balkanization", 2013). I have to confess that, despite living in Flagstaff, AZ, for almost two years, I had never heard of the term mexicanization before.

Linguists and lexicographers know, better than anybody else does, how deceptive dictionaries can be, how little they reveal about the term itself and how much remains hidden behind an entry, even in the OED. Jacques Barzun, in the exceptional From Dawn to Decadence: 500 Years of Western Cultural Life 1500 to the Present, explains the emergence and use of stereotypes as how one trait alone stands out in a figure or a period and that is all that is remembered. Barzun argues that the mind is an impressionable organ rather than a recording instrument. The mind as an impressionable organ, what an elegant way to describe how easy it is to distort our perception and cognition of what surrounds us!

In this book, Liridona Veliu looks at what characterizes the balkanization discourse on Twitter by using a corpus of almost two thousand tweets collected during a nine-year period, from 2009 to 2017, across different languages. Yet, Liridona´s work is not just an academic exercise. This book is an outstanding and scholarly effort to gain insight into how some ideas capture our criticality by using conventional expressions that become embodied with all sorts of connotations and prosodies. Chapter 2 is a must read for anyone interested in the term and its use during the 20th century. Veliu uses critical discourse analysis, a socio-cognitive approach (Van Dijk, 2000) and Hansen's (2006) work on identity construction to examine her corpus of tweets. The book features a careful analysis of, among others, the themes, the topics, the actors and the topoi that are relevant in the data analyzed. Her findings reveal that the term balkanization has come to be a proxy for division, data regulations, nationalism, war and, among others, race. Interestingly, the spaces associated with these archetypes, in the author´s words, are not mainly Balkan countries but, in decreasing order of frequency, the US, the Democratic Republic of the Congo and Cyberspace, the digital country we all inhabit in the 21st century.

The reader will find in this book a researcher that exposes her epistemological stance from the early paragraphs courageously, and who seems to come to terms with her choice of topic and methodological lens as a sort of self-imposed duty. In fields where it is not rare to find researchers that use apparently sophisticated methods with little understanding of the implications, Veliu's open stance and positioning resonates as a powerful effort to explore her own Balkan self. James Joyce made Stephen say in Ulysses that history is a nightmare from which he was trying to awake. I wonder how many different Balkan maps out there show the routes to our worst nightmares and the despair of our souls in the face of war and devastation. Yet, Veliu, far from oversimplifying her quest, argues that the balkanization discourse is a category of identity construction and othering in which 'the other' is not defined by what it is not, but by what it could or should be. As the author states: "'Balkanization' lives in the eternal negotiation of what could/should have been, but was not; what could/should be, but is not; what can/should be, but will not." This explains the widespread use of the term across ideologies, geographies and time.

The mind remembers tiny details, apparently trivial, like Liridona´s grandmother enumeration of every single family member who died in previous wars. Against the backdrop of horror and devastation, such level of detail can only perhaps serve us to maintain our own sanity. Yet, evoking her grandmother´s blue eyes and her detailed account of dead relatives in the middle of such madness is a powerful image, one that should remind us all that the horror is just one step away, maybe just one fake news away. The author is shocked that her grandmother does not submit to tears, and one may only wonder whether she was trying not to do so indeed to preserve and protect her from the insanity and the horror outside those walls that, like our memory, were fragile. Yet, they were the walls that kept them safe.

Pascual Pérez-Paredes[1]
August 19, 2018
Cambridge

[1] Dr Pascual Pérez-Paredes is a lecturer at the Faculty of Education, University of Cambridge, England.

Preface

'Balkanization' represents a discourse of dominantly pejorative characteristics used to describe a wide range of situations, circumstances, spaces, and people. Historically, such characteristics have included nuances of differences, barbarism, tribalism, underdevelopment, non-cooperativeness, disintegration, fragmentation, parcelization, instability, unreliability, dehumanization, devastation of civilization, and others; and have their roots on a preceding discourse, that of 'the Balkans', itself assigned to the Balkan Peninsula. Hence, 'the Balkans' discourse is a *conditio sine qua non* for understanding 'balkanization'. Not wanting to reproduce and fatalistically accept such discourses, I hence place both, 'balkanization' and 'the Balkans' within single quotation marks throughout the thesis, calling for questioning the conventionality they portray. This choice is based on Derrida's (1972) insistence to recognize that "... in a classical philosophical opposition we are not dealing with the peaceful coexistence of a vis-à-vis, but rather with a violent hierarchy" (p. 41) and to do this one must "... remain and operate on the terrain of and from the deconstructed system" (p. 42).

This then, is one of the most important intentions of this MA thesis (now turned into a book) – challenging 'the Balkans' in general and 'balkanization' in particular, since as Todorova (1997) says, I too believe that "... the reductionism and stereotyping of the Balkans has been of such degree and intensity that the discourse merits and requires special analysis" (p. 3). I question these innate characteristics conveyed through 'balkanization' and 'the Balkans' by first, identifying them in the closest present which is shaped by the speed and proliferation of information and knowledge in the era of social media; and second, by connecting their current manifestation to processes of historical events, hence demystifying and tracing their actualities back to longer processes of formation.

The epistemological position I occupy while pursuing this intention comes from a conceptual foundation based on genealogy and deconstructivism, which is then particularized in applying Critical Discourse Analysis (CDA) as a specific method of research on an empirical corpus of 1892 tweets that include the hashtag "balkanization". The tweets, as representatives of instantaneous communication through Twitter in particular and social media in general, are the data upon which my analysis takes place and through which I aim to claim the results of this study as reflective of what is conceptualized through the 'balkanization' discourse at the present time.

I pose the research question: "What characterizes the 'balkanization' discourse via Twitter subjectivities?" I found the need for such empirical scrutiny of 'balkanization' by identifying a gap of research on the current developments of the discourse which, as already stated, stands for an aphorism of 'the unwanted'; and as the research further proves, has been left to a historical past and an unobserved present. Should 'balkanization' be examined only retrospectively in time (which undoubtedly is influential and crucial in the current mutations of the 'discourse') it will remain in the vicious circle of restating what is already known and the impression of it being irrelevant due to belonging to the past only (which is not the case).

A bridge between historical examinations of 'balkanization' and present formations needs to be built for the same to further be examined in relation to any political processes conditioned by any meanings conveyed through 'balkanization'. In aiming to contribute to erecting that link, this thesis is a conjunction of a genealogical and historical account of 'balkanization' as presented in Chapter 2; and an empirical analysis conveyed on 'balkanization' through Twitter in Chapter 3. This is all preceded by a description of essential events in my life as an author that have formed my interest for the subject of research and have laid the foundations for the choice of the epistemology and theoretical framework, while a summary and final remarks are elaborated under the Conclusion and Future work section.

Abstract

'Balkanization', as a derivative of 'the Balkans', is part of a long-standing discourse of identity construction, otherness, and stereotyping whose application has moved beyond the geography of the Balkan Peninsula and has come to represent the pejorative in many of its forms and substances. As such, it epitomizes constructed sources of knowledge that shape worldviews and actions. In this thesis, I question 'balkanization' in its most current condition by examining manifestations of the same through the micro-blogging platform, Twitter. I do this while employing a qualitative genealogical approach of historicizing and deconstructing 'balkanization'; and by applying Critical Discourse Analysis (CDA) to 1892 tweets that include "#balkanization" and its lingual variations. The study reveals that first, ambiguity is the essential conceptual thread behind a diverse set of meanings that the 'balkanization' discourse is built upon; and second, that this ambiguity preconditions and is then preconditioned by a continuous growth of recontextualizing and applying the term as descriptive of various scenarios and spaces.

Keywords: *'Balkanization', (critical) discourse (analysis), Twitter, hashtag, subjectivities, genealogy, ambiguity, otherness*

Contents

1 'Balkanization' from Knowing to Questioning ... 1
1.1 Foundation: Through Life Episodes towards 'Balkanization' ... 2
1.1.1 I am Liridona ... 2
1.1.2 I am an Albanian from Macedonia ... 4
1.1.3 I come from 'the Balkans' ... 6
1.2 Research: 'Balkanization' through Twitter Subjectivities ... 8
1.2.1 'Balkanization': Irreconcilability itself ... 8
1.2.2 'Balkanization' through a spectacle of representation: Social media ... 9
1.2.3 'Balkanization' beyond technology: Twitter and subjectivities ... 12
1.3 Philosophy: Critique of Discourse ... 16
1.3.1 From genealogy to representation: Theorizing 'balkanization' ... 17
1.3.2 Sociocongitive discourse analysis: 'Balkanization' through critical activism ... 20

2 From Query to De-egypticization of 'Balkanization' ... 25
2.1 Questioning 'Balkanization': 'The Balkans' as a Discourse ... 26
2.1.1 'The Balkans' as the (un)defined: Onomastics, geography, and etymology ... 26
2.1.2 'The Balkans' myth: Beyond time and space, into ethicality ... 30
2.2 Constructing 'Balkanization': Europe's Other from Within ... 32
2.2.1 'Balkanization' in the aftermath of the First World War: Birth ... 32
2.2.2 'Balkanization' in the aftermath of the Second World War: Recontextualization. 34
2.3 Deconstructing 'Balkanization': Balkanism ... 43
2.3.1 Balkanism and Orientalism: Differences ... 43
2.3.2 'Balkanization' as a Western construct: Identity politics ... 47

3 'Balkanization' through Retrospection to the Present ... 51
3.1 Twitter: Mechanism and Data Collection ... 51
3.2 Analysis: Theory and Illustrations ... 57
3.3 Archetypes: 'Balkanization' through the Dominant and the Infrequent ... 66
3.3.1 Through archetypes: The pole of the dominant ... 68
3.3.2 Through archetypes: The pole of the infrequent ... 81

4 Conclusions and Future Work ... 97

Reference List of Sources ... 101

Reference List of Tweets ... 117

Appendix A ... 123

Appendix B ... 131

List of Abbreviations

ANT	Actor-Network Theory
CDA	Critical Discourse Analysis
CIA	Central Intelligence Agency
CSV	Comma-separated Values
COTF	Classroom of The Future
DRC	Democratic Republic of the Congo
DS	Discourse Studies
FPRY	Federal People's Republic of Yugoslavia
GIF	Graphics Interchange Format
NLA	Albanian National Liberation Army
NSA	National Security Agency
OED	Oxford English Dictionary
SFRY	Socialist Federal Republic of Yugoslavia
URL	Uniform Resource Locators
USSR	Union of Soviet Socialist Republics
WWI	First World War
WWII	Second World War

List of Tables

Table 3.1 "#Balkanization" and its Lingual Variations on Twitter 55
Table 3.2 Top Ten Archetypes Associated with "#Balkanization" 69
Table 3.3 Top Ten Spaces Associated with "#Balkanization" 70
Table 3.4 Bottom Ten Spaces Associated with "#Balkanization" 81
Table 3.5 Bottom Ten Archetypes Associated with "#Balkanization" 87
Table A Complete List of Archetypes Associated with "#Balkanization" 123
Table B Complete List of Spaces Associated with "#Balkanization" 131

List of Figures

Figure 3.1 Visual Conceptualization of the Methodology of Research 58
Figure 3.2 Word Cloud of 'Balkanization' Archetypes 59
Figure 3.3 Illustration of Applying CDA to Tweets 65
Figure 3.4 Temporal Depiction of Tweets Inclusive of "#Balkanization" and its Lingual Variations 67
Figure 3.5 Image Illustrating the "Data/Internet National Regulations" Archetype of 'Balkanization' 73
Figure 3.6 Image Illustrating the "National(ism/ity)" Archetype of 'Balkanization' 76
Figure 3.7 Image Illustrating Associations of 'Balkanization' with Azerbaijan 83
Figure 3.8 Image Illustrating "Gaming" Archetype of 'Balkanization' 90
Figure 3.9 Image Illustrating the 'Balkanization' in Art Archetype 94

1 'Balkanization' from Knowing to Questioning

Before reaching to the central research question of this thesis which aims at exploring conceptual connotations of 'balkanization' through Twitter subjectivities, I begin the first section of this chapter with revealing my own subjectivity as founding, accompanying and in turn being shaped by my role as an author of this thesis. The selection of life events and episodes I present below are those which I have identified as crucial in exposing how I have been born within 'the Balkans' and 'balkanization' discourses; how the process of normalizing the same has taken place; and how I have come to question the standardization of comprehension surrounding them which has inevitably resulted with questioning my own self.

I judge this information as crucial to be revealed due to three main reasons: the first reason holds on to moral foundations and me believing that it would be contradictory and greedy to reach towards others' subjectivities while obscuring my own; the second, in revealing how the subject of research is of a personal relevance to me by sharing my experience of the same, I aim at illustrating to the reader that this is not just a theoretical adventure on the ontology of 'balkanization', but is, in fact, an inquisitive need stemming from real life experiences and in turn shaping those; the third, revealing these personal experiences can also serve as a continuous reminder to the reader of how the same could have shaped the selection, analysis and interpretation of the research design and data, hence I encourage her or him to take the same with caution and critique by drawing on her or his own observations and reflections.

I consider this philosophy of subjectivities as important rather than hindering to processes of research and knowing, and I take it further forward throughout Chapter 1 (and the following chapters) where I elaborate on components of my research question and their importance in the present. In section 1.2 Research: 'Balkanization' through Twitter Subjectivities, I give a basic introduction to the 'balkanization' discourse (while I elaborate upon it in depth in Chapter 2), I expound on the role of media and social media in general and Twitter in particular as extremely influential and conditioning to power relations from the personal to the global, and I bring the two together (i.e. 'balkanization' and Twitter) by introducing the relation between them as an academic niche which, considering the relevance of social media in identity construction, requires research and empirical scrutiny.

Finally, in the third section of this chapter, in a rather 'funnel' fashion, I begin with the wide theoretical conceptualization of the epistemology and methodology as standing behind the inspiration, conduction and presentation of the findings of this research, for then to continue with an elaboration on the specific method of analysis and the sociocognitive approach to CDA. All this is rather what stands as relevant from a perspective of the process of research with a few important introductory insights into the crucial concepts of this thesis. Content and subject matter follow in the chapters after this one.

© Springer Fachmedien Wiesbaden GmbH, part of Springer Nature 2018
L. Veliu, *#Balkanization: A Critical Study of Otherness through Twitter*,
Masters of Peace, https://doi.org/10.1007/978-3-658-23824-7_1

1.1 Foundation: Through Life Episodes towards 'Balkanization'

Why should we cherish "objectivity", as if ideas were innocent, as if they don't serve one interest or another? Surely, we want to be objective if that means telling the truth as we see it.... But we don't want to be objective if it means pretending that ideas don't play a part in the social struggles of our time, that we don't take sides in those struggles.

Howard Zinn (1990, pp. 4-5)

I have always felt a strong connection to Zinn's view on objectivity, particularly to the above-written quote. His memoir and manifesto *You Can't Be Neutral on a Moving Train* (Zinn, 2002) has been a continuous reminder to me of how the complete detachment of the inner being of people from the supposed total neutral observation is just impossible and senseless in a world of infinite relations and connections. Moreover, it carries with itself the risk of robotizing and mechanizing living beings, hence dehumanizing them.

The scopes and the lenses through which we look at and observe different phenomena occurring around us are profoundly affected by numerous moments throughout our existence. It almost feels impossible to define something as an undeniable fact in all its characteristics. I do not believe that freedom from objections is found in academic objectivity, restrictions, and distinction of what is a fact or an indisputable reality *versus* a subjective observation. I consider freedom to be found within the honest explicitness of the belief that there is no such a thing as an observation, examination or study free of any kind of impartiality, emotional nonalignment, and bias. Precisely with this belief and assumption as an author, in this section of my perspective I list some crucial events and experiences of mine that have shaped my deep interest in '*balkanization*' and still accompany me through studying the same.

1.1.1 I am Liridona

I demanded freedom as the very second deed after my birth cry. I was named Liridona (From Albanian: *Liridona*: *Don(a)(ë)* - want; *Liri* - freedom). If considering that my name was decided before my birth or even before my conception, asking for freedom could, in fact, be considered as my very first deed. I suppose that it might sound unreasonable to claim an action as mine when others had undertaken it since I was not even there, but a task was planned for me, a request was formulated, an active appeal was established, and I would grow to be its bearer. My name was not meant to be merely descriptive and just an adjective. It was rather meant to be an effort, an endeavor, or an accomplishment that would result in changes. Hence, it is from this perspective in which asking for freedom was a deed in itself facilitated by my existence, that it can be considered mine just as much as anyone else's.

I was not the only one to be designated such responsibility. If looking at the history of Albanian names during the former Socialist Federal Republic of Yugoslavia (SFRY) era, especially during the early 1990s, in some regions less and in some others more, one can easily notice that the name which was given to me, Liridona (Male: *Liridon*), is often and noticeably manifested. My brother's name, who is a year younger than me, is Liridon. There were four Liridonas in my class during my primary school in a small town in Macedonia called Kičevo. Other Liridonas kept coming from Kosovo during the war in Kosovo (1998 – 1999).

The wave of Liridonas was strongly related to the struggle of Albanians within the SFRY as a minority for equal rights with the other bigger ethnic groups, such as Serbian, Croatian or Slovenian. This endeavor has fluctuated with different intensities depending on different political factors and triggered by different events. One of these crucial events is the 1989 hunger strike of the Albanians miners in Kosovo (which enjoyed the statute of a Socialist Autonomous Province at the time and was called the Autonomous Province of Kosovo and Metohija) against the Serbian initiative of constitutionally reducing the provincial autonomy of Kosovo (Popa, 2010). Raising a high sense of empathy, responsiveness and common identification among the Albanians in the former SFRY, who beside in Kosovo are living in other countries of the Balkan Peninsula such as Albania, Macedonia, Montenegro, Greece and others, a wave of a joint struggle to express the call for autonomy and freedom of decision in all possible ways spread in many years to come among the Albanians. The struggle was about to last.

Within the "bunch of Liridonas", I many times had to ask or outline which Liridona were people referring to. The margins of Liridonas referring to us as a singular entity, sufficient in and of itself and evidently self-explanatory, felt as a trap to my freedom to choose how to distinguish myself. We were a bunch of Liridona*s* and Liridon*s*, yet we were different, with different eyes colors, different hair length, different smiles, different voices, and personalities. Although I was too young to express or to even understand what this all meant to me, I simply craved to show that I was different and that as such, I should be recognized by others. I felt trapped within freedom.

Therefore, I feel that the interest in identity and identity construction has followed me since an early age. During my bachelor studies of Political Sciences at the South East European University in Macedonia, I felt a small victory to come across Heraclitus's concept of *pantha rei* (From Greek: *πάντα ῥεῖ*). Summarized as "everything flows" (Beris & Giacomin, 2014), *pantha rei* which stands for an impermanence, a continuous flow of change, hence of difference, gave me a comfort of freedom from prescription and generalization. There was nothing permanent, hence, there was no terminally and unchangeably frozen identity. Yet, impermanence seemed to be permanent then. This coincided well with Friedrich Nietzsche's (1968) "[e]verything becomes and recurs eternally – escape is impossible" (p. 545).

My interest was focused on establishing an unquestionable different self that would break any bonds and relations to everything and everyone else and would remain exceptional, exclusive and self-sufficient; in acknowledging the uniqueness of those relations for each of the different and unique Liridonas. There were many Liridonas and I could do nothing about it, but I also knew that I was one. In other words, I felt an urge to demonstrate that being different yet the same, should not be placed in hierarchical relations with being the same, yet different. This gave me one of my first important realizations: When differences are overlooked and unwelcomed, that is when identities are seen as incompatible. Hence, it is not differences that create disharmony, but rather their obliviousness, their unrecognizability and their incompatibility with communality.

The concepts of distinctiveness and differences seem to be tightly related to that of impermanence. Distinctiveness gains life in processes, rather than in unchangeable and static states that remain fixed permanently and eternally the same. Here again, my name comes into play. The "freedom" in my name is associated with another word: "want". It is not stating that I *love* freedom or I *like* freedom. My name stands for *wanting* freedom, and as long as this word remains within my name, I know I would always *have to want freedom*, meaning I will never have it.

It feels like a blessing and a curse, but more as a blessing. I have the privilege of having freedom in my name while being obliged to want it continuously; however, not that much as a constant reminder that it can be gone, but rather as a reminder that it can never be there at the first place. The ideal and infinite freedom cannot exist as long as there are borders and boundaries, but my search for it can never be suppressed either. Hence, it was made early clear to me that my internal urge of wanting freedom would rather be a search of breaking borders, limits, structures and entering new ones, but never achieving a constant state of being free as such a state was inexistent. What matters is *to want to want freedom* as long as I am alive.

Freedom, as everything else, is impermanent, though the quest for it remains a permanent one. I came to realize that the one freedom I could not have was the static one. Yet, my quest towards it was ingrained deeply in the different and impermanent shapes that freedom continues to gain. The path towards that impermanence of freedom, with the openness and flexibility of experiencing rather than possessing freedom, is the freedom I *want*. As Albert Camus in his *Myth of Sisyphus* manages to beautifully swap the sad story of a man punished by Gods to roll the round rock up to the mountain to only see it rolling down the hill perpetually and eternally, I too see the beauty of my name in the continuous challenge and the unceasing motivation to break borders, margins and selves with this. Camus (1955) concludes with "… the struggle itself toward the heights is enough to fill a man's heart. One must imagine Sisyphus happy" (p. 123). One must imagine Liridona happy.

1.1.2 I am an Albanian from Macedonia

The story of my name and the happy Liridona(s) has always been the symbolic analogy to the impossibility of isolating selves and subjectivities from contexts, hence the inspiration of many life choices, including academic interests. As already mentioned, the choice of my name was very much the result of the social and political context of the time. I was born on June 29, 1991, my mother tongue is Albanian, and I am an ethnic Albanian born and raised in Macedonia. Just four days before my birth, on June 25, 1991, Slovenia and Croatia had passed their independence acts as the first new countries to do so after the breakup of SFRY (see Sudetic, 1991). I came with a wave of disintegration, deconstruction, dissolution, rebellion, war, but also of change, rebirth and hopes for new beginnings.

As the only country among the six republics of the SFRY (Slovenia, Croatia, Bosnia and Herzegovina, Serbia, Montenegro and Macedonia) which gained sovereignty without resistance from the Belgrade-based Yugoslav authorities and army, Macedonia was referred to as an "oasis of peace" and as a rare successful example of conflict prevention (Džankić, 2016, p. 16; Battersby, Siracusa, & Ripiloski, 2011, p. 61; Hislope, 2013, p. 608). Nevertheless, the 'oasis of peace' did not last for too long.

I was nine years old when the so-called 2001 insurgency in the Republic of Macedonia took place. The attack towards the security forces of the Republic of Macedonia from the Albanian National Liberation Army (NLA) with the purpose of achieving greater rights, independence, and autonomy for the Albanian minority in Macedonia that constituted more than one-fourth of the total population of the country (Thomas, Mikulan, & Pavlovic, 2006, pp. 51-

54), opened the way to what some call a violent, military, armed, ethnic conflict (Kim, 2002; Engström, 2009; Ismaili, 2009; Daskalovski, 2004), and to what I simply called "war".

An unforgettable daily practice during that period was watching the TV news continuously. The jingles of the news that seemed all the same, scary and boring, in combination with the steam that derived from the cooked food in the kitchen (mostly beans) were encapsulated within the walls of my home and seemed terrifying. I still hate beans. Some of my friends stopped coming to school, while we all stopped playing in the schoolyard after our classes: from the walls of the school to the walls of our homes. I could not be blamed that I started hating (those) walls. It was not merely a dislike, but it was rather a detestation and an internal wish for destruction and for breaking up free. This was the first clear materialization of the struggle of reaching freedom, as well as the first of really wanting it.

Even when my imagination would reach in seeing those walls brought up to the ground, I felt a deep sadness and fear within me because destroying those walls meant destroying my home. I would have been left outside, completely unprotected, under the sun and the rain, under the bullets. Hence, I tried to get the middle ground and would often ask my parents whether we could escape the war, and come back when everything will be fine again. They often answered with "Everything is fine", but they did not answer my questions. After the walls of my home, there were country borders to defeat. This all resembled a box-within-a-box toy that I had no fun playing with.

Teachers started disappearing. They were leaving schools in attempts of escaping the war. "I do not understand" would my grandmother say, "it is not the first one, nor will it be the last". I found it very difficult to perceive that as a comfort. She would then stretch her memory back to the Second World War (WWII) (1939 – 1945), the First World War (WWI) (1914-1918), the Balkan Wars (1913 and 1913), the Yugoslav wars (1991 – 1999/2001), and a long list of names from brothers to neighbors whom she had lost during those wars. I was astonished by the firmness of her blue eyes that were easily expressing her focus in trying to remember correctly all the details, rather than shedding tears. With the same normality, she would then send me to the kitchen to check whether what she was cooking was burning, or not, while the jingle of the news would continue. She was illiterate, as she had never gone to school. She would then curse the teachers: "They are leaving you blind, escaping like cowards" she would say, "wars are for people". I would agree with her, of course. My exaggerated agreement which aimed at covering the deepest fears, would not escape her blue eyes. "Everything is fine" she would say, and would caress my hair, and I would feel traces of fear and hope all at once in her eyes, and a sudden realization that I was just a kid whom she loved and whom she would want to be outgrown by.

I felt like absolutely nothing could surprise my grandmother, and she was just one among the many who sounded like they had now come back from the future to experience what was going on again and again. While I was not sure about their fears, I was sure about the lack of pleasantness. They could not have chosen any of this. Was it "fate", but then was fate so peculiar in 'the Balkans' for which the sound of guns and crumbling walls asked for no explanation besides the self-explanatory "we are Balkans"?

Instead of answering this question, the dubiousness surrounding it would only get more intense with time. During my Erasmus studies in Ljubljana, Slovenia, from February until June 2013, I would have to travel a few times by bus from Macedonia to Ljubljana and the other way around. If sleeping, everybody would have to wake up when a border would be crossed and hoped that we would spend less time waiting initially, then less time being examined and controlled. The worst experience was when our baggage would be examined. Sometimes one could feel how human species feel the subordination not only to their fellow humans, but to the dogs beside them too. One would have feared to even look the dogs in their eyes while being continuously reminded of her nature and the freedom that had to be kept under control. I was in fear although not knowing what I did wrong. The others seemed also in fear of me, although never explaining what I did wrong.

The first time that I crossed the border Slovenia-Italy for a visit to Venice in May 2013, my journey was quite different. I found it to my enormous surprise that there was no one to stop and check me at the border. In fact, there seemed to be no border. Yes, officially, I had stepped in a different country, but what I had not known was that such transitions could, in fact, be unnoticeable. The borders could be invisible. This was made even more explicit to me after my arrival as a student to Switzerland on September 2013, when I was granted with an image of a different type of state borders, different thickness and boldness, especially in comparison with the borders of Balkan countries.

The first time I had to cross the Swiss-German border, I could not tell where the border was. Each time I would get off the plane at Basel's airport coming from Macedonia, I would often confuse the exit and *voila*, I would be in France. Remembering the exhausting controls while crossing the borders of Macedonia, Serbia, Croatia, and Slovenia during my studies in Ljubljana, I then started to question: Why would it be different in 'the Balkans' and for 'the Balkans'? The cry for freedom, the war, the boldness of borders – were they just because "we were Balkans", and if yes, who were 'the Balkans' then?

1.1.3 I come from 'the Balkans'

Just before completing my Master of Advanced Studies Program in Peace and Conflict Transformation at the University of Basel, Switzerland, I was triggered by an article which appeared in *20 Minuten* [From German: 20 Minutes] – one of the free daily newspapers and still the most widely read in Switzerland (WEMF, 2016). Its title, which was reading "*Der Balkan wird plötzlich cool*" [From German: "The Balkans are suddenly cool"] (Büchi, 2014), would encourage me to write my thesis on immigrants' portrayals in the Swiss public political discourse, where my study concluded that "nuances of xenophobia have been and are the most prevailing ones within the Swiss public political discourse on immigrants since 1990s onwards" (Veliu, 2015, p. i). At the time, 34.8 percent of the total population living in Switzerland was of an immigrant background (Swiss Federal Statistical Office, 2013), while by 2009 the number of immigrants from ex-Yugoslavia in Switzerland corresponded roughly to six and a half percent of the Swiss general population, about half of which were Albanians (mostly from Kosovo and to a slighter extend from Macedonia). The other half consisted of Serbs and Croats mostly, Macedonians, and Slovenians (Swiss Federal Statistical Office, 2010). I felt unwanted.

My reflections took me back to the conversations on visa liberalization towards the

Western Balkan countries[2] that raised a lot of dust regarding 'the Balkans' coming to Europe. These conversations had started even before my undergraduate studies. On December 2009, as announced in the Council of the European Union press release "The Council decided to grant visa free travel to and throughout the Schengen area for citizens of the Former Yugoslav Republic of Macedonia, Montenegro and Serbia..." (Council of the European Union, 2009). However, Council would refrain from adopting the same policy towards Albania and Bosnia and Herzegovina until 2010 since they would be considered as not fulfilling the necessary criteria (Council of the European Union, 2010).

Countries such as Sweden, Germany, Belgium, Switzerland, and Luxemburg became the main destination for a wave of asylum seekers from the Western Balkans. In relation to this, Marusic (2013) from the Balkan Insight writes:

> The European Union lifted visa requirements on Serbia, Macedonia and Montenegro in December 2009, allowing their citizens to travel freely into the EU's Schengen zone. Since then Serbia and Macedonia have received complaints about mass arrivals of asylum- seekers, mainly ethnic Albanians and Roma, filing applications in Germany, Sweden, Belgium, France and other countries. The EU has warned Balkan countries that if they don't cut the number of asylum seekers, visas may be re-introduced.

It was an accurate description that derived from the preceding Europe's panic from being inhabited by 'the Balkans'. As a response to this situation, in 2001 in a communication from the European Commission to the European Parliament, it was written that "... the Commission set up, as of January 2011, a post-visa liberalization monitoring mechanism under the framework of the Stabilization and Association Process, engaging with the countries concerned in a dialogue to assess the consistent implementation of the reforms and effective remedial measures" (European Commission, 2011). This preoccupation would further be followed by actual protection means. As in the "MEPs Adopt Visa Suspension Mechanism" BIRN (2013) writes:

> The European Parliament adopted "a protection clause" that will allow the Commission to suspend the visa-free regime for the Western Balkans, or other countries, that are deemed a source of excessive numbers of false asylum-seekers. The protection clause may be applied if the number of illegal immigrants from a certain country is considered a threat to the "public order" or security of individual EU states or the EU as a whole.

Shortly after the visa liberalization newly adopted policy, I was introduced to 'balkanization' by an Albanian academic and a former Professor of mine, Ali Pajaziti. Translated from Albanian, Pajaziti (2009) defines 'balkanization as the "... dispatch/division of a region or group into smaller and hostile parts: a geopolitical term used to denote the process of fragmentation and separation of a region or state into smaller hostile and non-collaborative parts"[3] (pp. 58-59). This added up to the confusion: While 'the Balkans' were pejoratively being looked at as a homogenous mass, all the same and to be feared of, hence unified from this perspective, they were at the same time being looked at as too different and fragmented to be

---

2 According to the European Union, the Western Balkans include the southeast European countries that are not members of the European Union, Albania plus the former Yugoslav countries such as Serbia, Bosnia and Herzegovina, Montenegro, Kosovo, Macedonia, not including Croatia and Slovenia that became members of EU (European Commission, 2013).

3 Translated by the author.

treated equally. I do not remember when for the first time 'the Balkans' entered my cognitive system, but by the time that all of this was happening, I realized that 'the Balkans' was not merely a geographic region that I read about in the geography and history books as the "Balkan Peninsula". 'The Balkans' were a threat (which meant I was a threat) that required (re)introduction of visas, protection clauses, and monitoring mechanisms. That is why, among others, this thesis is a very personal rebellion towards the naturalized pejorative portrayals of 'balkanization' as the main derivative of 'the Balkans', and an endeavor of deconstructing and understanding better its current conceptualization and apprehension.

1.2 Research: 'Balkanization' through Twitter Subjectivities

"You are what you tweet"
Germany Kent (2015).

I pose the research question: "*What characterizes the 'balkanization' discourse via Twitter subjectivities?*" The reasons upon which I built my decision to focus first, only on the concept of 'balkanization'; second, only on the hashtag; and third, only through Twitter as a channel, are further developed below while elaborating on the conceptual as well as the practical importance of all these three key notions of my research. This goes as well for my choice of including the concept of "subjectivities" in my research question.

The research question is also designed to assist me in my further research on 'balkanization' as part of my first year of Ph.D. studies at the Dublin City University in Dublin, Ireland. While tracing genealogically 'the Balkans' and 'balkanization', I was able to identify a gap in the academia (see section 2.3 Deconstructing 'Balkanization': Balkanism) which pointed out to a lack of research on 'balkanization' as a contemporaneous concept that continues to be forged at the present time. Most of the research on 'balkanization' is based on retrospective tendencies of historical explorations of the past, hence ignoring the ongoing process of its current construction. Filling in at least a part of that gap also stands for providing a missing component for my Ph.D. research that aims at discovering if and how does 'balkanization' influence the Euro-Atlantic integration processes of Western Balkans. That is, part of my contributions through this research is in taking forward those retrospective examinations of 'balkanization' into our current time, for the same to be taken forward towards the future and predictions of it through my Ph.D. research.

1.2.1 'Balkanization': Irreconcilability itself

Maria Todorova (1997), to whom if we are to approach 'the Balkans' as historiography and as a discourse the acknowledgment of the kick-off start may best be given, considers 'balkanization' "… the most important word and notion deriving from Balkan" (p. 32). According to her, 'balkanization' had its foundations established when "… the 'civilized world' (the term is introduced not ironically but as a self-proclaimed label) was first seriously upset with the Balkans at the time of the Balkan wars" (Todorova, 1997, p. 3). Todorova claims that the first written appearance of the word did not take place until 20 December 1918 (Todorova, 1997, p. 33), when the New York Times, under the title "Rathenau, Head of Great Industry, Predicts the 'Balkanization of Europe'" cites Walther Rathenau, a leading proponent of the idea for a Central European economic union:

> Black ruin will face us, and there will be a great tide of emigration probably to South America and the Far East and certainly to Russia. It will be most dreadful, and the result will be the *Balkanization* of Europe. The disappearance of Germany from a position of importance will be the most dangerous fact in history. Sooner or later the Eastern powers will press on the Western civilization. (Greenwall, 1918)

Hansen (2006), on the other side, wrongly places the usage of the word 'balkanization' for the first time in 1921 by the journalist Paul Scott Mowrer (p. 92). Although the Oxford English Dictionary (OED) traces back the first use of 'balkanization' to 1914 by E. H. Bradford Amer in the College of Surgeons Fellowship address ("balkanization", 2013), the definition that Mowrer (1921) gave to it is of a special importance as it seems to encapsulate very well most of the negativity conveyed through it and which stands for "... the creation, in a region of hopelessly mixed races, of a medley of small states with more or less backward populations, economically and financially weak, covetous, intriguing, afraid, a continual prey to the machinations of the great powers, and to the violent promptings of their own passions" (p. 25).

Through a thorough historiographical review, Todorova and many other authors, some of them contributing into building and some others into deconstructing it, encapsulate what the 'balkanization' discourse has historically conveyed, and which can be summarized in: *differences* (Braun, 1983; Glynn, 1993) *barbarism*, *tribalism*, *underdevelopment*, *non-cooperativeness* (Bideleux & Jeffries, 1998, p. 39; Goldsworthy, 1998) *political, economic and demographic disintegration* (Glynn, 1993; Frey, 1996; Frey, 1999), *territorial disintegration* (Hobsbawm, 1990), *parcelization* (Du Bois Edward Burghardt, 1945; Bell, Grosholz, & Stewart, 1996), *corruption, economic instability, breach of human rights, dehumanization* and *devastation of civilization* (Glynn, 1993; Rand, 1977), *gender enclaves, gated communities, divergence over time of human languages, programming languages* and *data file formats* (Weiss, 2006), *postmodernism* and *deconstruction* (Meštrović, 1994, p. 179), *threat to centralized and coercive systems* (Bell, Grosholz, & Stewart, 2013, pp. 257-258) etc.

Since in the review of literature artifacts section of this thesis (see Chapter 2) I present a more thorough description of how 'balkanization' came to be and the meanings associated with it, this section has the purpose to give an introductory glimpse on what does 'balkanization' stand for with the purpose of introducing 'balkanization' and further facilitating the transition to the second part of my research question which is Twitter. In my resonance with Todorova (1997) in "whether the Balkans are non-European or not is mostly a matter of academic and political debate, but they certainly have no monopoly over barbarity" (p. 7), is where my research interest and my endeavors to further challenging this assumed monopoly stem from.

1.2.2 'Balkanization' through a spectacle of representation: Social media

Claiming that 'balkanization', as well as the whole discourse on 'the Balkans' seem to be a mostly journalistic notion, or the product of travelers in the Peninsula (see Todorova, 1997, p.3), most of the scholars tend to focus in what has been produced in the past and its implications in the present, yet somehow neglecting to consider that 'balkanization' continues to be at least constructed *differently* today, if not different in meaning. Todorova states that "the

Balkans have a powerful ontology that deserves serious and complex study, and it is an ontology of constant and profound change" (Todorova, 1997, p. 184). While deconstructing incentives on 'balkanization' are taking place retrospectively, the process of the construction of 'balkanization' continues to develop congruently and inevitably, and I believe that not enough attention is paid to the constant and profound change of ontology that Todorova mentions. Moreover, considering the speed of the traveling of information nowadays, facilitated among others by social media, I am afraid that any endeavor of historical examination might end up as useless if not keeping up with the fast pace of knowledge production.

To realize the importance of the role that the social media have today does not need special proof. Slavoj Žižek, himself coming from Ljubljana and being referred to as "the man who knew too much" (see Jukić, 2013) with regard to casting 'the Balkans' as Europe's unconscious, on a different note talks about dating agencies' portrayals and imaginaries of selves based on external perception and validation (Big Think, 2015) as a hindrance to eventual live encounters (Ghost Pictures, 2015). Communication, according to Žižek, takes place in-between the perfect representational versions of selves, transplanted from real encounters to performance acts.

Already in 1967, Guy Debord, among others known as a French Marxist theorist, wrote his famous work of philosophy *The Society of Spectacle*, in which he introduces and further develops the concept of "*spectacle*". Through his claim that "all that once was directly lived has become mere representation" (Debord, 1995, p. 12) he highlights the importance of images in mediating and replacing real social interactions. In its most simplified sense, "the spectacle" stands for the mass media, which at the same time is the spectacle's "most stultifying superficial manifestation" (Debord, 1995, p. 19).

This superficiality of manifestation results not only with a minimized knowledge of one-another, but with the very minimized wish and need to reach towards that knowledge. What we come to know, according to Debord, is mere images, which being the only things we wish to know, become the only real things we know. "For one to whom the real world becomes real images, mere images are transformed into real beings" (p. 17) claims Debord (1995). Moreover, in relation to the historiography and geographic imprecisions of the Balkans, Debord's (1995) statement that the Spectacle facilitates societies on eliminating geographic distance "... only to reap distance internally in the form of spectacular separation" (p. 120) is crucial in exploring the role of social media in facilitating, eliciting, urging, supporting, or dissolving these spaces through the usage of the term 'balkanization'.

However, the role that social media and in particular Twitter might have on representing 'balkanization', goes back to the role of media in general. All of these concepts, similar to the ambiguity surrounding 'the Balkans', face high disputability. I, therefore, base my research on a narrow choice of definitions which seem to provide satisfactory explanations of their meanings, although while being aware of their dubiousness. Starting with "media", Campbell, Martin, and Fabos (2011), explain how the word "media", as a plural of the Latin word "medium", means

> ... an intervening substance through which something is conveyed or transmitted. Television, newspapers, music, movies, magazines, books, billboards, radio, broadcast satellites, and the Internet are all part of the media; and they are all quite capable of either producing worthy products or pandering to society's worst desires, prejudices, and stereotypes. (p. 12)

However, Campbell, Martin and Fabos remain unclear in defining what is worthy to be produced and if that shall be put into an antagonist position with the similarly unclear worst society's desires.

Similarly, Chris Livesey (2011) does not miss to point out the difficulties in defining mass media, by stating that mass media "… refer to channels of communication that involve transmitting information in some way, shape or form to large numbers of people – although the question of exactly how many a 'large number' has to be to qualify as a 'mass' is something that's generally left undefined…" (p. 1). Hence, all the other definitions of newly emerging concepts as derivative to these notions are, in fact, built upon these definitions, inheriting their haziness among others.

Social media is the case at hand. It seems like Obar and Wildman (2015) had to necessarily point out the difficulty of coming up with a rigid definition to a concept whose meaning is strongly related precisely with keeping up with change and modalities of information, so that they even add "currently" when defining social media as follows:

> Social media services are (currently) Web 2.0[4] Internet-based applications; user-generated content is the lifeblood of social media; individuals and groups create user-specific profiles for a site or app designed and maintained by a social media service; social media services facilitate the development of social networks online by connecting a profile with those of other individuals and/or groups. (p. 746)

While at Web 2.0 Internet-based applications and user-generated content, according to Procter, Voss, and Lvov (2015)

> … no longer are audiences the more or less passive recipients of news disseminated through a one-way channel but, thanks to modern information and communication technologies and, in particular, the global adoption of social media, they are connected to the newsrooms of the world and can interact with each other and also may take a more active role in setting news agendas. (p. 471)

Procter, Voss, and Lvov (2015) also state that "social media not only offers a window onto the phenomena of interest but also is inextricably implicated, through the agency of individuals and organisations (large and small) alike, in shaping these phenomena" (p. 489). This then, as Cheng (2014) states, "… has blurred the distinctions between the global and the local. People from every corner of the globe can participate in any discussion of any event, in any country and at any time" (p. 342).

These changes go deeper than superficial discussions on technological innovations and reach philosophical and ontological questions such as that of matter, form, and being. The Actor-Network Theory (ANT) developed by Michel Callor et al. (Carroll, Richardson, & Whelan, 2012; Caroll, 2011) and Bruno Latour (2007), by challenging the idea of *hylomorphism* [From Greek: *hulê* – matter; and *eidos* or *morphê* – form] and the clear distinction of form and matter as components of being, as developed by Aristotle (Apostle, 1979), is a

---

4 Web 2.0 is a term used to describe World Wide Web websites. There are a lot of unclarities with regard to its main characteristics, nevertheless according to Tim O'Reilly who coined the term Web 2.0. itself, its main features are: The Web as an application platform delivered as a service, to customers that can run the software by themselves; continuously updating content; harnessing collective intelligence through hyperlinks; democratizing the Web from an ease-of-publishing phenomenon into a conversational mess of overlapping communities; loose enforcement of copyright and right to privacy; simple and pragmatic to use, etc (O'Really, 2007).

classic example of fundamental challenges to historical truths by refusing differential treatment to human and non-human actors in a network.

What all this shows is that, as Bouvier (2015) states, "… we really need to produce studies that do not treat the online in isolation" (p. 158), as "… these changes point to wider shifts in culture: globalization, the demise of more centralized authoritative knowledge, shifts in a whole range of ideas and values" (p. 159). In a closer relation to my research focus, Bouvier (2015) further states that "… what is clear from studies of social media is that it is used for a combination of identity construction, the maintenance of social relationships and also to engage with more socially relevant matters" (p. 151).

Therefore, Weller (2014) et al. state that "… never before have researchers in the humanities and social sciences had access to such a rich tapestry of everyday, real-time communication" (p. 431). Similarly, Batrinca and Treleaven (2014), consider the social media data as "… the largest, richest and most dynamic evidence base of human behavior, bringing new opportunities to understand individuals, groups and society" (p. 89), while this further supports my argument on the importance of tracking the current mutations and shapes of the 'balkanization' discourse.

1.2.3 'Balkanization' beyond technology: Twitter and subjectivities

Keeping pace with social media is a challenge due to its wide-encompassing nature in terms of users as generators of content, the quantity of that content, and its continuously evolving nature. To narrow down my research within the constraints of an MA thesis, I chose to explore the usage of 'balkanization' in one among the ten most popular social media networks based on the number of their active users as stated by the statistical portal Statistica (2017): *Twitter,* which is ranked as the 10th with 319 million active users, but preceded, among others, also by some instant messaging services such as WhatsApp, WeChat or Facebook Messenger. My reasons behind choosing Twitter are a combination of the relevance and the many possibilities for observation that its data offer on one side; and the constraints of time, research focus and finances on the other. While I have already elaborated on the latter, the former requires further explanation as provided below.

Why Twitter? Besides me, although not as an active user, being familiar with Twitter and its functioning mechanism since November 2012, Twitter has been referred to as "… one of social media services on the Internet that are extremely popular in the world" (Hidayatulah, 2015, p. 153); "… the leading microblogging platform" (Weller, Bruns, Burgess, Mahrt, & Puschmann, 2014, p. 3); "… a global phenomenon… [which] provides a window on contemporary society as such, at national and global levels" (Weller, Bruns, Burgess, Mahrt, & Puschmann, 2014, p. 426); "… the fastest and most critical campaign tool for reaching and mobilising people, for gathering data and responding to public reactions" (Bouvier, 2015, pp. 157-158), or even as a "revolutionary machine" (p. xvii), according to Weller et al (2014), when paraphrasing Andrew Sullivan (2009), the American A-list political blogger, when he wrote in reference to the street demonstrations in Iran after the presidential elections of June 2009 that "The Revolution Will Be Twittered". Drawing on a significant set of literature, Zimmer and Proferes (2014) illustrate how Twitter has been used as a powerful tool for communication and coordination during global political and social protests, such as the 2007 Nigerian election protests, the 2008-2009 Iranian protests, the 2011 Arab Spring protests, and the Occupy movement; expressing and measuring consumer behavior and attitudes; detecting and tracking complex real-time events such as natural disasters and disease propagation; predict short-term performance of the stock; or in short, "... a valuable resource for tapping into the zeitgeist of the internet, its users, and often beyond" (p. 250).

Due to this, Twitter has been considered as "... an increasingly powerful tool for social science research" (Maddock, Starbird, & Mason, 2015, p. 1) which is "... becoming increasingly important for academic communities" (Ross, Terras, Warwick, & Welsh, 2011, p. 214); and hence it is "... appropriate to assume that this source would yield relevant and current data reflecting modern viewpoints" (Jones, 2014, p. 7). When in 2010 the U.S. Library of Congress declared that they were to obtain and retain the entire archive of public tweets (Raymond, 2010) as donated, Twitter Inc. added that "[i]t's very exciting that tweets are becoming part of history" (Adams, 2010). As Zimmer and Proferes (2014) state, this "... recognized Twitter's potential for research" (p. 251). This is proven also by the overall growth in all metrics of the Twitter-based research from 2007 to 2012, which according to them is reflected in "... the number of publications, the range of disciplines engaged in research on Twitter, the diversity of analyses performed, and the number of tweets and user accounts captured within dataset..." (Zimmer & Proferes, 2014, p. 257).

Williams, Terras and Warwick (2013) classified over 500 papers related to Twitter and microblogging research, published between 2007 and 2011, according to aspect (message, user, technology, concept) researched; method (analytic, design and development, examination, knowledge discovery); and domain (business, classification, communication, education, emergency, geography, health, libraries, linguistics, search, security, technical, and others) (p. 402). Weller et al. (2014) also describe how Twitter moved from a 'pointless babble' about one's lunch and a backchannel for interacting at an event, to "... being studied as data, which requires both contractual access as well as technical infrastructure to take in the tweets, store them, and analyze them" (p. xxi). The banal then revealed trends of identity construction and self-presentation, which are "... important not only in themselves, but rather as these serve to position people against others, as part of processes of evaluation and legitimization of wider kinds of identities and social processes" (Bouvier, 2015, p. 156).

When releasing the first tweet ever and typing "just setting up my twttr" (Dorsey, 2006), Dorsey and associates could not have guessed that what started as a side project at a San Francisco podcasting company Odeo, would become the above-described "powerhouse" (O'Reilly & Milstein, 2012, p. 5), nor that it would update the ancient golden rule of reciprocity into "tweet others the way you want to be tweeted" (Fitzpatrick, 2011). As a result of this, Twitter would also make microblogging increasingly relevant as an area of social networking services or online social network services, which Ross et al. (2011), based on extensive literature review of published work on microblogging and Twitter, define as

> ... a variant of blogging which allows users to quickly post short updates, providing an innovative communication method that can be seen as a hybrid of blogging, instant messaging, social networking and status notifications.... [T]he contents are short postings, these postings are kept together by a common content author who controls publication, and individual blog entries can be easily aggregated together. (p. 214)

This then connects us to another important component of my thesis: the concept of a hashtag in general, and "#balkanization' in particular. Efron (2010) explains how

> [m]icroblogging services allow users to post brief textual messages that are broadcasted.... Today, the most visible microblogging service is twitter.com where users post so-called tweets of no more than 140 characters.... Many tweets are marked with so-called hashtags. A hashtag is a character string preceded by a # sign. Hashtags often signal aspects of a tweet's meaning such as its topic or its intended audience. (p. 1)

According to Gregorio (2016), the hashtag was used decades ago, back in the days of Internet Relay Chat, circa 1988, but it was Chris Messina, an open source and open standards advocate, who first introduced it on Twitter on August 23, 2007. In a post on his personal blog, which he titled "Groups for Twitter, or a Proposal for Twitter Tag Channels", Messina (2007) called his idea for "improving contextualization, content filtering and exploratory serendipity within Twitter" using the pound or hash (#) symbol. He added that one other aspect that he liked

> ... about the emergent folksonomic approach to "grouping behaviors" on Twitter is that it doesn't rely on special Twitter accounts to be created that do the auto-friending thing (which requires action by a Twitter employee). Instead all tag channels automatically "add back" everyone who uses the tag, as well as those who simply "join". In terms of accelerating serendipity, this is a huge win for conferences and individuals. (Messina, 2007)

Starting from a tentative of content systematization, the hashtag has now reached to be, as Brightman (2016) states,

> .... more than just a word or phrase that started life on Twitter. It has evolved into a multifaceted tool to tag and track content, emphasize a point of view or galvanize public support through a host of social media platforms (and in some cases, not). The hashtag is part of our contemporary vernacular.

As this vernacular is us, then Kent's (2015) quote at the beginning of this section fits these insights. We indeed are, not only, but also what we share through hashtags and other mechanisms. This does not mean that what we choose to express is all we are, but it is a part of who we are, hence observing how it operates is as crucial as knowing who we are.

While Brightman (2016) emphasizes the one-dimensional role that hashtags have in constituting our views and becoming part of our 'lenses', going even further by drawing on examples such as #isthenipplepolitical, #tahrir, #winning, #BlackLivesMatter, #FirstWorldProblems, #rapedneverreported, Rambukkana uncovers the reflexivity of these views into real measures on the ground which then fire back again to forming individual experiences, as "to inscribe some hashtags into the world, to instance them in ink or through digital data, could get you killed; others could get you ostracized from social spaces you frequent, or get you fired; others might do nothing whatsoever" (p. 4) says Rambukkana (2015). According to Rambukkana (2015)

> [t]o use a hashtag is to imbue that actant with the properties of material action, to move it from the virtual to the actual, to make it an actor in its own right. To accelerate it into motion in this way, to imbue it with affect, allows it to affect in turn.... Hashtags, as a form of digital intimacy, are a way that things in the world touch other things in the world and form networks with them; they are multiple, open-ended, and contingent phenomena. (p. 5)

Bruns and Burgess (2015) too confirm this, by claiming that "[t]o include a hashtag in one's tweet is a performative statement: it brings the hashtag into being at the very moment that it is first articulated, and – as the tweet is instantly disseminated to all the sender's followers – announces its existence" (p. 23).

However, the impossibility of distinguishing between statements and acts which Rambukkana (2015) considers as "no longer possible" (p. 5) had, in fact, its conceptual elaborations laid out long before the appearance of the hashtag. This further leads my elaboration towards another conceptual cornerstone of my research question, *subjectivities*, which has preconditioned and been preconditioned by the epistemological position I chose to undertake (see section 1.3 Philosophy: Critique of Discourse). Mansfield (2000) provides with summarizing insights stretched through a significantly long time trajectory by choosing to focus on some of the most influential school of thoughts and theories regarding the self and subjectivity. He begins his introduction by asking:

> What am I referring to when I say the word 'I'? .... Where does my sense of self come from? Was it made for me, or did it arise spontaneously? How is it conditioned by the media I consume, the society I inhabit, the politics I suffer and the desires that inspire me? (p. 1)

Mansfield (2000) explains that the "'self' does not capture the sense of social and cultural entanglement that is implicit in the word 'subject'" (p. 2) and with this, he places himself in a particular ontological position which considers the subject as *constructed*. In turn then this preconditions also the choice of his epistemology as "genealogical rather than metaphysical" (p. 5) – one inspired by the nineteenth-century German philosopher Friedrich Nietzsche (1844 – 1900) and the twentieth-century, often described as a poststructuralist or postmodernist although himself rejecting the labels (Clegg & Bailey, 2008, p. 1286), Michel Foucault (1926 – 1984). Having had the terrain prepared by Nietzsche in his *On the Genealogy of Morality* (1997), Foucault (1980) disputes the existence of the individual as autonomous, independent and self-sufficient, but rather claims that

> ... it is already one of the prime effects of power that certain bodies, certain gestures, certain discourses, certain desires, come to be identified and constituted as individuals. The individual, that is, is not the *vis-à-vis* of power; it is, I believe, one of its prime effects.... The individual which power has constituted is at the same time its vehicle. (p. 98)

For Foucault then, the idea of unique subjectivities and individuals is not only based on a non-existing 'reality', but also intentionally created and used to serve a specific logic, system, and order of hierarchies. It is only through *language* as a mechanism of transforming contexts into individuals that 'subjects' come into existence. That is why Mansfield (2000) too sees "no strict and simple demarcation between the subject of the spoken sentence, the citizen in court, the searcher after truth and the person walking in the street" (p. 10). From this then, there is no real distinction between the Twitter user and her or his language; the citizen and the tweet or the hashtag.

Hence, Rambukkana's, Bruns's, and Burgess's claims go back to the fundamental questions of form and matter, human and non-human actors or actants whose well-established answers are no longer to be taken for granted. Beyond its technological aspect, the hashtag has an essential philosophical weight, and this is one dimension of its importance and inclusion in this thesis. Right there where the theoretical and the practical intertwine, where the cause and effect precondition each other, beyond the linearity of sequential historical events and towards a reflexive cycle of discourse and society, is where "#balkanization" needs to be examined.

The other nature of reasoning for focusing mostly on the hashtags is of a rather practical nuance. As Bruns and Weller (2014) confirm, 'although researchers in many disciplines have been making progress in the establishment of both theories and methods for studying Twitter, there is still a lack of comparability and compatibility across individual studies and there is a need for some commonly accepted standards in data collection, analysis, and interpretation. Similarly, while elaborating on the tools and methods of data collection (see section 3.1 Twitter: Mechanism and Data Collection), I explain extensively the difficulties of reaching to Twitter data due to constrains of different nature.

Focusing on the "#balkanization" only, instead of collecting and examining all the tweets that refer to 'balkanization' in general, enabled me to filter and narrow done the pool of data, without any major content loss. While the time factor was still obtained and the content was stretched through a wide diapason of time, I saw no major possible implications on the outcomes of my research. Further, as I conduct a qualitative analysis, the filtered data provide with a larger space for attention and an in depth examination of particular tweets that further elaborate but do not exclude general trends extracted from the totality of data. With regard to studying hashtags, Turner (2012) states that "... a hashtag that is not picked up by more than one user, that doesn't spread, will most likely be considered a failure by computer scientist". I, therefore, chose to believe in the potential of each and every tweet as an opportunity to learn, which considering that they formulate an empirical corpus of a total of 1892 tweets, might have been ignored even according to a quantitative criterion.

Hence, in weighting these difficulties *versus* the above described potential and importance of media and social media in general, as well as Twitter and hashtag in particular, I saw the weighing scale to favor the latter, or rather the possibilities for insightful contributions that the latter offer. While I do not aim to claim that I am filling in the academic gap of what characterized the 'balkanization' discourse in the present, nor that research of 'balkanization' on Twitter is representative of the 'balkanization' discourse today, I believe that it at least provides with some contemporary insights which are otherwise missing, and which due to the different limitations I face (such as time, financial resources, research focus of an MA thesis, and the complexity of data collection) are the only ones I can provide with at the moment.

1.3 Philosophy: Critique of Discourse

[Y]ou didn't question what you knew, did you? You might question a wrinkle – a feeling that came to you right out of the blue but you didn't question knowing
Bobby in *Hearts in Atlantis* by Stephen King (2009, p. 208).

As the title of this thesis reveals, I choose a critical approach to examine the 'balkanization' discourse as forged through subjectivities on Twitter. While extensive discussions (which I aim not to engage with) can be dedicated to what "critique" in fact is, it is from an understanding of what critique means that the epistemological position that I take in this thesis forms and reveals itself. Deriving from this then, it is essential to briefly comment on a conceptual cornerstone of this thesis for which one of the best sources to turn to would be Michel

Foucault's lecture "What is Critique?" (1997) delivered in 1978, at the French Society of Philosophy. Here, among others, Foucault (1997) states:

> After all, critique only exists in relation to something other than itself: it is an instrument, a means for a future or a truth that it will not know nor happen to be; it oversees a domain it would want to police and is unable to regulate. (p. 42)

Dedicating a commentary to this lecture of Foucault, Judith Butler (2002) further clarifies what the task of a critique according to Foucault would be, and which is indeed the inspiring foundation and aim of my research. Butler (2002) finds a critique's primary task in asking:

> What is the relation of knowledge to power such that our epistemological certainties turn out to support a way of structuring the world that forecloses alternative possibilities of ordering? Of course, we may think that we need epistemological certainty in order to state for sure that the world is and ought to be ordered a given way. To what extent, however, is that certainty orchestrated by forms of knowledge precisely in order to foreclose the possibility of thinking otherwise? (p. 214)

Hence, through the questioning of epistemological convictions that surround 'balkanization' now as formed by a historical process of forging which as such validate certain ways of knowing and exclude, ignore, or nullify others, is how this thesis presents a critical endeavor. Referring to Bobby's dialogue with himself in King's (2009) *Hearts in Atlantis* at the beginning of this section and the naturalized transferability of knowledge through time and space, I aim for questioning the knowing of 'balkanization' and unaccommodating to its hitherto conceptualizations.

Based on this then, this section presents a collection, summary, interpretation, and bridging of crucial conceptual formations that support my research methodology, as well as the process of data collection and elaborations. For this, I start with the wider epistemological framework that grounds itself in genealogical examinations as put forward by Nietzsche and Foucault, to move towards Critical Discourse Analysis (CDA) of Norman Fairclough, Theun van Leuwen and Ruth Wodak, social representation theory of Serge Moscovici and Stuart Hall, to the more specific sociocognitive approach to discourse analysis as put forward by Teun van Dijk which I employ as a research method in this thesis. This is all brought down to specific strategies of data collection through an examination of Twitter's functioning mechanism. This introduction to the theoretical foundation of research and the mechanics of data collection is aimed at giving a background of conceptual support to the data analysis while interpretation is presented in the subsequent chapters.

1.3.1 From genealogy to representation: Theorizing 'balkanization'

Research conducted on 'balkanization is of a mostly retrospective nature as the literature review best shows (see Chapter 2). The authors, although implicitly, have followed an epistemological inspiration grounded around the central notions of *deconstruction* and *genealogy*. An example of this is David Campbell, who in a critique towards the underprivileged discourse of the politics of identity that shaped the international response to the war in Bosnia (1992 – 1995), titled his book *National Deconstruction: Violence, Identity and Justice in Bosnia* (1998). He emphasized Foucault's (1990) argument that "the proper task of a history of thought... [is] to define the conditions in which human beings 'problematize' what they are, what they do, and the world in which they live" (p. 10). Following Campbell's model of problematizing and questioning the naturality of 'balkanization', der Derian (2009) claimed that "… the usage of 'balkanisation' seems to have enjoyed the standing of common wisdom and thus avoided critical scrutiny. A genealogy of the term is called for in order to understand how one meaning became paramount over contending definitions" (p. 100).

I too place my research within the broader conceptual frame of genealogy "as a mode of writing history or a historical method; it should be seen as a mode of evaluation, i.e. as critique; and it should be grasped as a textual practice or style specific for a genre" (Saar, 2002, p. 232). Based on the premise that genealogy always concerns subjects or selves in their very being, Saar (2002) brings up the historicized critical intention of genealogy in demystifying, denaturalizing, and desubstantializing the illegible, the diagnosable, and the controllable by drawing on the work of two of the most important figures in the history of thought: Friedrich Nietzsche and Michel Foucault.

When it comes to differentiating Nietzsche and Foucault in their genealogical endeavors, Laubender (2009) claims that a difference lies in that while "Nietzsche enacted his genealogical approach in order to achieve a more comprehensive picture of Judeo-Christian morality, Foucault uses genealogy as a means of deconstructing the traditional view of sex in Victorian society and reconstructing a new view of sexuality that pivots on the theory of discourses" (p. 16). Úna Crowley (2009) considers Foucault's genealogy as not "a replacement method for archaeology" (p. 341) as presented in his *The Archaeology of Knowledge* (Foucault, 1977). She finds Foucault's transition towards genealogy rather in the second part of his writings that include *Discipline and Punish: The Birth of Prison* (Foucault, 1975) and *The History of Sexuality* (Foucault, 1979; 1990). Michael Mahon (1992), by referring to an interview of Foucault by the Italian philosopher Giulio Preti, tells how to the question of "Which Nietzsche do you like?", Foucault replied that the one *of The Birth of Tragedy* (Nietzsche, 1999) and *On the Genealogy of Morality* (Nietzsche, 1997). Delving deeper into Foucault's Nietzschean inspiration, Mahon (1992) stresses that "the Nietzsche who is important to Foucault first, is the Nietzsche the genealogist, the one who problematizes truth as intimately entwined with relations of power, who sought a multiplicity of relations of forces at the origin of our taken-for-granted values and concepts and even the things we experience" (p. 2).

The most crucial article that manifests Foucault's relation to genealogy, is the author's own work titled "Nietzsche, Genealogy, History" (1977). Foucault already at the beginning of the article states the aim of genealogy in that "… it demands relentless erudition … it rejects the metahistorical deployment of ideal significations and indefinite teleologies. It opposes itself to the search for 'origins'" (p. 140). Foucault (1977) himself guides us towards what he considers "one of the most significant texts" (p. 140) on genealogy: Nietzsche's preface to the *On the Genealogy of Morality* (1997). It is through that willingness of looking beyond and deeper in/than the presumed, or what Nietzsche (1997) would call a "fundamental will to knowledge" (p. 2), that Nietzsche questioned what was unimaginable to question at the time, the value of morality: "So that morality itself were to blame if man, as species, never reached his highest potential power and splendour? So that morality itself was the danger of danger?" (Nietzsche, 1997, p. 8). For this, he poses what he calls "genealogical hypotheses" (Nietzsche, 1997, p. 5) and questions "what origin our terms good and evil have" (p. 4). As such, Nietzsche's examination emanates from genuine skepticism that further realizes itself in the search for descent.

Nietzsche's novelty and originality lie not only in rebelling against the conceptual firmness and concreteness of the concepts themselves, but also agains the traditional ways of knowing those concepts and the epistemology of reaching towards them which does not consider them in their way of becoming, but as, again, those which were already there. Therefore, in his other great work first published in 1889, *Twilight of the Idols* (2005), Nietzsche insurgents against the philosophers who, according to him, seem to fail in realizing that all of their conceptual knowledge is forged through processes of becoming:

> You want to know what the philosophers' idiosyncrasies are? .... Their lack of historical sense for one thing, their hatred of the very idea of becoming, their Egypticity. They think that they are showing respect for something when they dehistoricize it, *sub specie aeterni*[5] - when they turn it into a mummy. (p. 167)

In commenting on Nietzche's genealogy, Foucault (1977) importantly states that "where religions once demanded the sacrifice of bodies, knowledge now calls for experimentation on ourselves, calls us to the sacrifice of the subject of knowledge" (p. 163). And with this, Foucault calls for the troubling of any permanence and stationary despondency through historicizing it, through 'opening the mummy's sarcophagus' to speak in Nietzsche's terms, as only this can open the space for new understandings, views, and possibilities.

However, Foucault's uniqueness and novelty do not rely merely on his call for questioning the unquestioned and the unquestionable. Jacques Derrida's (1972) semiotic analysis known as *deconstruction*, by denying the silence towards Western's assumption on the metaphysics of presence, essential, or stable meanings and absolute truths, calls too for an enhanced necessity to critically and endlessly analyze (p. 42). Derrida's (1982) famous concept "*différance*" (p. 5), often misspelled as "différence" means both "to defer" and "to differ", noting the complexity and the possible misinterpretations of language. Moreover, before Derrida's and Foucault's endeavors, Martin Heidegger, known as a thinker of the continental philosophy, cannot remain unmentioned. He coined the term "destruktion" with the intention of questioning the very ontological concepts that we use as conceded in everyday meanings and going beyond the already built tradition of thought, and appeals for deconstructions of what has already traditionally been built and self-evidenced:

> Tradition takes what has come down to us and delivers it over to self-evidence.... If the question of Being is to have its own history made transparent, then this hardened tradition must be loosened up, and the concealments which it has brought about dissolved. (Heidegger, 1985, pp. 43-44)

However, as Stuart Hall (1997) states, Foucault's work "was much more historically grounded, more attentive to historical specificities, than the semiotic approach" (p. 43), and this is one of his most colossal contributions. Langer (1998) considers Foucault's approach "as a basic model or frame for discourse analysis from a critical perspective in which the concept of discourse is offering new answers in order to overcome the traditional dualisms of action-structure and micro-macro" (p. 2). Foucault transcending conventional semiotics equals the transition from language to discourse. According to Foucault (1977) discourses are

5 From Latin: Under the aspect of eternity. Used to describe what is universally and eternally true.

> ... practices that systematically form the objects of which they speak. Of course, discourses are composed of signs; but what they do is more than use these signs to designate things. It is this more that renders them irreducible to the language (langue) and to speech. (p. 45)

It must be said though that the Foucauldian notion of discourse faces a lot of criticism being called a "... slippery notion in Foucault's work" (O'Farrell, 2007); "... paradoxical and frustratingly unclear" (Howarth, 2000, p. 48); or "... (vague) in meaning" (O'Brien, 2013, p. 205), despite its crucial importance in pioneering a connection of language with representation.

Representation takes us a step forward in the epistemological journey of this thesis, bridging the gap between discourse and social structures. Hall (1997) considers Foucault's approach to have "radical implications for a theory of representation for "... it suggests that discourses themselves construct the subjects-positions from which they become meaningful and have effects" (p. 56). The social representation theory elaborated and applied by Hall, but previously established by Serge Moscovici, is built around the crucial concept of *social representation* which Moscovici (1973) defines as

> .... systems of values, ideas and practices with a two-fold function: first, to establish an order which will enable individuals to orient themselves in their material and social world and to master it; and secondly to enable communication to take place among members of a community by providing them with a code for social exchange and a code for naming and classifying unambiguously the various aspects of their world and their individual and group history. (p. xiii)

In further elaborating on social representations, Hall (1997) claims that the analytical process which considers social representations,

> ... involves making meaning by forging links between three different orders of things: what we might broadly call the world of things, people, events and experiences, the conceptual world – the mental concepts we carry around in our heads; and the signs, arranged into languages, which 'stand for' or communicate these concepts. (p. 61)

Meyer (2001) further emphases the linking role of social representations as collective frames of perceptions which "... perform the translation, homogenization and co-ordination between external requirements and subjective experience" (p. 21). What Hall calls "mental concepts" and what Meyer calls "collective/socially shared frames of perceptions", are the crucial transitioning notions to the more concrete approach of research that I apply to this thesis: the sociocognitive approach of CDA put forward by Teun van Dijk, which I extensively elaborate in the following subsection.

1.3.2 Sociocongitive discourse analysis: 'Balkanization' through critical activism

Van Dijk avoids using the traditional term "Critical Discourse Analysis" because it suggests that his approach (2009) "... is a method of discourse analysis, and not a critical perspective or attitude in the field of discourse studies (DS), using many different methods of the humanities and social sciences" (p. 63). However, a decade and a half prior to this statement he expressed his acknowledgments to the founders of CDA Norman Fairclough, Theun van Leuwen, and Ruth Wodak when writing about its principles and applying the same on racism in the British House of Commons (van Dijk, 1993, p. 281).

Built upon the above-mentioned Foucauldian contributions to the history of thought, CDA emanates from acknowledging the co-constitution of language and social structures. By drawing on Fairclough and Kress, Wodak (1995) claims that "dominant structures stabilize conventions and naturalize them. That is, the effects of power and ideology in the production of meaning are obscured and acquire stable and natural forms, they are taken as 'given'" (pp. 204-205). Enhancing the incorporation of genealogical and archaeological components within CDA, she calls (for) the breaking of conventions and stable discursive practices acts of 'creativity', which again by referencing Fairclough and Kress, she state that "would require a theorization and description of both the social processes and structures which give rise to the production of a text, and of the social structures and processes within which individuals or groups as social-historical subjects create meanings in their interaction with texts" (Wodak, 1995, p. 204). What this puts forward as one of the most distinguishing elements of CDA, is reflexivity, or what Fairclough (1995) calls *critical language awareness*, and which according to Willig (2008), can be both, personal and epistemological:

> Personal reflexivity involves reflecting upon the ways in which our own values, experiences, interests, beliefs, political commitments, wider aims in life and social identities have shaped the research. It also involves thinking about how the research may have affected and possibly changed us, as people and as researchers.... epistemological reflexivity encourages us to reflect upon the assumptions (about the world, about knowledge) that we have made in the course of the research, and it helps us to think about the implications of such assumptions for the research and its findings. (p. 10)

The emphasis that Willig puts on language as a tool of constructing and not merely mirroring reality, is what Paul Gee (1999) calls the "magical property of language" (p. 82) as the virtue of language through which it both, creates and reflects the contexts in which it is used. This again connects us to the reflexivity of discourse, which as Fiske (1996) states, although

> … used privately and individually, it remains inescapably social, so those who share discourse are likely to form social and political alliances, for they will share broadly an understanding of the world and the way that their interests can best be secured within it. We use discourse, then, both to form our sense of the social world and to form the relations by which we engage in it. (p. 6)

Wodak and Meyer too, as quoted in Tenario (2011), identify the reflexive component of discourse within the "Foucauldian tradition, in which discourse is an abstract form of knowledge, understood as cognition and emotions" (p. 185) as one of the three main trends of the diverse approaches to discourse definition, the two others being the German and Central European tradition and the Anglo-American tradition.

Langer (1998) however, considers the semantic haziness and terminological flexibility surrounding the notion of discourse to be the reason for attracting the attention of both, social theorists and researchers in linguistics and other branches of the humanities. Despite sharing their interest though, different fields of thought, approaching discourses through dimensions (linguistics, sociological or psychological) separately, have ended inconsiderate to the possibility of learning from each other. An example of this is the studies of media communication and discourse analysis, which as van Dijk (1985) claimed, were "two vast fields of research that, despite their common interest for text, talk, and communication, seem to virtually ignore each other" (p. v), and this is why Van Dijk's definition of discourse is the most applicable one to express the dimensions of 'balkanization' upon which I will focus my research and further analysis. He identifies three dimensions of encountering discourse(s) from the perspective of critical analysts: language use – not limited only to spoken language; the communication of belief – people use language in order to communicate ideas or beliefs and they do this as a part of more complex social events; and interaction in social situations-transcends using language or communicating ideas (van Dijk, 1997, p. 2).

The three dimensions of discourse that van Dijk (2009) identifies are reflected in his "triangular sociocognitive account" (p. 64) as an approach to CDA, focused on all three discursive, social, and cognitive components, the last being his novelty in the study of discourse, and as such, further developing and transcending the hitherto work of CDA and Foucauldian discourse analysis. Wodak (2006) herself acknowledged the significance of integrating sociocognitive theory in CDA and considered unjustified the reasons of many scholars for rejecting or excluding them. She claims that

> … [on] top of explaining why certain events, experiences, utterances, and so forth were perceived and reproduced in specific, prejudiced ways, [I] was and am concerned to date to explain how such meanings become widely accessible and why and how they are tied to specific ideologies in certain periods of time in specific socio-political contexts. This is an issue where theories on collective memories as well as collective experiences over time would need to be theoretically linked with relevant empirical results. (Wodak, 2006, p. 184)

These collective experiences "… are transferred from generation to generation and obviously stored as mental models and common sense knowledge" says Wodak (2006, p. 185), connecting us back to the social representation which van Dijk incorporates in his approach, hence completing the overview on the epistemological mosaic of this thesis. While Van Dijk pays tribute to Moscovici and his associates for coining the term social representations, he claims that his notion is, in fact, different. While social representations are part of the social memory, van Dijk's (1990) mental models

> … are cognitive representations of personal experiences and interpretations, including personal knowledge and opinions, and are located in episodic memory. Models represent the interpretations individuals make of other persons, of specific events and actions, and essentially are the cognitive counterpart of situations. When people witness a scene or an action, or read or hear about such events, they construct a unique model of that situation or update an old model. Models, thus, are also the referential basis of text understanding. (p. 166)

Following this definition, my analysis of the 'balkanization' discourse through Twitter aims at uncovering the general trends revealed by the available data as an entity in itself, while drawing on and connecting it to specific tweets as examples of individual interpretations and as the cognitive counterpart of the normalized, adapted, naturalized, and decontextualized perceptions of 'balkanization'.

Despite of describing mental models as rather encompassing but not reducible to social representations, van Dijk (2000) importantly states that "social representations cannot be reduced to mental models" either (p. 23). He explains that

> … in everyday situations people may live, express or enact different ideologies... however, there is no doubt that also across different situations, not only one social actor, but many social actors, may have and express and use the same or very similar opinions. This similarity cannot simply be explained by similar circumstances, but need to be accounted for by more permanent mental structures, shared with others, as they are represented in social memory. (van Dijk, 2000, p. 23)

Deriving from this then, the notion of ideology becomes relevant in analyzing and interpreting the data. Van Dijk (2000) considers discourse to play "... a fundamental role in the daily expression and reproduction of ideologies" (p. 4). At this point, due to the many controversies and the pejorative connotations surrounding the concept of ideology that have fueled some avoidance or phobia for using the term, it is of a high relevance to clarify that van Dijk approaches ideology with a rather sharp and explicit explanation of his own. By tracing back the term to its invention by the French philosopher Destutt de Tracy (1803) at the end of the 18th century as "science of ideas" (van Dijk, 2000, p. 6), van Dijk's (2000) general definition of ideologies is as "fundamental beliefs of a group and its members" (p. 7) to constitute what he calls the *cognition element*. Mediated by *mental models* as "the most important interface between ideologies and discourse" (van Dijk, 2000, p. 24), the cognition element then connects to discourse as "language use, text, talk, verbal interaction, and communication" (van Dijk, 2000, p. 10) and the social component as the "political, cultural and historical aspects of ideologies" (van Dijk, 2000, p. 10).

However, despite Van Dijk being considered as "one of the outstanding researchers of last 30 years in the field of social texts" (Langer, 1998, p. 16) and "a world leading scholar of discourse studies" by SAGE Publishing in a biography titled "Teun A. van Dijk: Pompeu Fabra University, Spain" (2017) who has "attempted successfully" (Wodak, 2006, p. 182) to bridge mediation and society, his approach has also been the subject to criticism. Tenario (2011) considers there to be "a slightly deficient explanation of how to apply some of the rules identified by van Dijk in discourse practice; thus, method and conclusions are open to multiple interpretation" (p. 191). Langer (1998) considers that by focusing on existing discourse structures, van Dijk "does not take account of texture, that is what at all can be a topic in the discourse (and what cannot be said)" (p. 19), while adding Fairclough's criticism to van Dijk's overestimation of the reproduction of power relations, ideology, and underestimation of the interpersonal function of language. Nevertheless, these disagreements in the academia, as van Dijk claims, "only prove that also among critical scholars there is no consensus on the politics, theories or methods of critical inquiry" (1993, p. 281).

With this, I wrap up the main information on the conceptual foundations of this thesis inclusive of an introduction to the main composing elements of the research question and the epistemology of research, preceded by my personal perspective as an author. The following chapter begins with applying what has been elaborated until now upon 'balkanization' and 'the Balkans' as the wider research interest. Before proceeding with taking forward the endeavor of addressing the niche of scrutinizing 'balkanization' as a contemporaneous discourse via Twitter in Chapter 3, Chapter 2 provides with the means of engaging critically with 'balkanization' in the present but by first using history as a vessel of analysis. This is what essentially the task of genealogy is and upon which I elaborate in-depth in the next chapter.

2 From Query to De-egypticization of 'Balkanization'

By debunking the process of becoming of 'balkanization', in this chapter, I employ a genealogical approach that is grounded and centered on the purpose of destabilizing its metahistorical definition. This has called for historicizing and contextualizing the concept through a review of sources and literature which led me in tracing 'balkanization' as part of 'the Balkans' discourse, itself leaking from the Balkan Peninsula as a name and as a geography. This, although examined and discovered in a retrospective manner due to 'balkanization' being a derogative of 'the Balkans' and not the other way around, is placed as a first section of this chapter as it represents my wider research interest which is conceptually, historically, and cognitively fundamental and preconditioning to the 'balkanization' discourse.

From there, proceeding with a review of literature on 'balkanization', two main prevailing tendencies that follow a chronological criterion revealed – one, works that have gradually constructed and designated a meaning to 'balkanization' after WWI; and two, literature that challenged and questioned the conceptual connotations of 'balkanization' naturalized by then, and which did not appear until the end of the twentieth century and the beginning of the twenty-first century. Balkanism, as representative of the latter tendencies, is extensively elaborated under the Deconstructing 'Balkanization': Balkanism section. Further, the constructing tendencies have different nuances if comparing those of post-WWI and of post-WWII. If until WWII 'balkanization' had a connection with the Balkan Peninsula, after WWII, the expression started to be detached completely from the region and applied to a wide range of other fields of thought and disciplines. However, it is important to state that a strict division of these different tendencies based on a temporal criterion is not possible. Different tendencies intertwine up until now. The chronological criterion only represents the peak of such different patterns of elaborations on 'balkanization'. As such, one should be careful in taking for granted this structure as definite classification, as it should be the case with any categorization in general.

From the perspective of considering the importance of deeply exploring the historic pathway that 'balkanization' has undertaken in order to place it now in a very contemporary context, I rather believe that the literature review holds nearly the relevance of a research method for this thesis. This due to it exceeding the mere collection and summary of sources, into analyzing, systemizing, and drawing conclusions from the same, as a precondition to a better understanding of the nature and emphasis in its current comprehension. Onwuegbuzie (as cited in Onwuegbuzie, Leech and Collins, 2012) states that the literature reviews is rather a complex process as "… an interpretation of a selection of published and/or unpublished documents available from various sources on a specific topic that optimally involves summarization, analysis, evaluation, and synthesis of the documents" (p. 2). Cooper (1998) too, states that

> … literature reviews can focus on research outcomes, research methods, theories, applications, or all these. Literature reviews can attempt to integrate what others have done and said, to criticize previous scholarly works, to build bridges between related topic areas, to identify the central issues in a field, or all these. (p. 3)

However, questioning whether a literature review can be considered a research method or not is not the aim of this chapter. Rather, the purpose is providing with the conceptual founda-

© Springer Fachmedien Wiesbaden GmbH, part of Springer Nature 2018
L. Veliu, *#Balkanization: A Critical Study of Otherness through Twitter*,
Masters of Peace, https://doi.org/10.1007/978-3-658-23824-7_2

tion of 'balkanization' indeed by integrating what others have said and researched on 'balkanization', looking critically upon their work, identifying the central issues that come out of this process in order to explore what current characteristics are being added, revoked or mutated to 'balkanization' through Twitter today, hence building bridges between the mostly retrospective approach of research on 'balkanization' with the very present one. It is from the perspective of which reviewing literature artifacts of the 'balkanization' discourse stands not for a mere collection of sources and their revision, but for an analysis which ends with specific conclusions on conceptualizations of the 'balkanization' discourse which are only then possible to be seen as changed or mutated in the present, that this chapter presents not just a review of literature, but already a part of research.

2.1 Questioning 'Balkanization': 'The Balkans' as a Discourse

"This is our world, although the people who drew this map decided to put their own land on top of ours. There is no top or bottom, you see"
Odenigbo in *Half of a Yellow Sun* by Chimamanda Ngozi Adichie (2006, p. 12).

The geographic imprecision of 'the Balkans' is followed by discourses that transcend its uncertain spatiality as a subject of analysis. These discourses on 'the Balkans' follow a long historical path and take diverse shapes. Leading my way towards the core of this research, 'balkanization' that is, I look upon crucial concepts that have contributed to shaping what today is meant by 'balkanization'. As the linguistic variations are quite diverse, it is the right moment to clarify the usage of some terms and notions within the context of this thesis while giving an overview of their place in academia and wider. Within the frames of *the Balkan Peninsula* and *'the Balkans'* as elaborated below, is where my research interest for 'balkanization' is rooted in.

2.1.1 'The Balkans' as the (un)defined: Onomastics, geography, and etymology

According to Klapka, Halás, and Tonev (2013), a region is "a limited spatial system and an expression of an organizational unity that differ it from another region" (p. 94) which they consider an "objective reality" (p. 94). The geographic region of 'the Balkans' seems to fit as much as to conflict with this definition. This because objectively there does exist a piece of land called "the Balkan Peninsula", and which is a spatial reality where there seems to be a system of common and similar cultural, historical, and geographical unity. At the same time, as the further elaborations witness, the limits of this spatial system, its unity, and expression of organization are highly disputable and they rather confirm to Joseph Babatunde Fagoyinbo's (2013) elaborations who, differently from Kapka, Halás, and Tonev (2013), states that "geographic regions and sub regions are mostly described by their imprecisely defined and sometimes transitory boundaries" (p. 37).

However, Klapka, Halás, and Tonev (2013) state further that geography and spatial science usually recognize two types of regions – formal and functional. By referring to Ullman, they explain how while

> ... the formal region is organised (or 'tied together') vertically, the concept of site being of interest, the functional region is generally organised by horizontal relations in space in a form of spatial flows or interactions of various kind (persons, goods, material, energy, information etc.) between parts of a region, the concept of situation being of interest.... This type of an organisational unity of a functional region infers that it usually has a heterogeneous inner structure in comparison to formal (or homogeneous) regions. (p. 95)

In the line between that heterogeneity and homogeneity that Klapka, Halás and Tonev refer to, is where the Balkan Peninsula, as an imprecisely defined geographic region, meets with the homogeneity of perceptions that is afterward reflected back into the formality of the region *per se* in terms of practical defined measure on its territoriality. As this chapter concludes, but also as this thesis later infers, it is precisely within that "imprecisely defined" description that the discourse of '*the Balkans'* and further that of 'balkanization' is positioned. However, let us take this forward one step at a time.

The Balkan Peninsula takes its name from the Balkan mountain range [also known as *Stara Planina* (from original Bulgarian and Serbian Cyrillic: *Стара планина*)] (see Todorova, 2997, p. 22; Gray & Sloan, 2004, p. 114) that stretches from the Serbia-Bulgaria border to the Black Sea parallel to the river Danube, and constitutes the eastern border of the Balkan Peninsula. As such, it is obviously of a great significance for the onomastics and etymology of the peninsula as well. One starts facing the first ambiguities on 'the Balkans' even by looking at the meaning and the origin of the word "balkan". Maria Todorova claims that it is widely accepted that "balkan" as a word was brought to the peninsula by the Ottoman Turks. Todorova, who comes from Bulgaria and is currently a Professor of History at the University of Illinois at Urbana-Champaign, is often mentioned throughout this thesis. Her book *Imagining the Balkans* is groundbreaking work that transcends, but does not exclude, the region's geographical imprecision, by coining *balkanism*, which among others, stands for an academic endeavor and studies on the discourse on 'the Balkans' as "... created and imported from the West" (Todorova, 1997, p. 57) which creates the region as much as it describes it. According to her then, it is from the word "balkan" that the term "Balkan Peninsula" derives, and which was firstly coined and used by the German geographer August Zeune in his 1808 who erroneously believed of the Balkan Mountains as the northern frontier of the peninsula (Todorova, 1997, p. 25).

Before being named Balkan Mountains, Haemus was the ancient Thracian word used to describe the same mountains. Marinow (2014) states that Haemus turned into a political border between Bulgaria and Byzantium and remained the most lasting demarcation element between the two (p. 17). Todorova confirms the same, by adding to this that the earliest mention of the word "balkan" comes from the Italian humanist writer and diplomat Filippo Buonaccorsi Callimaco in 1490 (p. 22). Since then and throughout the eighteenth century, Haemus and Balkan were increasingly used interchangeably.

With regard to the etymology of the word "Balkan", besides Todorova's (1997) explanations on "balkan" standing for "mountains" (from *balkan* in Turkish); mud (from *balk* in Turkish); or big, high, or proud house (from *Bala¯-Kha¯na* in Persian) (pp. 27-32), many of other ideas seem to circulate in some scholar and informal sources. "Balkan" has been associated by Elizabeth Gowing (2011) with honey and blood (from Turkish: *bal* means honey; *kan* means blood). The same claim has been supported by Mary Chen (2016) and her story on the journey in Sarajevo, and even adopted for a movie written, produced, and directed by Angelina Jolie (2011) titled *In the Land of Blood and Honey.* Considering this and followed by some other misconceptions in its descriptions (see Todorova, 1997, pp. 25-30), Todorova (1997) claims that "… the reason why Balkan became one of the most often used designations (alongside Southeastern Europe) has little to do with precise geography" (p. 25) and that, in fact, its definition "… has followed a set of geographic, political, historical, cultural, ethnic, religious, and economic criteria, and most often a combination of criteria" (p. 25).

Through a retrospection that I believe comes the closest to the different positions taken on the geography of Balkan, Todorova (1997) summarizes the vagueness of the Balkan Peninsula's geographic borders. She states that

> … [t]he standard approach of geographers distinguishes between a *stricto sensu physico* geographical definition, and one employed for more practical purposes. The first accepts as the undisputed eastern, southern, and western borders the Black Sea, the Sea of Marmara, the Aegean, Mediterranean, Ionian, and Adriatic Seas. The northern border is most often considered to begin at the mouth of the river Idria in the Gulf of Trieste, following the southeast foothills of the Julian Alps, and coinciding with the Sava and the Danube Rivers. Accordingly, some geographers treat as Balkan, besides Albania, Bulgaria, Greece, and all countries of the former Yugoslavia, only the Dobrudzha part of Romania and the European part of Turkey. Others, well aware that the political-geographic and physical-geographic boundaries do not coincide, tend to include all of Romania (sometimes even Moldova), but Turkey is excluded. (p. 30)

I think that this summary statement is a cohesive and comprehensible one, not because of its success in placing 'the Balkans' into a geographical spatiality, but rather in terms of summarizing the implicitness of the borders into two main approaches: the physical-geographic approach, and the political-geographic one, which seem to be mutually constructed rather than independent.

Todorova (1997) elaborates on some authors' different approaches, such as Cvijic, Hoffman, and Viljavec (pp. 30-31) who while defining 'the Balkans' geographically have, in one way or another, ended up in inevitably including cultural and geopolitical criteria. She herself chooses to consider as 'the Balkans' Albanians, Bulgarians, Greeks, Romanians, and most of the former Yugoslavs among which Slovenes are not included, but Croats are (due to parts of Croat-populated territories were under Ottoman rule), while she states that Turks are also considered (Todorova, 1997, p. 31). However, she does not clarify in depth the reasons for excluding Slovenes, which considering that Slovenia was a part of SFRY leaves some space for contestation. Further, Todorova in this definition and in other parts of her book, at times seems to base her statements in an interchangeable perception of nations and countries, which in a Balkan context is a matter of sensitive debates.

Reviewing online dictionaries and websites, it is vivid that in their attempts of trying to define the Balkan geographically, they as well cannot help but unavoidably intertwine their explanations with many ethnic, cultural, historical, religious, and political considerations. Examples of this are the website of the Washington based Center for Educational Technologies, home to the NASA-sponsored Classroom of the Future[6] ("The Balkans", 2001); the online Encyclopedia ("Balkan Peninsula", 2016; "Balkans", 2016); the online World Atlas ("The Balkan Peninsula - Map & Details", 2002); the English-Online website ("The Balkans,

[6] "The Classroom of the Future (COTF) program at Wheeling Jesuit University serves as NASA's principal research and development centre for education technologies and provides technology-based tools and resources to K-12 schools" (NASA-sponsored Classroom of the Future, 2016).

2016"); the Encyclopaedia Britannica (Danforth, 2015); and the Michigan State University website, in which Sowards (2008) states that "… one can't understand the Balkans without understanding its ethnic groups, and one can't understand the ethnic groups and their history without knowing the influence of the region's geography". He then continues by stating that "… even the geographic extent of the 'Balkan' region is a matter of controversy…. But the presence of contradictory themes is itself characteristically Balkan" (Sowards, 2008).

The relevance of detecting and revealing this ambiguity is not only of a denotation nature, but also of a signifying relationship. This is one of the reasons that even the etymological and onomastic imprecisions on 'the Balkans' do matter in all the other discursively constructed designations related to them. Most of these designations have been externally assigned to the region and its people. While Ottomans decided to name its mountains as Balkan Mountains, even though they already had a local name; while Auguste Zeune as the first named the place a peninsula; while Filippo Buonaccorsi Callimaco is the earliest to mention the word "Balkan"; and while German literature was struggling on whether Southeast Europe would be a more proper definition to use (see Todorova, 1997, p. 28); the locals who were being signified had no place at the table of discussions.

'The Balkans' were initially externally signified, and this then became the only naming version of themselves that they knew. A prove of this is that in the Balkan languages themselves, the word "balkan", with some variations of plural or singular, is used as a self-designation. In Albanian, the noun appears only in the singular as "*Ballkan*" to refer to the region. The same situation appears to be in Croatian too as "*Balkan*"; or "*Балкан*" in Cyrillic for Serbian, Macedonian and Bulgarian. "*Ta Valkania*" and "*Balcani*" are used in Greek and Romanian, and they are both used in plural (Todorova, 1997, p. 32). As Todorova (1997) states, the use of the noun in the region can be ascribed from neutral to pejorative connotations. A bold example of the latter is the expression "*Balkanci smo*" (From Serbo-Croatian: We are Balkans), which Todorova states is a self-criticizing derogative used only in Serbo-Croatian (p. 32), but which, in fact, extends to Albanian and Macedonian as well. The only positive example is the "Bulgarian derivative 'balkandzhiya' (female 'balkandzhiika') which indicates someone who possesses a special ethos: independence, pride, courage, honour" (Todorova, 1997, p. 32).

Although the aim of this section is to get familiar with preceding discourses to that of 'balkanization', while on the semantics of 'the Balkans' it seems fit to comment that the empirical analysis of the tweets revealed quite a few lingual and grammar variations of 'the Balkans' and 'balkanization' in local languages, all within the same externally designated signifier: "balkan"; "balkana"; "balkanizacija"; "balkanizacije"; "balkanizaciji"; "balkanizaciju"; "balkanizovan"; "balkanske"; "balkanski"; "balkanskih"; "balkanskimi"; "balkanskom"; "balkansku"; "balkanu"; "балкан"; "балканизација" and "балканот". In other words, the people of the Balkan Peninsula know to call themselves only as others have called them. This, as we will see, is of no usual or accidental nature, as in their attempts of defining 'the Balkans' geographically, the signifiers were constructing 'the Balkans' conceptually.

The second reason for dwelling deeper into the ambiguities on the meanings and geography of 'the Balkans' is not in their precision, definition, or exactness, but rather in the abstruseness itself. I believe that while the ambiguities on etymology and geography might have not preconditioned, then they have certainly facilitated the discourse on 'the Balkans', which in turn has validated them. In other words, the heterogeneous ideas on what is meant by 'the Balkans' and where do 'the Balkans' begin and end, somehow give support to a homogeneity, semantics, and solidarity of thought – "We all agree/decide that we cannot agree/decide on 'the Balkans'". The undefined then becomes defined as 'the undefined'. It is either the lack of or the excessiveness of definitions that generates a definition of 'the Balkans'. Hence, rather than an opposite or an 'other', 'the Balkans' seem to be 'less' defined by what they are, than by what they are not. With this, the Balkan Peninsula transforms into 'the Balkans'.

2.1.2 'The Balkans' myth: Beyond time and space, into ethicality

As such, the geographic, onomastic and etymological abstruseness surrounding what is meant with "balkan", "Balkan Peninsula", and "the Balkans", only further emphasizes the ambiguity not only as a loyal companion, but moreover as a foundation of the discourse of 'balkanization' as described in the next sections, itself a derivative of 'the Balkans' discourse. Hence, 'the Balkans', as a part of a long-length discourse of identity construction and stereotyping that did move beyond formality into functionality, is a crucial component of this thesis. Hence, my choice of putting both, 'the Balkans' and 'balkanization' within single quotation marks, is expressing a call for questioning the conventional meanings of the terms, which among others, have the element of indefinability as part of their definition.

In order to differentiate the formal Balkan Peninsula from the functional discourse on *'the Balkans'* (again, contested spatiality is an undivided component of 'the Balkans' discourse, but nevertheless a separate one), I refer to the geographic region, altogether with its imprecisions, as "the Balkan Peninsula". I make this choice due to the general practice of referring to geographical regions, including states, in the singular form of a noun (unless they are federations or confederations). In a novel by Christopher Bollen (2015) titled *Orient*, one of the characters, Ted, admits that there is something he can never tell his students: "... but, do you know what geography really is? .... It's not the shapes of countries or a list of trade routes. Geography is a snapshot of war, plain and simple. It's a record of the state of hostile powers at a moment of suspended animation" (p. 33). Chimamanda Ngozi Adichie (2006), whom I quote at the beginning of this section draws our attention to challenging the presumed naturality of maps, borders, and territories, in that the same are products of complexed webs of interactions, crafted and made by people to serve (someone's) purposes, based on narratives that deny a voice to those whom they are crafted for (see Adichie, 2009), and as such, I believe, deserving of investigation, deconstruction, and academic scrutiny.

Along the lines of spaces that discourses acquire, Hansen (2006) explains how "spatiality, temporality, and ethicality are analytical lenses that bring out the important political substance of identity construction" (p. 42). Further, she stresses the importance and the impact of territory in building abstract discourses referring to Samuel Huntington, famous for his *Clash of Civilizations* (2011):

> ... discourses which evolve around the construction of political subjects such as 'terrorists,' 'barbarians,' 'tribes,' 'heathens,' 'savages,' 'homosexuals,' 'women,' 'civilization,' 'the international community,' 'humanity,' and 'the people'; and identities are often constructed as a mixture of the territorially bounded and the abstract political. (Hansen, 2006, p. 43)

From this then, we are left to understand that geography is a materialization of meanings, and as such, it cannot be seen as disassociated from time and judgments. 'The Balkans' are a bold example of this. Arguing on the power and significance of geopolitical reasoning, Tuathaigh (1999) states that in 'the Balkans' "[g]eography helped making the conflict inevitable" (p. 114). By basing his statement on how the region is composed of values separated by high mountains that fragment the area's ethnic composition, Tuathaigh (1999) is only one of the many authors which cannot disassociate the geography of the Peninsula from the stigmas attached to it, and hence facilitates the transition from the Balkan peninsula to 'the Balkans' as a discourse.

Entering here slowly into the temporal realm, it is not until the nineteenth century that pejorative nuances are attached to the discourse on 'the Balkans'. According to Todorova (1997), this transition as founding of the political connotations added to 'the Balkans', began by the end of the nineteenth century to refer to states that had emerged out of the Ottoman Empire: Greece, Serbia, Montenegro, Romania, and Bulgaria (p. 32). From spatiality, Hansen (2006) further elaborates on the importance of recognizing the role of temporality in the creation of discourses by stating that

> … temporal representations locate a contemporary foreign policy question within a historical discourse, but they are, from a poststructuralist perspective, precisely discourses: framings of meaning and lenses of interpretation, rather than objective, historical truths. (p. 6)

On these lines, Erik de Lange (2016), currently a Ph.D. candidate with a research interest in threat perceptions and securitization methods, makes a bold statement: "Time has been peculiar in the Balkans" (p. 10). De Lange (2016) claims that "… along the disputed borders of the Balkans runs not a geographical but a temporal boundary" (p. 10). I believe that precisely this lack of a geographical boundary requires the geographical analytical lenses in recognizing it as such, as it afterward becomes the discourse that transcends these imprecise boundaries but does not exclude them.

The temporality of 'the Balkans' gains clarity in conjunction with its ethicality and its nuances of otherness. It is here where Western countries and Europe come into play. Todorova (1997) importantly states that "'Europe' when used as distinctive from 'the Balkans'… was a synonym for progress, order, prosperity, radical ideas, that is, an image and an ideal, a Europe belonging to Time (understood as development)" (p. 43), and Hansen (2006) further reaffirms this by stating that the"… confluence of spatial and temporal identity implied that 'the Balkans' would be unable to break these patterns and progress toward more civilized and Western forms of behavior" (p. 85). Todorova (1997) well encapsulate the impossibility of dividing the geography of 'the Balkans' from its ethical and temporal portrayals, by concluding:

> The Balkans are usually reported to the outside world only in time of terror and trouble; the rest of the time they are scornfully ignored…. If one were to make more of the frozen vision of the Balkans than merely define it as the product of casual, dismissive, or hectoring journalism, one could argue that this image is more than a stereotype. It appears as the higher reality, the reflection of the phenomenal world, its essence, and true nature, the "noumenon" to the "phenomenon," to use the Kantian distinction. None of the politicians, journalists, or writers who have specialized in passing strictures on the Balkans have ever made a claim for a philosophical basis of their argument, yet this is what they have achieved. The

frozen image of the Balkans, set in its general parameters around World War I, has been reproduced almost without variation over the next decades and operates as a discourse. (p. 184)

Deriving from the abstraction materialized into the context of the Peninsula, or the context of the Peninsula abstracted into the narratives built around and about it, it is this invention that I refer to as the myth of 'the Balkans'. Joseph Campbell (1991) says that "... mythology is not a lie, mythology is poetry, it is metaphorical" (p. 206). With a vast contribution on the study of myths, Campbell (1991) among the different functions that myths serve, summarizes four – the mystical, cosmological, pedagogical, and with a relevance to this thesis is the fourth function, the sociological one – which supports and validates a certain social order. As such, the myth of 'the Balkans' built upon an ambiguous geography, time, and ethicality, is carried and incorporated into 'balkanization' as explained in the following section.

2.2 Constructing 'Balkanization': Europe's Other from Within

.... you looked around and saw everybody either married or busy and happy and thinking and being creative, and you felt scared, sick, lethargic, worst of all, not wanting to cope. You saw visions of yourself in a straightjacket, and a drain on the family, murdering your mother in actuality, killing the edifice of love and respect built up over the years in the hearts of other people.

Sylvia Plath (2000, p. 154)

The Balkan wars and WWI founded the first grounds of giving birth to 'balkanization'. Initially, the concept will be linked to the Balkan Peninsula and the events occurring there. However, the fabrication of 'balkanization' followed its most important switch after the WWII, although no crucial differences in meaning would take place. The visions of 'balkanization', deeply ingrained in pejorative versions of 'the Balkans' only developed further by stationing the term to a variety of disciplines which only inherited and adopted its meaning, but kept the essential derogatory connotations conveyed through it.

As the section reveals, such connotations would become a defining element of how 'the Balkans' would come to be known as. The red disparaging thread of the 'balkanization' discourse will remain as the discourse will gain greater dimensions in terms of applicability. Through this, 'the Balkans' will be placed "... in a *cognitive straightjacket*" (Todorova, 2010, p. 176), and rather not a pleasant one as the elaborations below expose. This is what I also refer to through Plath's quote at the beginning of this section.

2.2.1 'Balkanization' in the aftermath of the First World War: Birth

As already mentioned before (see subsection 1.2.1 'Balkanization': Irreconcilability itself), as the Daily Express correspondent of The New York Times, Greenwall has been known to facilitate the first ever written appearance of 'balkanization' in 1918 during his interview in Berlin with Walther Rathenau, a German statesman who also served as a Foreign Minister during the Weimar Republic[7] (Schuster, 2012). This preceded the British monthly magazine

[7] Weimar Republic [From German: Weimarer Republik] is how the German state between 1919 and 1933 is/was unofficially called. Its constitution was drafted and the Repulic was proclaimed on November 9, 2017 in the city of Weimar, hence the name (see Lee & Lang, 1998).

The Nineteenth Century, which accused Great Britain of pursuing a policy aimed at the 'balkanization' of the Baltic provinces in 1920, and in the same year the Public Opinion equalized an "unhappy Balkanized world" with a condition in which every state is at issue with its neighbors (Todorova, 1997, p. 12).

Paul Scot Mowrer's (1921) definition of 'balkanization' as one of the most iconic ones (see Todorova, 1997, p. 34; Hansen, 2006, p. 92), was preceded by him stating that

> … the Christian states of the Balkans were no sooner liberated from the Turks than they began fighting among themselves. Cleanout ethnical and natural boundaries being impossible, each felt that his neighbor was encroaching. The peoples were uneducated and primitive, that is to say, easily aroused and easily led. They were consciously weak, that is to say, jealous, covetous, intriguing, afraid. Their economic fragility, the ruinous condition of their finances – always hopelessly in debt – combined with their feuds to make them an easy prey to the machinations of the great powers. (p. 23)

After eleven consecutive years of experience as a special European correspondent for The Chicago Daily News, Mowrer (1921) states that "… it is necessary to look more carefully into the nature of the *malady* which is afflicting 'Balkanized Europe'" (p. 4) as he examines numerous nations that had arisen after WWI.

In 1923, Leon Trotsky who in 1912 was sent from Vienna to the Balkan Peninsula as a military correspondent of the newspaper Kievskaya Mysl, would be among the first journalist to facilitate the introduction of 'balkanization' to the public by writing that

> … victorious France is now maintaining her mastery only by Balkanizing Europe…. Britain's traditional mask is of hypocrisy. As a result, our unfortunate continent is cut up, divided, exhausted, disorganized and Balkanized – transformed into a madhouse…. Europe is compelled, either to remove these frontiers, or to face the threat of complete economic decay. (Jordan, 2007, p. 61)

Besides receiving the clear message of 'balkanization' being equalized with a "madhouse", Trotsky's and the other authors' conceptualizations of 'balkanization' are only a few among the many examples of wrongly attributing 'balkanization' to the dispatch of the Ottoman Empire and the proliferation of countries that came out from it. As Todorova (1997) states, "when the term was coined, at the end of WWI, only one Balkan nation, Albania, was added to the already existing Balkan map; all others had been nineteenth century formations" (p. 32). It is the context of the time characterized with the disintegration of the Habsburg and Romanov Empires, which analogically, retrospectively, and projectively facilitated the coining of the word. According to this then, 'balkanization' which was coined to express a present reality of 'the Balkans', has, in fact, its inspirational roots in hindsight. This tendency of 'looking back' at 'the Balkans' is strongly intertwined with a temporal criterion of the linear and European vector of time of the prosperous civilized and the backward barbarian. In Rathenau's and Mowrer's statement, there are already explicit traits of this. "'Balkanization' not only had come to denote the parcelization of large and viable political units, but had also become a synonym for a reversion to the tribal, the backward, the primitive, the barbarian" (p. 3) says Todorova (1997).

It is also important to emphasize that "balkanization" entered the wider dictionary initially as a journalistic notion, but it transcended journalism and entered academia throughout the twentieth century. An example of this is Aurel Braun (1983) who treats Albania, Bulgaria, Greece, Romania, Turkey, and Yugoslavia as too dissimilar in terms of ethnicity, culture, economy, political systems, and national self-conception for them to be treated systematically. As a scholar of Political Science and International Relations, Braun adopts a classical realist attitude of seeing these countries determent to fragmentations and divisions. He considers the pre-WWII history of these countries as too frequently justifying this image; therefore, Braun's (1983) prophecy is that "... if the Balkan swords have been returned to their scabbards, they are yet to be turned into ploughshares" (p. 1).

Bideleux and Jeffries (1998) who by disagreeing with what they call "Balkan historians" such as Peter Sugar (1997) and Wayne Vucinich (1965) and while not describing what they mean by that, both call for a consideration of various cultural, demographic, economic and even natural-environmental factors, but this not with the intention of giving a critical view on 'balkanization' but instead with the intention on stating that it then

> ... becomes clear that much that has been attributed to 'the Ottoman Impact' was already in existence or incipient or merely inherited and perpetuated (rather than initiated) by the Ottoman rule. The Ottoman conquest presented the Balkan peoples with a convenient and superficially persuasive scapegoat, which has helped divert attention from the way in which their own cultures, institutions, rulers and histories must 'share the blame' for their deteriorating predicament, and indeed, for the ease with which the Ottomans subjugated the Balkans for several centuries. (p. 39)

In other words, for Bideleux and Jeffries, the state of division and disintegration of 'the Balkans' is the cause and the effect itself. Perhaps, as they quote Stavrianos (2000), "... the location and the accessibility of the peninsula which encouraged frequent and prolonged invasions" (Bideleux & Jeffries, 1998, p. 30) might have also had an impact. Hence, there is no other more classical element than nature itself to naturalize 'balkanization'. Should one aim at simplifying Bideleux's and Jeffrie's observations, one could end up with the impression that among others, the geography of the Peninsula and the inherent nature of the people living there, are naturally made to be as they are – deteriorative. From this then, the contextualization of 'balkanization' within the Balkan Peninsula has on one side kept constrained the term from being applied to other fields of thought, but has on the other used the geography itself for naturalizing more the supposed impossibility of the region for any unification and harmony. This opens the way to the importance of the spatial criteria in the constitution of 'balkanization' which gains its visibility further on as the expression was slowly taking a distance from 'the Balkans' geographically and being applied to other spaces.

2.2.2 'Balkanization' in the aftermath of the Second World War: Recontextualization

The first ascriptions of 'Balkanization' as detached from the Balkan Peninsula had already taken place during the WWII, although the trend will gain its visibility after the end of the war. In 1941, the U.S. Supreme Court while handling a case of "appeal from a judgment affirming a conviction and sentence for transportation of liquor without permit", stated that "the absence of local restrains on interstate business would end up in "balkanizing American commerce, trade, and industry" (Duckworth v. Arkansas, 1941). 'Balkanization' of trade is again mentioned in another case ruled by the U.S. Supreme Court, to describe "trade barriers so high between the states that the stream of interstate commerce cannot flow over them" (H. P. Hood & Sons, 1949), while in another case of 1979 "economic Balkanization" was described as that which "had plagued relations among the Colonies and later among the States under the Articles of Confederation" (Hughes v. Oklahoma , 1979).

However, following the aftermath of WWII, it would have been expected that the creation of SFRY that proved a counter-process to fragmentation, would dissolve or challenge the connotations related to 'balkanization'. The SFRY, as a federation symbolic to the slogan of the Communist Party of Yugoslavia "brotherhood and unity", presented the world with an image of a peaceful and harmonious coexistence of more than ten ethnic groups and a contrary trend to disintegration. Whether or not Yugoslavia stood up to the image of a hybrid socialist paradise prophesized by its leader Tito, or it was merely an idealized and romanticized propaganda beneath which nuances of chauvinism were 'sugar-coated', is a matter of other discussions which do not cast doubt on the fact that in 1945 the Federal People's Republic of Yugoslavia (FPRY) was officially established and it joined together six federal states known as People's Republics.

Completely contrary to this though, with the wind of decolonization processes of the time, there were some other series of writings on 'balkanization' which not only contributed to the reinforcement of the meaning that had until then been built, but also to a certain extent to the detachment of 'balkanization' from 'the Balkans' as a region, or better said from any geographical connotation related to the Balkan Peninsula. With detachment, I do not mean the breakage of any ties of meanings between 'balkanization' and the Balkan Peninsula, as again, this would hot have been possible considering that onomastically 'the Balkans' are a geography among others. With detachment, I refer to a disregard to that geographical component or a lack of its presence while placing and using 'balkanization' into a set of other different contexts and settings.

An example of this is William Edward Burghardt Du Bois, known as a famous American Pan-Africanist who mostly dedicated his writings to the black people everywhere in their struggle against colonialism and neo-colonialism. He uses 'balkanization' to denote the parcelization of the colonized territories as a result of foreign influences with the intention of keeping them easily under control and rule (Du Bois Edward Burghardt, 1945, p. 72). As quoted in Bell, Grosholz, and Stewart (2013), Kwame Nkrumah, who served as the first president and prime minister of Ghana, drew on Du Bois's writings and considered 'balkanization' as one of the most important tools of neo-colonialism, while considering as its counterpart a process of political and economic integration (p. 237). Further, Godfrey Mwakikagile (2010) who is a specialist in African studies, states that to him and to Kwame Nkrumah as a great crusader for African unity, "balkanization and colonization are twins" (p. 544). Represented as an undesirable state, 'balkanization' is again characterized by an image of separateness and foreign vulnerability, this time even situated in a completely different continent, the African one.

Similarly, Hama (1974) applies 'balkanization' hand-in-hand with imperialism and neocolonialism. He considers 'balkanization' an evident and natural opposition to a unified Pan-African cooperation, an obstacle to an independent Africa, a *major problem* (Pallister, 1977) to be more precise. As such, in the writings of all these authors, 'balkanization' did not only stand for an opposition to unity, integration or harmonious relations, but further as a hindrance to prosperity, development, and independence.

The tendency of equating 'balkanization' with colonization reached the twentieth-first century too. In 2011, Lubo Mitev, himself a Bulgarian, wrote in his blog on "The Balkanization of Africa". Stating incorrectly that 'balkanization' derived from the events that saw the splitting of Yugoslavia into seven states (while the construction of 'balkanization' took place quite prior to that), Mitev (2011) asks whether balkanization can be applied to the international relations' then actuality of South Sudan's endeavors for independence, the protests in Egypt, and Tunisia. He wraps up by saying that "... whether North Africa is experiencing a revolution cannot be doubted. Yet, whether this will lead to balkanization, can be. One can only hope that, if any breaking up of territories does occur, it will not have the same consequences as it did in the former Yugoslavia" (Mitev, 2011).

Of an interesting focus here is the prism of 'balkanization' as antagonistic to independence. Although I will not go deeper into elaborating on this now, it is worth noticing that it seems almost oxymoronic that 'balkanization' stands for both, a lack and disrupt of sovereignty, self-government, and autonomy, but also for the absence of communal harmony, common, and collective functionality. 'Balkanization' is an obstacle to individualism and self-sufficiency, as much as one to collectivism and unity. It is an inadequate for both, particularism and universalism. As mentioned before and as further seen, this puts 'balkanization' and 'the Balkans' on a different category of othering, one that relies on confusion and ambiguity more as transcendental rather than replacing of pejoratives.

Continuing further, equating 'balkanization' with the German word "*Kleinstaaterei*" (a system of mini-states), Eric Hobsbawm (1990), considers both words as parts of the dictionary of political insults (p. 21). He elaborates on Mazzini's principle on nations based on their sizes, from which the concept of *Grossstaten* [From German: large-scale nations] emerged, the only ones to which the principle of nationality applied. As opposed to these large-scale nations, *Kleinstaaterei* [From German: small-scale nations] as a pejorative notion used by the German nationalists to denote the territorial fragmentation of Germany evolved. Hobsbawm includes 'balkanization' in the middle of elaborating on his argument, notes the interchangeability between it and "kleinstaaterei" and the pejorative nuances that both still retain, and as such, almost naturally places 'balkanization' in a complete different context which is not only physical as he is referring to Germany, but also one of a political theory on nationality. We will further see that similar to this fashion, 'balkanization' being decontextualized does not refer only to it being physically 'transplanted' into another space, but also timely and conceptually expanded and transformed into a wide encompassing term of different phenomena.

Best descriptive of this is Ayn Rand's lecture titled "Global Balkanization" (1977). She picks 'the Balkans' and 'balkanization' as examples of tribalism, products of irrationalism and collectivism, a history of endless and bloody warfare, and enormously anti-intellectual freedom, to 'scold' the world which is "moving towards disaster" (Rand, 1977, p. 3). Rand (1977) begins her lecture by asking the audience: "Have you ever wondered about the process of the collapse of a civilization? .... The specific means by which the accumulated knowledge and achievement of centuries vanish from the Earth?" (p. 3). She is quite bold in warning of an upcoming 'apocalypse' which is threatening the Western civilization, jeopardizing objective reason, self-interest, individual rights, laissez-faire capitalism, and ethical egoism among others, all essential components of the philosophical system she developed and called *Objec-*

tivism[8]. It is of no surprise that she not even once sees in this change of the geopolitical scene of the time a potential for improvement, or even a normality of change that naturally accompanies systems of different kinds. Instead, her lecture is associated with a strong, continuous and unapologetic tone of belittling, condescending, patronizing and even ridiculing nuances. Her article is not just a matter of a different point of view and personal values and principles, but of a language of offense and denigration.

Refereeing to a list of examples of movements seeking for political independence and autonomy, among which she mentions the continuous disputes between Serbs and Croats and the unresolved ferment among Macedonians, Rand (1977) chooses to describe these incentives as coming from "tribes and sub-tribes, which most of the world has never heard of – since they have achieved no distinction to hear about" (p. 4). However, she goes further in correcting herself and stating that there is a certain kind of distinction that these "tribes and sub-tribes" have achieved – "*a history of endless, bloody warfare*" (Rand, 1977, p. 4). It indeed is true that in her lecture she also includes a few other European examples, such as the Corsicean, Basques, and Bretons movements in France; Welsh and Scottish "nationalists" in the United Kingdom; Catalonians in Spain; French-speaking Walloons and Dutch-speaking Flemish in Belgium, and others (Rand, 1977, p. 4). Nonetheless, Rand picks particularly 'the Balkans' as specimens to learn from:

> As to the stagnation under tribal rule - take a look at the Balkans. At the start of this century, the Balkans were regarded as *the disgrace of Europe*. Six or eight tribes, plus a number of sub-tribes with unpronounceable names, were crowded on the Balkan peninsula, engaging in endless wars among themselves or being conquered by stronger neighbours or practicing violence for the sake of violence over some microscopic language differences. (pp. 12-13)

On a similar line, in an article of Patrick Glynn "The age of balkanization" (1993) in an American monthly magazine of opinion and a pivotal voice in American intellectual life, 'balkanization' transcends the territorial divisions and denotes social separatism and fragmentation, divisions by ethnic group, race, religion, gender, and sexual orientation. He also expresses his lack of surprise for this situation touching first 'the Balkans' among others, while he states that "the most dramatic manifestation of the change is found, *of course*, in the countries that used to be known as Yugoslavia and Czechoslovakia" (Glynn, 1993). Glynn (1993) draws an analogy between 'balkanization' and Quebec's secessionism in Canada, Scottish separatists in the United Kingdom, tensions between the north and the south in Italy, rebellious youths and ethnic hatred in Germany, France and Britain, the growing threat to the US's 'melting pot', the controversial doctrine of "multiculturalist education", and the "postmodernist" philosophy. From his long list of denunciations and complaints, the only question left to ask seems to be whether there is anything 'good' left that 'the Balkans' stand for.

Glynn (1993) seems unable to answer this, but he surely answers who stands on the other 'good' dichotomous side of the barbarians, and that *of course* – to use Glynn's language, would be America as "the most rationally constituted of nations" and the West. Hence, he concludes: "We are now in an age that will move either toward ever greater fragmentation and violence or toward the ever wider spread of the tolerance and rationality by which *we in*

8 Objecitvism is considered a comprehensive philosophy, including an epistemology and a theory of art, developed by Ayn Rand, based on "conception of metaphysical realism, rationality, ethical egoism (rational self-interest), individual rights, laissez-faire capitalism, and art" (Badhwar & Long, 2010).

the West have learned to live and prosper" (Glynn, 1993). He finds that the root of the problem lies in "the very large and very deep question of human identity" (Glynn, 1993), which as the master-idea of Western civilization is essentially relaying in the faculty of reason and intellectual seriousness, and which 'the Balkans' seem to obviously lack. "The ferocious wars in the Balkans is but one manifestation of a reemergent barbarism apparent in many corners of the earth" says Glynn (1993).

Glynn's relatively short article is a bold and explicit elaboration on quite a few elements associated with 'the Balkans' and 'balkanization' – the negativity of standing as the 'other' of civilization, as the threat to it, a prey of uncontrollable reason and a believer of myths, a disgrace and an undeservedly assigned burden to the West and the U.S. which different from 'the Balkans' stands for "... the heir and the perfecter of the great Roman idea of *civis*" (Glynn, 1993). Glynn's article is associated with a tone of defensiveness, melancholy for 'the old times', and a dislike to those who challenge 'the order'. He is quite visibly upset even to postmodern tendencies of eliciting a disintegration of what he calls "general truths" (Glynn, 1993) and which tendencies he deliberately describes as 'balkanized' in nature, but this leaves us to think of a deep personal rebellion to the changing world towards which Glynn himself has expressive reluctances.

A similar trend of relating 'balkanization' with nuances of dehumanization that shake the very foundations of 'human nature' and a panic from the destruction of any human achievement hitherto, is put forward by Harold Bloom (1994). Also from the United States, Bloom relates 'balkanization' to an apocalyptic image of literature. "Finding myself now surrounded by professors of hip-hop; by clones of Gallic-Germanic theory; by ideologues of gender and of various sexual persuasions; by multiculturalists unlimited, I realize that the Balkanization of literary studies is irreversible" he declared (Bloom, 1994, p. 517). Going a step further than Glynn, Bloom further adds to 'balkanization' nuances of kitsch, bad taste, and lack of aesthetics. In defining literature as "not merely language; it is also the will to figuration, the motive for metaphor that Nietzsche once defined as the desire to be different, the desire to be elsewhere" (1994, p. 12), Bloom seems to contradict as much as to support his quest for a *status quo* on one side, as well as his revolt towards the threatening change he writes about. As Todorova (1997) comments on this, "Bloom introduced 'balkanization' to mourn everything he detested in his discipline" (p. 36).

Glynn, Rand, and Bloom, present a chaotic and anarchic future that threatens the systematic, the civilized, and the functional "Western canon". They all sound overwhelmed by a wave of *saudade* [From Portuguese: A profound nostalgic and melancholic emotional state due to the loss of something or someone that one loves and which might never return] towards a magnificent past that is doomed to hit the iceberg, and while the captains refuse to leave the ship, the others seem careless to even notice that they are drowning. However, what leaves for a lot of skepticism and incredulity towards their claims, and what the Western countries could have questioned, is the nearly narcissistic nuances associating the three of them in their self-perceptions as the saviors, the awaked, the enlightened, and the courageous to face this new and threating wind of time. Hence, Glyn's, Rand's, and Bloom's articles are about them as personas and personalities before they come to be anything about 'the Balkan' and 'balkanization'. This does not demand any special effort to notice.

In between the field of economy, trade, and literature, and the essential idea of humanity and civilization, 'balkanization' has been applied to a wide range of different fields of thoughts and disciplines. In the famous *Politics* (published initially in 1997) of Andrew Heywood, a principal examiner for political ideologies and global politics, 'balkanization' is unsurprisingly defined in terms of fragmentation of a political unit in a collage of antagonistic entities, to which Heywood (2013) adds "as has often occurred in the Balkans" (p. 368). He further takes this definition and applies it to quasi-autonomous non-governmental organization "quangos" which he considers a "notoriously loose and confusing term" (Heywood, 2013, p. 368). Elaborating on one of the criticisms of quangos, Heywood (2013) states that "they foster balkanization by making public administration more disjointed and less systematic" (p. 368).

William H. Frey (1996), a demographer, added a demographic feature to 'balkanization' relating it with the newly emerging demographic division as result of the impacts of post-1965 immigration to the United State across regions of the U.S. which, according to Frey, gave rise to separate immigration and internal migration patterns. In another article titled "Immigration and Demographic Balkanization: Towards one America or Two?", Frey (1999) continues to hold on to his argument that the immigration of the time in the U.S., along with the ongoing internal migration movements

> … are creating a demographic balkanization that portends increasing divisions across broad regions of the country. If the new trends continue, today's multi-ethnic immigrant gateway regions may very well turn into individual melting pots in which different Hispanic, Asian, African American, Native American, and Anglo groups coexist and intermarry while still retaining some elements of their own national heritage. (p. 79)

Frey is of particular interest due to conveying through 'balkanization' a regional divide between areas with a diverse population as a result of the immigration flow on one side, and homogenous population of regions where internal migration prevails, as it analogously encapsulates again that dissolution and enforcement of dichotomies transmitted through 'balkanization' – enclaves of the same substance patterns inside (homogenous or heterogeneous), but irreconcilable among each other. As such, it remains an undesirable state, as Frey (1999) states that "some readers may view this new demographic balkanization with trepidation since it does not conform to the single 'one America' ideal" (p. 89).

Srdjan Jovanović Weiss (2006) lists a number of 'balkanized' spheres such as the balkanization of law which denotes perceptions of emerging gender enclaves in a traditionally male profession; balkanization of international law that refers to the problem of many different countries' interpretations of laws that are supposed to be applied internationally; urban balkanization in the sense of gated communities, while by allowing some part of society to exclude itself spatially there's a chance for conditioning a further social fragmentation processes of inequality that will in effect become social exclusion; also Internet balkanization indicating the Internet being divided into separate enclaves or sometimes used to refer to the divergence over time of human languages, programming languages, and data file formats.

Weiss, who originally comes from Serbia, is famous for his work in architecture and design by revealing the potential constructive aspects of 'balkanization' specifically in these fields. 'Balkanization' "also has positive aspects, it depicts political self-determination: not in order to fight, but rather to maintain its differentiation, its autonomy … it is a chance for the small" says Weiss (2011). He focuses on 'balkanization' as a spatial-political concept through a prism that conjuncts post-communist architectural projects and political text (Weiss, 2007). Weiss (2017) considers the "architecture of balkanisation" a strategic force in the reorganization of territories and looks at spatial strategies acts as processes of 'balkanisation' which then produce knowledge through their specific organizational and operational practices. While Weiss (2011) expresses architects' disappointment with how desolate corporate architecture has become, he asks "what would happen if we unleashed the Balkanization *virus* onto corporate monoliths".

Whether Weiss decontextualizes 'balkanization' or not, is more contentious in his case as he does talk about the architecture of these post-communist countries known as 'the Balkans'. In this way, Weiss keeps strings attached to the geography of the region, although conceptually speaking, he does provide with new knowledge contexts, those of architecture and design in which he applies 'balkanization'. However, as already said (see subsection 2.2.2 'Balkanization' in the aftermath of the Second World War: Recontextualization), decontextualization, in this case, does not refer to a complete extrication of 'balkanization' from the geography of 'the Balkans'. This is impossible even semantically in the first place, and then conceptually as well, as the negativity (or positivity in Weiss's example) conveyed through it has inevitably the geographic disintegration as a baseline. Hence, recontextualization might be a better term to use.

An example of this is also Grubačić (2010), an academic with a Yugoslavian background, who elaborates on how 'balkanization' essentially came to be a manifestation of pejorative metaphors based on stereotyping on 'the Balkans', but he himself then decontextualizes the word and further builds on 'the Balkans' as a metaphorical threat to the centralized and coercive systems (p. 210). He recognizes that "'the Balkans' and 'balkanization' are presented and projected to the world opinion as nothing but 'historical residue of 'primitive nationalism'" (Grubačić, 2010, p. 210), and asks "[w]ho are the real barbarians?" if comparing the courageous example of Yugoslavia to the Euro-American massacres of Arab and Jewish people, Amero-Indians, and historical legacy of feudal wars, colonialism, slavery, and genocide (Grubačić, 2010, p. 211).

Although acknowledging the Eurocentrism in constructing an otherness through 'balkanization' instead of deconstructing of what or why is there a need for distinguishing "real barbarians", Grubačić is convincingly looking for another context to place 'balkanization', undress it from the quintessential barbarism that it stands for by putting it 'somewhere else, just not here'. Therefore, he distinguishes between "balkanization from above" which he calls "political balkanophobia" and considers it to be an invention of European colonial modernity that represents the elite response towards autonomous processes from below with the intention of territorial unification of regional identity; and "balkanization from below" giving to it democratic nuances as an alternative process to centralization, remarkably threatening for the emerging large, centralized, and coercive systems (Grubačić, 2010, pp. 257-258). As such, Grubačić presents one of the classical examples of deconstructing and constructing 'balkanization' at the same time.

Even prior to Weiss and Grubačić, Stjepan Meštrović (1994) approaches 'balkanization' through a poststructuralist and deconstructivist angle, yet in itself much constructing and decontextualizing simultaneously. Meštrović (1994) recognizes 'balkanization' as an "alleged evil" (p. viii) constructed by the West, intended to denote to those people in 'the Balkans' who seem to slaughter each other, as opposed to the civilized Americans, French, and British. According to him, there is no good reason to understand 'balkanization', that is the breaking up of a unit into increasingly smaller units that are hostile to each other, as something that must apply only to 'the Balkans' (Meštrović, 1994, pp. viii-ix). However, Meštrović (1994) does not seem to revolt against the reductionism associated with 'balkanization', but to rather further develop it in a way, by considering 'balkanization' a genuinely postmodern phenomenon – if one understands postmodernism to be a rebellion against the grand-narratives of Enlightenment, and if one has it in mind how postmodernism vanquished Enlightenment rationalism and left democracy without secure philosophical foundations with its doubt and deconstruction. He wraps up with a prophecy:

> Western Balkanization threatens not only the existence of the UN, NATO, the EC and a number of other globalizing organizations. It also threatens race relations, the relations between the sexes, and the very fabric of liberal institutions built on the remnants of the Enlightenment tradition.... I predict that the process of Balkanization in the former Yugoslavia has not yet run its course and will probably cause still more fragmentation and violence ... and finally, that a form of Balkanization will tear apart and affect both East and West. (Meštrović, 1994, p. 179)

However, other examples are not as dubious as that of Weiss, Grubačić and Meštrović. An article published by the U.S. Chamber of Commerce Foundation as the non-profit branch of the business-oriented American lobbying group United States Chamber of Commerce was titled as "Say No to the Balkanization of the Internet" (Cooper R., 2015). The article refers to how the international community accesses and shares digital data while stating that a 'balkanized' Internet is

> ... one that lacks a centralized authority guiding Internet development but is instead composed of a confusing and cumbersome patchwork of laws, rights, access, and all the minutia that make-up cyberspace.... Balkanization raises virtual borders in what was intended to be a vehicle for sharing knowledge without regard for national borders. (Cooper R., 2015)

Referring to the leak of confidential information and the 'cloud memory' as quite recent phenomena, Cooper (2015) is determined to defend the Internet from being 'balkanized' and transformed into a prey of national regulations and surveillance. He says that this would be "a bad thing. It would frustrate innovation, slow economic growth, and limit individual freedoms".

Although the following two examples might belong to literature that has followed as questioning this application of 'balkanization' to the Internet challenges of the twentieth-first century, placing the same here is relevant for the logical flow of the argument. As a response to the above-mentioned dangers of "Internet balkanization", Sergio Alves (2014a) calls for ending the use of the term if not for its tongue-twisting nuances, then at least for its pejorative connotations as he refers to Todorova's work on this. Alves (2014a) will reappear again as shared in one of the tweets under Chapter 3 where the 'balkanization' of the Internet will further prove to be one of the most prevailing connotations associated with the 'balkanization' discourse. Similarly, although not from the same prism of historical sensitivity towards the derogatory nature of the word, but rather from its debatable nature, Maurer and Morgus, in an article titled "Stop calling Decentralization of the Internet 'Balkanization'" (2014), call "to move from the alarmist "Balkanization" to a more detailed analysis of fragmentation and diversity".

As seen, chronologically 'balkanization' became a description of many phenomena and processes that were born as attached to 'the Balkans' as a region, but then grew to be attached to political and social situations as detached geographically from 'the Balkans'. Among the above-mentioned decontextualized notions, the diverse features added to it include class and race differences in an Indian context. Although in lack of more precise information, it is worth mentioning a "Political Ideologies: Syllabus" (2013) of the Rai University, which addresses 'balkanization' as a caste-ridden and racially conscious divided society into clusters, each entitled with disproportional possessions, careers, or other types of opportunities.

Quite surprising as much as not, the *National Post* upgraded even the field of gastronomy by adding to its jargon 'balkanization'. In a published article titled "Deconstructed Dish: Burgers get Balkanized", Pollack (2011) quite impatiently waiting to try an unusual Bosnian recipe for burgers, says: "so I dig in, and it's foreign and familiar all at once". What Pollack brings as especially visible, is precisely that naturality of the word 'balkanization' on, literally, the dining table. As we can see, she is just one of the many doing this.

While opposing tendencies to these naturalizing propensities also exist (as the next section shows), most of the literature below resembles retrospective examinations. By no means are such examinations essential in understanding the pathway which brought to this decontextualization, however, there seems to be a lack of 'monitoring research' on how the term is being used today. Parallel to these genealogical endeavors, 'balkanization' seems to continue to be constructed as attached or detached from 'the Balkans', but nearly always as a pejorative. The most recent U.S. elections proved this. The internet seems overflowed by articles that speak of a "balkanized America" referring to Donald's Trump victory through 'balkanizing' the American electorate (Rothman, 2016); the American media (Evans, 2016; Herzfeld, 2017; Rushlau, 2017) the American education (Liberalteacher, 2016), that can result with 'balkanizing' the global financial market (Weber, 2017), politics (Suntrup, 2017), 'balkanization and encouragement' of race-based decision-making (Clegg, 2017), and even with civil war (Berman, 2016). We see that 'balkanization' and 'The Balkans' continue to frighten, while reading, among others, Berman (2016) who states:

> When the battle leaves the playing field and enters the realm of Balkanization, we have entered a dangerous place, that America only emerged from 150 years ago. Yes, that's the Civil War to which I'm referring … today's politics of Balkanization is arguably much worse than the relics of the bloodiest conflict ever to take place on American soil.

These and other cases call for a critical examination of the 'balkanization' discourse who is indeed inclusive of retrospective genealogical scrutiny which reveals a process of becoming (as presented in the next section), but also transcending into the current mutations that the discourse is going through (see Chapter 3), hence avoiding the risk of being stuck in historical investigation of the past only.

2.3 Deconstructing 'Balkanization': Balkanism

After an awkward pause, Bast extended his hand. Chronicler hesitated for a bare moment before reaching out quickly, as if he were sticking his hand into a fire. Nothing happened, both of them seemed moderately surprised. "Amazing, isn't it?" Kvothe addressed them bitingly. "Five fingers and flesh with blood beneath. One could almost believe that on the other end of that hand lay a person of some sort".

Kvothe in *The name of the Wind* by Patrick Rothfuss (2008, p. 45)

The end of the twentieth-century brought a deconstructing angle on 'balkanization', built on a postmodern and poststructuralist tradition of thought. These tendencies have necessarily called for a search of descent of the concept, tracing back its path of becoming, hence of naturalization and habituation. As leading all these deconstructing incentives is Todorova (1997) who considers 'the Balkans' as a discourse of producing knowledge and power over the Balkan as a region. By revealing how a deceptive intellectual tradition constructed and discursively created 'the Balkans', she considers "Balkan" and what derives from it, including 'balkanization', as *nomen nudum*, the taxonomical term used to denote a name "which has no standing because it was introduced without publication of the full description demanded by the rules governing botanical and zoological nomenclature" (Todorova, 1997, p. 37). By questioning the naturality surrounding the different semantic variations of the same such as 'the Balkans' or 'balkanization' which are the product and the molders of discourses on/of the same, Todorova established the term "balkanism" and a tradition of critical examinations on 'the Balkans' and 'balkanization' as revealed below.

Todorova first coined the term *balkanism* in her book *Imagining the Balkans* (1997). In another section of a book "Balkanism and Postcolonialism, or On the Beauty of the Airplane View" (2010), she stated that she found to her

> ... surprise and delight that balkanism was an uninhabited category, something exceptionally rare in humanities. I have no claim to have coined it (so in that sense it is not a neologism) but the only person who had employed it before was an obscure early twentieth-century author who had used it (in its plural form as balkanisms) as a synonym for the pejorative attributes of the Balkans as a region. (p. 176)

2.3.1 Balkanism and Orientalism: Differences

Todorova (2010) claims that balkanism expresses the idea that explanatory approaches to phenomena in Southeastern Europe, that is, 'the Balkans', often rest upon a discourse (in the Foucauldian sense) or a stable system of stereotypes (for the ones who shun the notion of 'discourse')" (p. 176). After this followed a general academic wave of debates on balkanism as an academic field or discipline while exploring its connections with the Orientalism of Edward Said. Said (1979) as a public intellectual, considered as the founder of postcolonial studies (Young, 1990, p. 1), famous for his book on *Orientalism* (1979), considers Orientalism as "... a style of thought based upon an ontological and epistemological distinction made between 'the Orient' and (most of the time) 'the Occident'" (p. 2), a pervasive Western tradition, both academic and artistic, that has produced knowledge and hence facilitated the hegemony of the West towards the Orient.

Clarifications on this point are also essential to this thesis in order to position balkanism in the academia. While Todorova recognizes Said's work and states the obvious similarities between balkanism and Orientalism in that both are discursive formations and metaphors which shape attitudes and actions towards their subjects ('the Balkans' in the case of balkanism, and the Orient in the case of Orientalism), Todorova (2010) summarizes the differences between the two in the geographic and historical concreteness of 'the Balkans' unlike the traveling and mostly metaphorical and symbolic nature of the Orient; the mostly Christian composition of 'the Balkans' versus the largely Muslim Orient; and the lack of a colonial predicament for 'the Balkans' (pp. 176-177). Todorova objects the application of the postcolonialism of 'the Balkans' as she does not consider the Ottoman, Habsburg, or Romanov empires as colonial ones. While she acknowledges their legacy, especially the longest one that of the Ottoman Empire, she lists several features which question colonialism in 'the Balkans', such as

> [f]irst, there is no abyss or institutional/legal distinction between metropole and dependencies. Secondly, there is no previous stable entity which colonizes … Thirdly, there was no amelioration complex, no civilizing mission obsession comparable to the French or the English colonial project. Fourthly, there is no hegemonic cultural residue from the Ottoman Empire comparable to the linguistic and general cultural hegemony of English in the Indian subcontinent and elsewhere, or of French in Africa and Indochina. (Todorova, 2010, p. 179)

Todorova (1996) insists on balkanism as a distinct discourse, "seemingly identical, but actually only a similar phenomenon" (p. 10) to Orientalism. In contrast to Said's unbridgeable dichotomy of the West and the East, she considers 'the Balkans' to be a transitory concept, "a bridge between East and West, between Europe and Asia … between stages of growth, and this invokes labels as semi-developed, semi-colonial, semi-civilized, etc." (Todorova, 1996, p. 10). Although she never addresses 'balkanization' as a term, Suzana Mileska (2007) approaches what she calls "Balkan subjectivity" and 'the Balkans' as a "neither", claiming that "… neither is not about going through an ultimate process of acquiring some kind of a desired identity opposed to the pre-destined one, but is marked by a restless chain of negotiations" (p. 181). Todorova (1996) goes even further by adding that on certain aspects balkanism has evolved even against or despite Orientalism. 'The Balkans' being after all in Europe, white, and predominantly Christian, have even served as a "substitute for the emotional discharge that Orientalism provided, exempting the West from the charges of racism colonialism, Eurocentrism and Christian tolerance against Islam" (p. 21).

However, Neuburger (2004) states that "Orientalism holds an untold explanatory context in the Balkans" and that "orientalization and mongrelization of and within the Balkans were not mutually exclusive" (p. 5). Along the same lines, to Todorova's claim that balkanism is an independent rhetorical paradigm and not "merely a sub-species of orientalism" (1994, p. 454; 1996, p. 10), Milica Bakić-Hayden and Robert M. Hayden (1992) express their disagreement by considering balkanism as a "variation on the orientalist theme" instead (pp. 1-15). Bakić-Hayden (1995) agrees that "while it is important to recognize the specific rhetoric of balkanism, however, it would be difficult to understand it outside the overall orientalist context since it shares an underlying logic and rhetoric with orientalism" (p. 920). She calls this gradation of 'Orients' "nesting orientalism" which as she states,

> … is a pattern of reproduction of the original dichotomy upon which Orientalism is premised. In this pattern, Asia is more 'East' or 'other' than eastern Europe; within eastern Europe itself this gradation is reproduced with the Balkans perceived as most 'eastern'; within the Balkans there are similarly constructed hierarchies. (Bakić-Hayden, 1995, p. 918)

According to Katherine Elizabeth Fleming (2000), Milica Bakić-Hayden and Hayden managed to "rehistoricize" Said through comparing a colonial world to a postcolonial one as "… language of orientalism still retains its force in noncolonial settings, pointing out that now, in the postcolonial world, it has not as a discourse of power disappeared along with the institutions of colonialism" (p. 1224). However, in her endeavors of reflecting on the links between Orientalism and balkanism, Fleming, agreeing with Todorova, puts the emphasis of the differences between the two on the lack of history and tradition of West European academic interest in 'the Balkans' that is comparable to the Orient. She sees these differences in terms of chronology, longevity, style, aim, and quantity, and even suggests that

> … we must view the term academic with caution, for the vast majority of such writing is in actuality produced not by academicians in the strictest sense of the term but rather by Balkan 'experts' whose expertise derives from their experience as journalists, travellers, or political strategists. (Fleming, 2000, p. 1226)

Hence, Fleming (2000) argues that "Orientalist cannot simply be a catchall category" (p. 1231), and she agrees with Todorova in that Orientalism and balkanism "are not the same thing" (p. 1225). Importantly she concludes that "while it is Said who has made it possible for us to even consider such a discourse as 'Balkanism', Said's model alone cannot show us what it is" (Fleming, 2000, pp. 1232-1233).

Fleming (2000) also considers Vesna Goldsworthy's (1998) call on attention upon West's influence on the Balkan and the 'imaginative colonization' which "compared to traditional imperialism or economic colonialism, appears to be an innocent process: a cultural great power seizes and exploits the resources of an area, while imposing new frontiers on its mind-map and creating ideas which, reflected back, have the ability to reshape reality" (p. 2) to have a valid premise, but to also be ultimately a bit overblown (p. 1221). However, according to Goldsworthy herself (1998) "the process of literary colonisation, in its stages and its consequences, is not unlike real colonisation" (p. 2). "The Balkanisation of the Balkans continues to take place precisely because 'Balkan' always refers to someone other than ourselves" says Goldsworthy (1998, p. ix) as she pulls together different literary pieces related to 'the Balkans' and examines those in relation to colonial and imperialist implications. In her introduction, Goldsworthy (1998) claims that her book "seeks to explore the way in which one of the world's most powerful nations exploited the resources of the Balkans to supply its literary and entertainment industries" (p. 2).

Although accusing this constructed otherness of 'the Balkans', some years after her book was published, Goldsworthy herself wrote an article where she considers globalization as possible of promoting and enabling 'balkanization'. As it appears, she follows the discourse she intended to deconstruct, while describing 'balkanization' as "a particular kind of fragmentation where the fragments are mutually hostile and in competition with each other" (Goldsworthy, 2003) and considers the supposed nationalism of these entities to possibly be growing as a response to globalization, in relation to 'the other' American, European, or Asian.

Comparably to Goldsworthy's emphasis on colonialization, the Croatian philosopher and semiotician Srećko Horvat (2013), in an interview for Revolting Europe referred as a "process of self-colonization" to the internalization of the inferiority by 'the Balkans'. The interview which is given right after Croatia became the twenty-eighth member of the EU elaborates on EU's membership processes considered by 'the Balkans' themselves as the "promise of civilization" that will allow them to escape their "own demons, nationalism and balkanization" (Horvat, 2013). Therefore, he refers to Croatia's EU member state status as a "pseudo-integration" that derived from the imaginative blackmail of "If we do not enter in the EU, we will remain in the Balkans" (Horvat, 2013).

However, again defending Todorova's instance on differentiating balkanism from orientalism due to essential differences in their lack or presence of colonial history, Andrew Hammond (2007) argues that while the similarities of balkanism and orientalism are indisputable, the divergence of these two discourses lays in a few elements – the lack of a role as a clear and powerful opposite that the Orient plays in relation to Europe and European civilization, hence 'the Balkans' is 'the other' from within Europe which "… represent a Europe disfigured by the presence of the 'non-European', serving to illustrate the ease with which the self can be subverted" (p. 205); the lack of antiquity due to the absence of an imperial culture which has having resulted not only with the absence of any positive comments, but also with the idea that "… the region has nothing worth commenting on at all" (pp. 206-207); the next difference has to do with the gendering of the two regions and the propensity to feminize the Middle East, while on the other side emphasizing the patriarchy of 'the Balkans', its maleness and 'noble savagery'" (p. 208); finally, the third difference is related to the second one and lays in the lack of sexual allure that travelers found in the region where, as Hammond says, "… even the Balkan female is defeminized" (p. 210).

In terms of semantics, Hammond uses interchangeably "South-East Europe" and "the Balkans", himself not distinguishing between the two. He refers to neologisms such as "to balkanise", "balkanised", and "balkanisation" only once in his article, confirming that they refer to "… the process of dividing a unified entity into radically smaller and mutually hostile units" (Hammond, 2007, p. 213). Hammond (2007) well summarizes this into "… pitting heterogeneity against singleness" (2007, p. 213) which rose as a result of the region's nations fighting against the Ottoman Empire and for their independence. This, for the empirical powers and Britain in particular, for which fragmentation would be something to fear, "… was viewed not as a libertarian triumph, but as a descent into barbarism and tribalism" (Hammond, 2007, p. 213).

Nevertheless, Hammond aims to challenge Todorova's claim that 'the Balkans', with their "unimaginative concreteness, and their almost total lack of wealth" (Todorova, 1996, p. 12), have only exceptionally been associated with any nuances or romanticism. For this, he refers particularly to Edith Durham's *High Albania* (1985), but ceases to elaborate in depth the type of romanticism that he believes 'the Balkans' are associated with and does not mention romanticism throughout the rest of his article. Moreover, considering his claims that 'the

Balkans', different from the Orient, have even been stripped away from femininity and sexual allure which he deeply elaborates, it indeed seems that 'the Balkans' have rarely been romanticized.

Lene Hansen (2006) too acknowledged 'the Balkans' as romanticized, by identifying three discourses: the Byronian Romanticism that constructed 'the Balkans' as a romantic image that should stay as such, and not be transformed but instead supported by the West in its struggles for freedom from the Ottoman Empire; the civilizational Enlightenment discourse in which 'the Balkans' yes, is different but also capable for political and economic transformation as the West, therefore again the West had a responsibility to help; and finally, a 'balkanization' discourse in which 'the Balkans' are seen as fundamentally different, isolated, threatening and incapable of any transformation associating them with an apocalyptic fatalism (p. 115).

Deriving from all of this, if considering balkanism as an academic field of its own (which I believe most of the above-written suggests), this thesis could be a balkanist research. Nevertheless, the importance of all the above-elaborated lays in acknowledging the strong connection between balkanism, Orientalism, and postcolonialism, rather than in its complete detachment and exclusionary position. The claims of the authors in distinguishing balkanism from orientalism are ones of distinguishing and disputing the total sameness between the two, the melting of one into the other, and as such, I see them as very reasonable.

2.3.2 'Balkanization' as a Western construct: Identity politics

Beyond the discussions of whether balkanism sets the ground for essential differences in relation to Said's Orientalism, others ought to follow Todorova's quest for questioning 'the Balkans' and what came with/after it. As already mentioned before (see section 1.3 Philosophy: Critique of Discourse) an example of this is David Campbell (1998) who refuses to assume "a pregiven, externally existing entity called Bosnia" (p. ix). The failure of the international community in their 1995 response to the War in Bosnia, according to Campbell, is first based on a conceptual failure, identity politics, which itself is based and grown as a part of the history of thought of the West. "What the cultural fundamentalism of Europe and the balkanization fears of America reveal is that the opposition to multiculturalism is enabled by the belief that there can and should be a necessary alignment between territory and identity, state and nation" (p. 167) says Campbell (1998). By understanding 'balkanization' as "the way in which differences are raised into 'cultural ramparts' and a social field is split 'into sects, groups, little nodes of power'" (Campbell D. , 1998, p. 167), the Western diplomacy, lacking an understanding of heterogeneous communities and inflexible in challenging its own dogmas, found itself confused in addressing the Bosnian case who seemed to not fit their discourse of national identity, nor that of multiculturalism. For Campbell (1998) "balkanization stems from the desire for a bounded community and the nostalgia for a politics of place rather than a problematization of identity politics" (p. 169), but the rigidity of perception and stereotyping is what made the international community to see this possibility as impossible for 'the Balkans'.

James der Derian (2009) claims that "… it takes only a cursory knowledge of the history of international relations to find some fault with this definition…. Nor does it take an acute sensibility to sniff out the presence of great power *telos* operating in this definition" (p. 100) of 'balkanization' which he described as the "… break-up of larger political units into smaller, mutually hostile states which are exploited or manipulated by more powerful neighbours" (p. 100). Der Derian then, problematizes the naturality of 'balkanization' and takes the effort of tracing back the discourse on 'balkanization' through an exploration of Marxist lexicon in which 'balkanization' and the national rivalries associated with it were perceived as the leftovers of the feudal system.

In a simplified summary, Campbell, der Derian, and Todorova, consider 'the Balkans' as Europe's internal other, which enabled the West to identify itself as a civilized, progressive, developed, and a superior one. Therefore, 'the Balkans', as Keyserling states (quoted in Todorova, 1997) "hadn't it existed, it would have been created" (p. 116). Unwrapping the different layers added to 'balkanization' along the way seems to resemble at least a process of cutting the distance of knowing 'the other' of 'the West', if not that of getting closer to it. As Rothfuss (2008) illustrated at the beginning of this section through the encounter of Kvothe and Bast, tracing back 'balkanization' is an attempt of de-demonizing 'the Balkans, of discovering that indeed "on *the other* end of that hand" (p. 45) there are human beings too. This is where *balkanism* comes in as an academic-explanatory approach to the discourse of 'balkanization' and 'the Balkans', part of Todorova's contribution. Although Todorova (1997) mentions *genealogy* only once while arguing "for the historicity of balkanism, which was shaped as a discourse in the early decades of the twentieth century, but whose genealogy can be traced to patterns of representation from the sixteenth century onward" (p. 193), her work and that of other authors presented above, is essentially a genealogical vocation that goes deep and back into the roots of 'balkanization' while on the way historicizing and looking upon it critically. As such, it requires a destabilization of any absolute truths, which is the core task of genealogy.

Through a genealogy of 'balkanization', Todorova and other authors which deconstructed the naturality of the discourse by tracing it back to its processes of formation and the many actors involved in those, reveal a red thread in their conclusions and which is based around the ambiguity surrounding 'the Balkans' and 'balkanization'. Whether romanticized or not, products of colonial exploitation or not, geographically concrete or not, 'the Balkans' and 'balkanization' are a subject of persistent, relentless, continuous, insoluble, and conclusionless discussions. Caught in between 'the West' and its 'other', 'balkanization' seems to stand for a category of othering, which different from the Orient, is built as a transitory phenomenon and a 'neither/nor'. It is precisely this ambiguity of definition that enforces pejorative connotations of meaning. Associated with nuances of, among others, abstruseness, differences, barbarism, tribalism, underdevelopment, non-cooperativeness, political, economic and territorial disintegration, fragmentation, parcealization, instability, unreliability, dehumanization and devastation of civilization, 'balkanization' remains to be an equivalent to a call for evacuation, fabricated externally and assigned as an extra layer to the prejudices that were already hunting 'the Balkans'.

The retrospective scrutiny applied to the 'balkanization' discourse by Todorova and others is important, but not enough. The trajectory of research should always maintain a correlation between present and past as an accompanying element. With "the present" I rather refer to a continuous now that is taking place simultaneously as I am studying 'balkanization' and writing about it. The following chapter is a tentative of getting as close as possible to the 'balkanization' discourse as presently continuing while acknowledging its important ties to the past. This acknowledges the genealogical foundation of this thesis. As Foucault says in an interview with Kritzman (1988), "… I set out from a problem expressed in the terms current today and I try to work out its genealogy. Genealogy means that I begin my analysis from a question posed in the present" (p. 262). This is exactly what has this chapter communicated. The second part of my contribution is in taking this endeavor forward and focusing in examining it in the present through van Dijk's sociocognitive discourse analysis.

I consider this to be necessary and crucial in times where the presumed naturality surrounding 'balkanization' is further enhanced by the fast pace of information flow and knowledge production. As Castells (2010) suggests, "… flows of messages and images between networks constitute the basic thread of our social structure.… [I]t is the beginning of a new existence, and indeed the beginning of a new age, the Information Age" (pp. 508-509)". Nevertheless, he does not consider this "… necessarily an exhilarating moment. Because, alone at last in our human world, we shall have to look at ourselves in the mirror of historical reality. And we may not like the vision" (Castells, 2010, p. 509). For this then, 'balkanization' not only that has no reason to be exempted from examinations and acquaintances under this and any new wave of meaning and comprehension production, but it, in fact, demands such investigations due to, as the next chapter reveals, being still an active and thriving discourse which conditions interaction on the many different levels of communication.

3 'Balkanization' through Retrospection to the Present

Having applied a genealogical account to the 'balkanization' discourse, it is time that following the same epistemology but now through a specific method of sociocognitive discourse analysis on empirical data, linkages and avulsions in the historical development of the discourse are reviewed. Again, it is of a crucial importance to emphasize that, as Garland (2014) rightfully suggests,

> ... genealogy is motivated not by a historical concern to understand the past ... but instead by a critical concern to understand the present. It aims to trace the forces that gave birth to our present-day practices and to identify the historical conditions upon which they still depend. Its point is not to think historically about the past but rather to use historical materials to rethink the present. (p. 20)

In addition to the literature artifacts examined above, tweets present another historical material that would help us to better rethink the present always in connection with the past.

In the first section of this chapter I describe the process behind the formation and structure of the empirical corpus of this thesis and the different challenges and difficulties accompanying it, from data collection to ethical consideration on presenting the tweets; while in the second sections I outline the theoretical framework of analysis, as well as provide with exemplifications of how the same was applied in practice (see Figure 3.1 and 3.2 under section 3.2 Analysis: Theory and Illustrations). Parts of the results of data analysis are elaborated in the third section of this chapter where I had to take a decision of presenting the most relevant information to the reader due to space limitations. Such relevance does not refer to degrees of importance of some observations as opposed to others, but rather to the most expressive and demonstrative trends of data analysis that could convey a comprehensive summary of the 'balkanization' discourse through Twitter in the space allowed for this thesis while supported by my epistemological position.

3.1 Twitter: Mechanism and Data Collection

> *... a new paradigm rising in the social media era, of trusted authoritative scientific sources giving way to science being communicated through total anonymity – faceless Twitter accounts run by nameless individuals reaching millions of people. Welcome to the brave new world of science communication.*
>
> Kalev Leetaru (2017)

As the Twitter's functioning mechanism was decisive in choosing the tools and strategies for data collection, I need to reclaim back to Twitter's association with microblogging. Boyd, Golder, and Lotan (2011), explain how Twitter is an example of social networking sites and blogging characteristics intertwined together, as "[l]ike social network sites, profiles are connected through an underlying articulated network, but these connections are directed rather

© Springer Fachmedien Wiesbaden GmbH, part of Springer Nature 2018
L. Veliu, *#Balkanization: A Critical Study of Otherness through Twitter*,
Masters of Peace, https://doi.org/10.1007/978-3-658-23824-7_3

than undirected; participants can link to ('follow') others and see their tweets, but the other user need not reciprocate" (p. 2).

At the same time, like blogs, Twitter lists users' messages called "tweets" in a chronological reverse order in both, the users' profiles and Twitter's "home" stream, its central feature. However, in 2016 (Kamen, 2016) Twitter Inc. introduced an algorithmic change on the timelines. The switch to a chronological format of the "home" stream is now possible only manually, as it was declared by Twitter Inc.: "Tweets you are likely to care about most will show up first in your timeline. We choose them based on accounts you interact with most, Tweets you engage with, and much more" (Twitter Inc., 2012). Diverse strategies are applied by different users in deciding whom to follow – some focus in following thousands, while others retain a smaller circle of friends or people whom they know; for some Twitter is a platform for entertainment, while for others it serves a networking tool; private and public figures have of course different aims of using Twitter. However, the user profiles and tweets are public by default, while users can choose to protect their messages at any time if they wish so.

Although mentioned before, as the aim of this subsection is to get familiar with Twitter's working apparatus and its components, it is worth repeating that a tweet cannot exceed the 140-character threshold. This remains as such, since, as Boyd, Golder and Lotan (2010) state, "the system was originally designed for tweets to be shared via SMS" (p. 2), while now tweeting is made available through a diverse range of mechanism: mobile phones, PCs, tablets, even through some desktop and website programs. Twitter's Creative Director Biz Stone encouraged embracing ones constrains, by reminding us how "[d]etractors initially said Twitter's 140-character limit was constraining – but that unleashed a new form of wit and creativity, and power for activists" (Rao, 2014). However, later Twitter Inc. altered the tweets' limit, by tweeting that photos, videos, GIFs, polls, and Quote Tweets to no longer count toward the 140 characters (Twitter Inc., 2016), and other trimming suggestions are available to be considered (O'Reilly & Milstein, 2012, p. 37). Furthermore, currently Twitter is considering to upper its character limit to 280 characters (Rosen, 2017).

Twitter's three important features are replying to a message, retweeting it, and liking it by clicking on the heart-shaped sign available below every tweet. The use of "@user" syntax serves for referring to specific users and addressing messages to them, and it is an essential condition for any conversation to take place among the users. O'Reilly and Milstein (2012) explain how people quickly developed a way of having conversations on Twitter by using the "@" symbol followed by an account name (connected to an account page), and how Twitter swiftly incorporated this convention which was not there at the beginning (p. 47). Wenger, White, and Smith (2009) describe how the "interaction between the inventiveness of the community and the developers built upon each other – all within a matter of days" (p. 20) during the South by Southwest Conference in 2007.

Retweeting was not introduced to Twitter users until 2009 (Bunz, 2009). Before a whole retweeting system was built, retweeting someone used to require to manually copy and paste their tweets, and use the "RT" and the "@username" attributions before clicking the "update" button. However, Boyd, Golder and Lotan (2010) argue that

> [n]ot all retweets are an accurate portrayal of the original message. When people edit content to retweet, they may alter the meaning of the original. Even when the content was not altered, taking a tweet out of context can give it a life of its own. (p. 9)

They draw attention to the possibility of misinformation through alteration or misinterpretation, and again point on the importance of the practice beyond its functional dimension in that "[s]preading tweets is not simply to get messages out to new audiences, but also to validate and engage with others" (Boyd, Golder, & Lotan, 2010, p. 1).

Finally, a keyword preceded by the hashtag sign "#" is used to designate topics and categorize web content. While I have extensively elaborated on the importance of tagging (see subsection 1.2.3 'Balkanization' beyond technology: Twitter and subjectivities), it is worth mentioning that the practice of using hashtags has its own history that precedes Twitter, and it may stem from an older computer programmers practice (Boyd, Golder, & Lotan, 2010, p. 2). A topical hashtag may be used for a tweet to be made visible to others that follow that particular hashtag, but this does not mean that all users who post on a hashtag will also follow that conversation. Weller et al. (2014) consider the hashtag conversations to take place on a macro level, as markers that help create a thread of information and have a potential to reach well beyond the user's existing number of followers (as it can be found by anyone by a simple search on Twitter); the @replying practice is considered as the micro level that enables users to communicate on a more personal level and direct contact; while the follower-followee network holds the meso-level in between (Weller, Bruns, Burgess, Mahrt, & Puschmann, 2014, p. 16). They call for studies that will go beyond of researching (on) only one of these layers, and will contribute for a more multilayered understanding of Twitter as a communicative tool (Weller, Bruns, Burgess, Mahrt, & Puschmann, 2014).

However, to follow Weller's and his colleagues' suggestion proved to be quite a challenging endeavor. They themselves explain how any research done on Twitter to this point has relied on collecting the data through any of the three different Twitter data interfaces – the Streaming API, the REST API, and the Search API (Weller, Bruns, Burgess, Mahrt, & Puschmann, 2014, p. 56). Nevertheless, this did not in any way make things easier for me as a researcher who lacks computer language and programming skills, but that is yet interested in observing social phenomena among and through the three different Twitter communication levels that they mention. The Twitter Analytics (https://analytics.twitter.com/) tool provided by Twitter Inc. is meant for personal use mostly as it does not provide with any possibility for extracting a structured set of historical data on a particular hashtag ("#balkanization" in this case).

While it is understandable for research on Twitter to require an interdisciplinary approach, the same proved to be very costly and sometimes was even considered as impossible with regard to reaching access to historical data (but instead, only to a portion of those) by different providers which I contacted, among those Bradwatch (https://www.brandwatch.com/); Node XL (http://www.smrfoundation.org/nodexl/); Talkwaelker (https://www.talkwalker.com/); Hashtagify (http://hashtagify.me/); Trendsmap (https://www.trendsmap.com/); and even GNIP as Twitter's enterprise API platform and data reseller (https://gnip.com/).

It was through the help of Martin Cassai that such complications where surpassed. Martin created a software that would automatically extract all the information I needed from single tweets through a technique called web scraping (see Mitchell, 2015). The software enabled us to copy all the required data directly from the Twitter webpage and then save the results into a comma-separated values (CSV) file organized into columns with information on users and their tweets. Not all the extracted data became part of my analysis. Information such as those on the number of followees and users following, as well as biographical description proved to be irrelevant. Others such as gender or location of users, which would have added an interesting dimension to my analysis, were unfalsifiable, hence also excluded from the analysis. This is also why spatiality as a dimensional archetype of the analysis (see section 3.2 Analysis: Theory and Illustrations) is rather extracted manually by me while detecting the geographies to which the hashtags in every tweet text were referring to, rather than the places that the users had chosen to assign as their locations.

Although the first tweet that included the word 'balkanization' took place in June 2007 (see Example 1) the first tweet that included the "#balkanization" did not take place until October 2009 (see Example 2).

> *Example 1:* At what point does 'community' cease to exist cuz of balkanization? http://tinyurl.com/yserpb (Rice, 2007)
>
> *Example 2:* Why are there no meetings of the Congressional White Caucus? Just askin'… #tcot#balkanization#tocra (ResistTyranny, 2009)

After extracting all the historical data that included the hashtag, the empirical corpus of my research resulted with a total of 1896 tweets on Twitter, stretched through a diapason of nine years, from October 3, 2009, when the first tweet that included "#balkanization" was tweeted, to August 4, 2017 as the timely threshold of finalizing the collection of data and beginning with the analysis.

As explained before (see section 1.2 Research: 'Balkanization' through Twitter Subjectivities), due to limitations of time and resources I focus on tweets that include only the hashtag "balkanization" and its lingual variation, such as "balkanisation", "balkanizacija" and "балканизација" (see Table 3.1 below). The search on "#balkanization" revealed 1480 tweets in English, 363 of which used "#balkanisation" instead. The difference between the "z" and the "s" versions has two explanations – the latter represents the British English version of the term as opposed to the American English one, and it also appears on tweets written in French (352 tweets in total). The French tweets where hence translated to English by Leonora Saliju, an archaeologist studying and working in Fribourg, the French-speaking part of Switzerland; and by Trime Halili, currently living and working in Macedonia. Both Saliju and Halili are holders of DALF C1 language certificates. The corpus holds also 17 tweets in Slovenian, 11 tweets in Croatian, 9 tweets in Serbian, 7 tweets in Bosnian as translated by me; 3 tweets in German as translated by Verena Wulf; 3 tweets in Italian by Alma Rondanini; 3 tweets in Bulgarian by Christine Andreeva; 1 tweet in Hindi by Harikrishnan Sasikumar; 1 tweet in Turkish by Meltem Öktü; and 1 tweet in Spanish by Yessita Herrera, all native speakers respective to the languages translated from. The search also resulted with four tweets in languages I was not able to recognize, hence decided to exclude from my empirical corpus also due to the insignificant implications they might have on the overall analysis. This then reduces the empirical corpus to a final of 1892 tweets.

Table 3.1 "#Balkanization" and its Lingual Variations on Twitter
Note. The numbers in the cells stand for the number of tweets of each lingual variation of "#balkanization" in respective languages.

Language	Variations				Total
	#balkanisation	**#balkanizacija**	**#balkanization**	**#балканизација**	
English	363	5	1112		1480
French	352		3		355
Slovenian		17			17
Croatian	1	9	1		11
Serbian	1	7		1	9
Bosnian		7			7
Unknown	2		2		4
Italian	1	1	1		3
German		1	2		3
Bulgarian			1	2	3
Macedonian				1	1
Turkish			1		1
Hindi	1				1
Spanish	1				1

At this stage, it is important to state that I do not aim to conduct a generalizable study, but rather a reliable study and analysis. Due to this, I do not believe that considering only tweets that include the "#balkanization" compromises the results of my analysis. On the contrary, the tweets that chose a hashtag instead of the word per se are the ones that become part of the wider network and reflect deeper interests of shared beliefs and perceptions. As Paul Gee (1999) states,

> … a discourse analysis is based on the details of speech (and gaze and gesture and action) or writing that are arguably deemed relevant in the situation and that are relevant to the arguments the analyst is attempting to make…. ultimately it is the purposes of the analyst that determine how narrow or broad the transcript must be. The validity of an analysis is not a matter of how detailed one's transcript is. It is a matter of how the transcript works together with all the other elements of the analysis to create a "trustworthy" analysis". (pp. 88-89)

However, the collection and interpretation of data for this MA thesis did give rise to some ethical dilemmas which need to be elaborated and which are already familiar to the academic community, as Zimmer and Proferes (2014) well summarize them in questions such as "what disciplines are engaging in Twitter research and what amount of scrutiny of research ethics is typical within these fields? .... Are subjects notified or given the opportunity to opt-out of being studied? How are research ethics boards evaluating such projects?" (p. 251). Maddock, Starbird, and Mason (2015) too draw our attention to "… how definitions of public and private information apply to internet data, and whether an avatar or profile is a person" (p. 2).

Finding myself in between Twitter's Terms of Service (Twitter Inc., 2016b), Twitter's Privacy Policy (Twitter Inc., 2017), and Display Requirements (Twitter Inc., 2015) on one hand, and the rights of users as ethical human subjects who have not explicitly agreed on their personal information to be used for this research on the other, I decide to follow the argument of "but the data is already public" (Zimmer, 2010). The first reason for this choice is already elaborated under the Research: 'Balkanization' through Twitter Subjectivities section where I expand on the importance of recognizing subjectivities as initiators, instruments and at the same time products of the power/knowledge relations who cannot be disassociated from the language they use due to it being the mechanism of materializing themselves into particular social orders and *vice versa*. This also goes along Leetaru's (2017) line of argument quoted at the beginning of this section where he refers to a new world of science of communication based in faceless and anonymous scientific sources which he considers as "… most frightening". I do agree with his claim on requiring a 'face' to authorship along the lines of identifying the author as ingrained in her or his work, but I believe that such anonymity is also a symptom of current developments of communication and as such, it can be a source with a vast potential for observation. In other words, we should work with what we have and make the most out of these new characteristics of identities and subjectivities in performance, instead of imposing a specific view of how the same should be and based on that inflict a specific course to the development of science and research.

The second reason is of a rather legal nature: In a study on republishing public social media data collected during Hurricane Sandy in the U.S. in 2012 conducted by Bica and Anderson (2016), they claim that "… anonymizing the tweets would be in direct violation of the Twitter Terms of Service" (p. 2). They rightfully claim that "Twitter not only provides ample warning to all users about their privacy rights and the potential uses of their data, but instructs researchers who collect and use this data to do so in a personally-identifiable way" (Bica & Anderson, 2016, p. 4).

Twitter indeed requires from anyone that aims in displaying Twitter content to "[d]isplay real, unmodified Tweets from real accounts" (2015), including full name; avatar; and username of any user. Further, the decision is also led by Twitter's Terms of Service which among others, state that

> [b]y submitting, posting or displaying Content on or through the Services, you grant us a worldwide, non-exclusive, royalty-free license (with the right to sublicense) to use, copy, reproduce, process, adapt, modify, publish, transmit, display and distribute such Content in any and all media or distribution methods (now known or later developed). This license authorizes us to make your Content available to the rest of the world and to let others do the same. (Twitter Inc., 2016b)

In addition to this, Twitter's Privacy Policy states that what a user shares on Twitter: "may be viewed all around the world instantly" (Twitter Inc., 2017).

Another note on ethics that needs to be made clear is in relation to Twitter's legal obligations to remove deleted tweets from the research content. In its Developer Documentation, Twitter requires developers to clean "… the referenced Tweet from memory and any storage or archive, even in the rare case where a deletion message arrives earlier in the stream that the Tweet it references" (2012) once they receive a status deletion notice. Maddock, Starbird and Mason (2015) reveal the challenges they faced with regard to tweet deletions while researching online rumoring behavior during crisis and disaster events. They explain how removal of deleted tweets causes methodological concerns, and raises legal and ethical alarms – the first due to Twitter, Inc. request, and the second due to traditional human subjects research where "a participant's withdrawal requires researchers to remove this material" (Maddock, Starbird, & Mason, 2015, p. 4). It is here where I find it relevant to state that the empirical corpus of this MA thesis is constituted by existing tweets as of August 4, 2017, and does not include any deleted tweets that have used "#balkanization" or any of its lingual variations until that date.

3.2 Analysis: Theory and Illustrations

So far as we have any information about man, we know that he has always and everywhere been under the influence of dominating ideas. Anyone who alleges that he is not can immediately be suspected of having exchanged a known form of belief for a variant which is less known both to himself and to others.

Carl Gustav Jung (1969, p. 62)

As elaborated under the Philosophy: Critique on Discourse section, the content of the tweets has been analyzed through the CDA socio-cognitive approach as proposed by Teun van Dijk (2000). I have analyzed the data by putting van Dijk's (2000) model of CDA through Lene Hansen's (2006) work on identity construction. Together they constitute the methodological theory behind the data analysis and interpretation of the empirical corpus of tweets as depicted in Figure 3.1 below. Following the methodological model of Figure 3.1, I have analyzed the tweets through discourse levels and respective categories, such as *meaning (topics, specification or vagueness, implication, local coherence, synonymy, paraphrase, contrast, examples* or *illustrations, disclaimers, comparisons)*; *propositional structures (actors, modality* and *topoi)*; *formal structures*; *argumentation (generalization, false analogies, begging the question, authority* and *counterfactuals)*; and *rhetoric (alliterations, metaphors, irony* and *hyperbole)* as defined by van Dijk (2000).

However, due to the analysis requiring some other categories but the ones identified by van Dijk (2000), I decided to additionally add *exclusive disjunction, imperatives, colloquia, exclamations,* and *conditionality* as discourse categories part of the discourse level of *meaning*; *expletives, rhetorical question, labelling, idioms,* and *predictions* as part of *rhetoric*; and *emoticons* as part of *formal structures*. I have also excluded particular discourse levels and categories as envisioned by van Dijk (2000), such as *similes* and *litotes* due to the rarity of their appearance and the difficulty of their identification; and *sentence syntax* as a discourse level, due to the large empirical corpus and time constraints which did not allow for a thorough examination of "word order, active and passive sentences, and nominalizations" (van Dijk, 2000, p. 54).

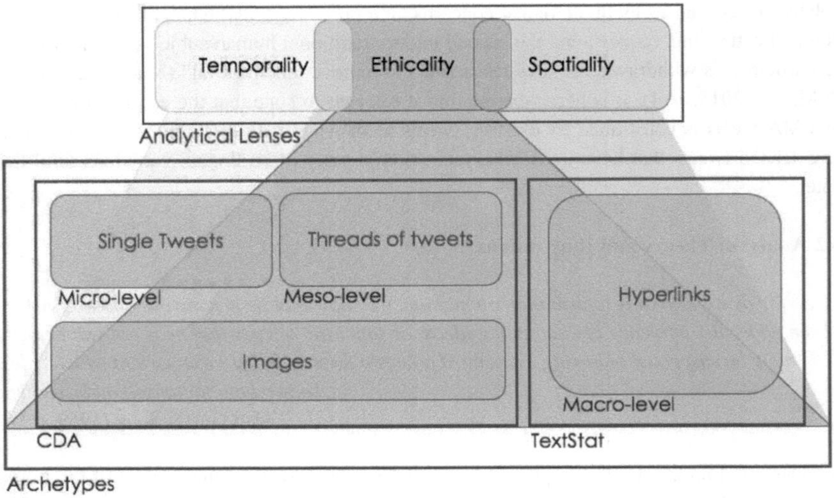

Figure 3.1 Visual Conceptualization of the Methodology of Research. Own illustration of the author.
Note. Temporality, ethicality and spatiality present the three main analytical lenses as adapted from Security as Practice: Discourse Analysis and the Bosnian War by L. Hansen, 2006. Archetypes present meanings associated with 'balkanization' from tweets examined through CDA as adapted from Ideology and Discourse: A Multidisciplinary Introduction by T. van Dijk (2000).

Van Dijk (2000) confirms that these discourse categories overlap, and that their relevance lies in them being merely practical and analytical categories. Not every tweet text has been examined through every discourse category and level. I find it important to mention that this structure of research as provided by van Dijk (2000) has been applied by him in larger pieces of text and speech. An example of this would be a debate in the British House of Commons, held on March 5, 1997 (van Dijk, 2000) in which van Dijk illustrates all the categories and levels of analysis within the same debate. However, this was not possible to be done in singular tweets, of course, due to the text of tweets hitting the 140 characters' threshold. This has resulted at times with a few categories, and at times with one category per tweet.

The second step after putting each tweet through an examination of its discourse levels and categories is the extraction of the prevailing *topics, topoi, themes,* and *actors*. The purpose of using topics, topoi, themes, and actors is not specifically aimed at systemizing the analysis of the discourse. Rather, such components help in better knowing what to look for while applying the thorough analysis of discourse levels and categories to every tweet. To have in mind these four components of discourse is something that takes place before and after looking for the discourse levels and categories in every tweet, as the same are helpful in both, identifying and organizing meanings. Following this, I extract the prevailing topics, topoi, themes, and actors out of the analysis of the tweets and refer to them as *archetypes*. The final results of this analysis are illustrated in Figure 3.2 below.

Figure 3.2 Word Cloud of 'Balkanization' Archetypes. Own illustration of the author.
Note. Most frequently appearing archetypes are in bigger sizes.

Van Dijk differentiates between *topics* which "represent the gist or most important information of a discourse, and tell us what a discourse 'is about', globally speaking … the information that is best recalled of a discourse" (van Dijk, 2000, p. 45); more "abstract *themes*, typically expressed by single words, such as 'Immigration' , 'Discrimination' or 'Education' which are broad categories" (p. 45); and *topoi* which are "like topics as earlier defined, but they have become standardized and publicized, so that they are typically used as 'ready-mades' in argumentation" (p. 53). Different from topics and themes, topoi seem to rather have a more evaluative nature, as van Dijk (2000) gives the example of immigrants being called "threats" or "burdens" (p. 53). Further, as van Dijk (2000) states, "[m]odels of actions more specifically feature participants who are *actors* in various roles" (p. 21). Such actors are personalities appearing in the forms of individuals and public figures, members of groups, or groups. However, their names are not mere semantics, but rather represent recognizable ideologies. In other words, actors are meanings in themselves due the ideological 'luggage' reflected in their actions.

Van Dijk does not elaborate whether such categories as *topics, topoi, themes,* and *actors* are the result of previous analysis of discourse structures and levels, but the definitions he provides of them allow me to use such categories as a pattern for clustering the analysis of singular tweets into what I call *archetypes.* At this point, I want to clarify on the choice of using the word "archetype" to convey the most prevailing meanings associated with "#balkanization". The word might cause some conceptual correlation to the famous *Jungian archetypes* (Jung, 2010), further elaborated and defined by Fesit and Feist (2008) as (emotionally) repressed experiences inherited from our ancestors which become highly developed, but which we do not have to be experienced individually. As Papadopolus (2006) suggests, "Jung's theory of archetypes introduces a complexity that enriches his earlier formulations of teleology, by offering a bridge between the personal realm and the wider collective structures" (p. 31). He explains that archetypes have an "organising effect … on the knowing process, on one's very consciousness" (Papadopolus, 2006, p. 32). Relating this to 'balkanization' then, the archetypes conveyed through "#balkanization" are first, indeed part of the collective (un)consciousness; second, I am examining them through indirect symbols from which I only after extract archetypical meanings; and third, they are given material expression by individuals and cultures once they enter consciousness and find materialization by giving justification to particular social orders as opposed to others.

As such, without going deeper into Jungian philosophy, I found the word quite expressive and descriptive to the preceding theoretically and epistemological supportive logic behind the analysis of the tweets. The term seems to also be analogous to van Dijk's (2000) elaborations on *mental models* as "episodic representations of the daily events we participate in, witness (in reality or on TV), or read about" (p. 21). Corresponding to the organizing feature of Jungian archetypes, such mental models "represent the way [I] see and understand events" (van Dijk, 2000, p. 21). Further, again analogously to archetypes' tides to ancestors' implications, van Dijk (2000) states that "such a representation is often influenced by previous experiences (old models), and the ways these may bias [my] current perceptions and interpretations" (p. 21).

Finally, van Dijk (2000) makes sure to clarify that due to ideologies residing on a higher communal level i.e. being socially shared, we would not expect to be looking for them in the mental models which he considers as "*personal* and *subjective*" (p. 21). However, this is not the case. These mental models, which I choose to call *archetypes*, are the ones that facilitate the relation between ideologies and discourse, hence precondition and are in turn influenced by socially shared cognition. As van Dijk states (2000), "[s]uch mental models are not only important for the representation of our personal experiences. They are also the basis of the production and comprehension of action and discourse" (p. 24).

Applying this conceptualization as a research method on the semantics of the empirical corpus of 1892 tweets, presents, as van Dijk (2000) states, only a "small selection of the information represented in the model that is used to understand such discourse" (p. 25) of 'balkanization' in this case. Identifying the different discourse categories and levels on the text of each tweet that included the "#balkanization" is only one component of the analysis. Van Dijk (2000) would consider this as part of the *micro-level* of description or analysis which "usually describes social actors, and the social interaction between these actors in social situations" (p. 31) as opposed, or rather relational to, the *macro-level* where "we talk about groups of social actors, institutions, organizations, whole states or societies, and their relationships" (p. 31).

In between the micro, and the macro level, there should be an addition of "*intermediate* or *meso-levels*" (p. 31) upon which van Dijk (2000) does not elaborate in depth. At this stage it is important to clarify that I have extracted the above-listed archetypes not only from the tweets that included #balkanization, but also from the threads of tweets in which they were participating as a comment to some other user's status; were retweeted by other users and hence initiated or not a discussion of their own; or from tweets commenting on other tweets that included #balkanization, but that did not necessarily use the hashtag themselves. While this conditioned a larger amount of work and further expanded the empirical corpus, I found it crucial for the contextualization of meanings and the minimization of the limitations that the 140-character threshold presented. I consider this as part of the meso-level of analysis, the one mediating between on one side the personal subjectivities of individuals, and on the other the macro picture where the same are summarized (i.e. the whole discourse surrounding "#balkanization").

Van Dijk (2000) also makes it clear that the division of macro, micro and meso-levels "is merely a practical distinction that has led to much controversy. In reality macro and micro aspects of society are often intermingling" (p. 31). Considering that all the analysis takes place around the "#balkanization" itself, this is what already gave me access to the macro level. As already mentioned (see section 3.1 Twitter: Mechanism and Data Collection), Weller et al. consider the hashtag a representative of the macro level of conversation due to its potential of reaching beyond the exchange between followers and followees (Weller, Bruns, Burgess, Mahrt, & Puschmann, 2014, p. 16), and which as such, automatically provides the space for global searchable talk.

However, in order to get a better grasp of the macro level and increase the validity of my research, I decided to upscale the level of my analysis and reach beyond the text of the tweets. This is where *intertextuality* comes into play. Following the refugee crisis of 2015 in Europe and the Brexit referendum in June 2016, Bennett (2016) examines UK migration policy discourses through Twitter. Due to first, Twitter being considered "elite-dominated and unrepresentative form of communication" (Bennett, 2016, p. 5), upon which point he does not elaborate in depth but I would assume he refers to access to Twitter being preconditioned by access to the Internet; and second, "as these texts are often 'source' texts of discourses that then are mediated and recontextualized via Twitter" (Bennett, 2016, p. 6). Bennet (2016) states that the hyperlinked references to the mainstream media should also be included in the analysis. While I believe that this does not neutralize elitist nuances of Twitter, and nor does it fully explain the recontextualization of text via Twitter, it does richen the overall analysis by providing better contextualization of statements, hence exposing the link between text and context, micro and micro level of discourses, subjectivities and social orders.

Due to this then, the empirical corpus of research widened to include not only tweets but also hyperlinked texts to articles and news of mainstream media. However, for every hyperlinked text to be submitted to a thorough analysis of discourse categories and levels as the tweets' texts have, would be impossible. Such analysis would not be unfeasible due to the time, length and technical as well as financial constraints of this MA thesis. However, instead of excluding it as a research component, I decided to rather reach towards hyperlinked references to text by using the *concordance* feature offered by TextSTAT (Hüning, 2007) as a simple text analysis tool. TextSTAT is a web crawling[9] software through which I was able to combine all the hyperlinked texts extracted from the tweets into an empirical corpus that was then categorized according to the language criterion. All links shared in any of the 1892 tweets were extracted and formulated another empirical corpus, complementary to that of the tweets' texts which resulted with a total of 700 hyperlinked references to text, out of which 586 in English; 101 in French; 10 in Balkan languages (Croatian, Macedonian and Slovenian); and 1 hyperlinked reference for each, German, Italian and Chinese text.

Through the concordance feature, TextSTAT provides with, I was able to contextualize the textual content surrounding 'balkanization' in each of these hyperlinks, which was helpful in sparing time from reading all the 544 hyperlinks. Due to it providing also with the future of a frequency list extracted from the totality of the links, it was also helpful in identifying the context of a word that resulted in a high frequency, should it have attracted my attention. Another note of relevance to be made here is related to TextSTAT's inability to extract frequency out of repeating links i.e. TextSTAT will count only once the exact same Uniform Resource Locators (URL). Should multiple tweets share the same hyperlinked references to text, it is only once that TextSTAT will take into consideration the same repeating URL and it is only one count of frequency that it will display. This then reduced the corpora of hyperlinked texts to a total of 544 hyperlinked texts in English; 97 in French and 10 in Balkan languages. Due to the low implications that they could have to the overall results of analysis and due to the different research constrains of this MA thesis, I have excluded the three links in German, Italian and Chinese.

Aside intertextuality, for a more inclusive analysis, another component has been examined: *multimodality*. As Benett (2016) states, "Twitter is a new genre that allows for novel methods of legitimization that often include a high-degree of multimodality" (p. 6). Images, GIFs (Graphics Interchange Format), as well as hyperlinked references to other images, videos, songs, and so on, accompany tweets. Most often associated with the work of Kreus and Van Leeuwen (1996) on text analysis and meaning making, multimodality is becoming increasingly important in the latter development of critical and discursive studies. Both, Benett

9 A web crawler is a software application and one of the main components of web search engines which is automated to run often simple and repetitive tasks over the Internet.

(2016) while examining UK migration policy discourses through Twitter, and Kreis (2017) in her analysis of anti-refugee discourse on Twitter, elaborate on the importance of their research as being multimodal among others.

Iedema (2003) refers to multimodality as a "discourse analytical term" (p. 32) which "was introduced to highlight the importance of taking into account semiotics other than language-in-use, such as image, music, gesture, and so on" (p. 33). Along those analogous lines although not the same, van Dijk (2000) also mentions the importance of *formal structures*, already included in the discourse levels considered in this thesis, as "the form of a clause or sentence, the form of an argument, the order of a news story, the size of a headline, and so on" (p. 53). However, Iedema (2013) explains in depth why current social research needs to unavoidably rise above semantics in order to be able to better identify the text and context link. Due to this then, I have extended my analysis into including also the different images (107 in total), songs references (3 in total) and video references (49 in total).

Although he acknowledges the importance of multimodality in examining representation [which complements my choice of theoretical framework as proposed by Serge Moscovici and Stuart Hall (see section 1.3 Philosophy: Critique of Discourse)], Iedema (2013) also states that "multimodality runs the risk of a somewhat objectifying view on the representations under consideration" (p. 32). To avoid such risks, he suggests what he calls "resemiotization" which has also a view on the "social unfolding of the processes and logics of representing" (Iedema, 2003, p. 50). Although I will not go deeper into elaborating on "resemiotization", Iedema's point has already been taken into consideration as I have applied the analysis not only to the text of the tweets and the ethical component reflected by the same in correlation with spatiality and temporality throughout the thesis, but also through the genealogical examination of 'balkanization' (see Chapter 2). In other words, no formal structure of a tweet has been decontextualized and analyzed as an isolated unit of analysis, but has rather been examined in correlation not only to the text of tweets, but also to an extended context of the thread of that specific tweet located in time and space, hence historical context.

The time of the tweeting was an easy component to extract. However, it is important to state that the spatiality of tweets has again required my personal analysis. Due to the places from where the users have tweeted although being unfalsifiable (i.e. the location of users can be chosen by them and does not have to correspond with their actual coordinates), the opportunity of drawing any observation with regard to which part of the world tweets most on 'balkanization', were excluded. What remained as a possibility was seeing which spaces 'balkanization' was mostly used in association with the tweets' texts. Hence, I have manually extracted from tweets the spaces to which the "#balkanization" is used in relation to or as a description of. This includes not only countries and geographic regions as physical constructs, but also mental spaces or fields of thought.

With this then we reach towards a crucial and final note on explaining the logic behind the analysis of the data for this thesis. Both, the examination through the discourse levels and categories as proposed by van Dijk (2000) of the tweets, thread of tweets and images related to "#balkanization", as well as the TextSTAT analysis of all hyperlinked texts related to the same, are part of the *ethical* lenses of analysis. Ethicality is only one of the three main analytical lenses, alongside *temporality* and *spatiality* as adopted from Lene Hansen's (2006) elaborations on identity construction through a consideration of how "identity is always spatially, temporally, and ethically situated" (p. 32). Hansen (2006) calls ethicality an "analytical lens" (p. 42) of an equal ontological status as spatiality and temporality "that bring out the important political substance of identity construction, not explicitly articulated" (p. 42).

Hanses (2006) provides with an in-depth analysis of the genocide discourse in Bosnia during the war and the humanitarian intervention, by reaffirming the importance of ethics and policy correlation and concluding that

> … the Balkan Other is, as in the Balkan discourse, combined with an articulation of ethical identity that constructs all 'parties' as responsible for the war and hence leaves the West in a political space unencumbered by moral considerations. A potential Western intervention should be based not on moral concerns related to the Balkans or the Bosnians but on the consequences the war might have for European and Western security. (p. 152)

Hansen's post-structuralist theory of identity and foreign policy in combination with the Western debate on the Bosnian War was not only epistemology applicable to my research, but also very specifically to the subject of analysis (i.e. 'balkanization' as derivative of 'the Balkans').

As the archetypes are a result of semantical, multimodal and intertextual discourse analysis, it is here where the ethical and moral references are extracted from. Spatiality and temporality remain components that are extracted from the tweets, and then further put in relation to ethicality. Bringing the three components together does not only follow Hansen's model of analytical lenses, but it also adheres to the many times repeated importance on the contextualization and historicization of text that genealogy requires. Therefore, the examples of tweets provided in the elaborations below (see section 3.3 Archetypes: 'Balkanization' through the Dominant and the Infrequent) are archetypical representatives of the 'balkanization' discourse which are carefully presented as situated in space and time.

In finally bringing together ethicality, temporality and spatiality as the three dimensions of identity construction, with this I summarize the theoretical mechanism and methodological support behind the data analysis (see Figure 3.1 below). An illustration of applying the same can be found in Figure 3.3 below. The image presents an example of applying the methodological conceptualization components of this thesis. Multiple elements of analysis have been identified under the three main analytical lenses – first, ethicality is revealed in identifying several discourse categories, such as metaphors ["hostage" (Westra, 2017)]; exclamation and praise have been identified in "Great response Michelle!" (Westra, 2017); generalization and vagueness appear as part of "… all" (Westra, 2017) supposedly refereeing to all companies in the virtual reality industry which claim is not supported by any sources; vagueness appears as no clear explanation is given about what is clearly meant with "… the #balkanization of the industry" (Westra, 2017); and the whole statement of "… all being held hostage" (Westra, 2017) appearing as an example of modality in stating a questionable position as an indisputable truth. Considering this analysis and comparing it with analysis on other tweets that include the "#balkanization", I have extracted two archetypes – one which is a theme and that is the "fight(s/ing)" archetype; and another which is a topos and which is the "data/Internet national regulations" archetype.

Figure 3.3 Illustration of Applying CDA to Tweets. Own illustration of the author.
Note. Adapted from Westra (2017) and Demonkid (2017).

Further, Figure 3.3 reveals two other components of ethicality – first, intertextuality is expressed in the article "Facebook's Oculus Fights Sales Ban for VR Rift Headset" (Korosec, 2017) shared through the first tweet (Demonkid, 2017) which has been extracted and added as part of the TextSTAT empirical corpus and examined through its concordance feature. Second, multimodality is expressed through the image shared by John Westra (2017). Analyzed as part of the formal structures the image presents a discourse level in itself. It shows what appear to be four industrial chimneys as symbols of the four companies (Daydream, HTC, Oculus, and Samsung) built of concrete. As immoveable, the four chimneys i.e. the four companies, visually supports Westra's (2017) claim on the companies being held "hostage". A grey and dark ambient as opposed to their names written in a colorful format, surrounds the companies, hence externalizing agency for a dull and unpleasant situation.

While temporality is clearly placed in June 2017, spatiality on the other side is, as explained above before, extracted from the spatial connotations used in correlation to "#balkanization" and which in this case is cyberspace. Note that several tweets and archetypes can share the same space. In fact, that is that which conditions an eclectic and agglomerative view of the 'balkanization' discourse, by opening the space for drawing links of connectedness and comparison. By adding spatiality and temporality to the CDA analysis of the ethical archetypal dimension, we complete the methodological prerequisites as sat before. Importantly, this also reflects the micro level of analysis taking place within the tweet of John Westra (2017); the meso-level of analysis being extended beyond the tweet that includes "#balkanization" to the tweet towards which it is expressed as a response [i.e. that of Demonkid (2017)]; and the macro level of analysis being accessed not only through the hashtag per se, but also through the hyperlink which connects the tweets to the wider space of information and knowledge production. It is by the format of this example that all the tweets have been analyzed and examined. As depicted in Figure 3.2 above, this has resulted in a list of 204 different archetypes. Constrains of this thesis do not allow for an elaboration on each of those archetypes separately. Therefore, I have added the full list of archetypes sorted by their frequency in Appendix A. Selected information that I consider crucial to present to the reader are summarized and interpreted in the following sections.

3.3 Archetypes: 'Balkanization' through the Dominant and the Infrequent

"There is a lake between sun and moon...
In the silence between whisper and shout
The space between wonder and doubt...
The gap between actor and act
The lens between wishes and fact"
Pye Dubois (1992).

Before beginning to present examples of specific archetypes, the general trend of the fluctuations of the total numbers of tweets as inclusive of "#balkanization" ever tweeted (see Figure 3.4 below), deserves some attention. From the current data, the peak of the number of tweets that have used "#balkanization" was reached in 2016. The relevance of depicting this trend lies in that it reveals a continuous rise of tweets that have used the hashtag throughout the years, but with a quick decline in 2015 for which my analysis cannot account. As the data covered a period that stretched exactly until August 4, 2017, it is difficult to comment on whether the increasing trend has continued until the end of the year. However, considering the number of tweets tweeted until August 4, 2017 (661 tweets in total) it is valid to assume that the same tendency has been endured.

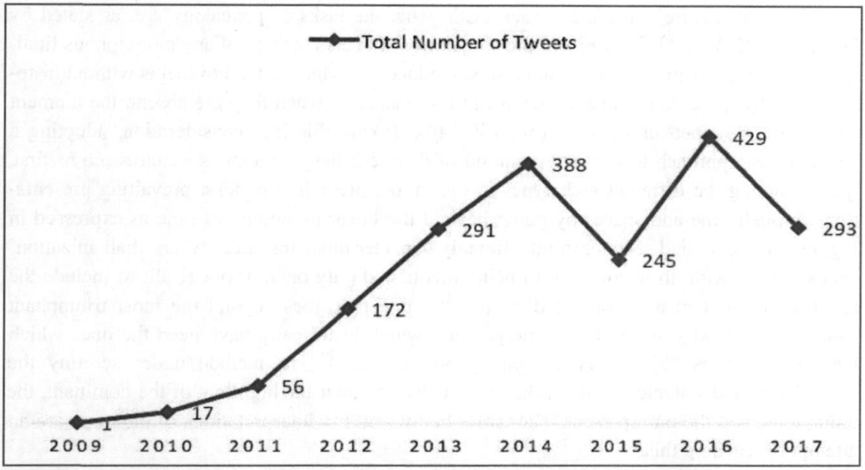

Figure 3.4 Temporal Depiction of Tweets Inclusive of "#Balkanization" and its Lingual Variations. Own illustration of the author.
Note: The time span covers a period from October 3, 2009 to August 4, 2017. Points in the graph line stand for the total number of tweets in respective years as expressed in the X-axis.

The archetypes presented below derive from the analysis applied to the data set consisting of a total of 1892 tweets which have used "#balkanization" and its lingual variations in languages stretched through a diapason of time from October 3, 2009, to August 4, 2017. The examples of archetypes and tweets come from two main strands of data interpretation which required a practical and exclusionary decision to be presented as such, and which were a helpful way in deciding what to exclude from presenting in this thesis. First, I elaborate on the top ten most prevailing archetypes and spaces stretched through a diapason of nine years since the first tweet which used "#balkanization" took place in 2009. Second, I reach towards the other end of the spectrum and that is the archetypes and spaces that have come up as the rarest in relation to the "#balkanization" and which typically were mentioned only once. In attempting to reach the two poles of the discourse, I hence chose the top ten and the bottom ten of archetypes associated with 'balkanization'.

In the two sections following, I present the main findings deriving from the analysis restricted to a specific number of examples and elaborations due to thesis limitations. It is important to clarify that claiming that the elaborated archetypes below are more relevant than those which I have not elaborated upon, would not only be incorrect as frequency in itself cannot do justice to such a claim, but it would also be epistemologically self-contradictory. Hence, before dwelling deeper into some of the specific examples out of the 204 archetypes that have resulted from the data analysis, I would like us to once more go shortly back to the genealogical foundation of this thesis. This will also help me explain the logic behind the choices I have made on which information to elaborate for the reader and which other to rather leave aside from the main body of text but nevertheless include them in the appendices (see Appendix A; Appendix B).

This will require considering back again what the tasks of genealogy are, as stated by Foucault (1977): "… it must record the singularity of events outside of any monotonous finality; it must seek them in the most unpromising places, in what we tend to feel is without history…. Finally, genealogy must define even those instances when they are absent, the moment when they remained unrealized" (pp. 139-140). Taking this into consideration, adopting a genealogical approach to the interpretation of data, enables as much as requires me to first, 'jump' among the different archetypes in their most prevailing or least prevailing presentations through time and spaces by going beyond the linear monotony of time as expressed in Figure 3.4 above; and second, to intentionally consider those instances where 'balkanization' appears to be with no history due to being mentioned only once or not at all; to include the less/least present in a history of discontinuity, one that goes beyond the most triumphant forms of knowledge which have emerged and which historically have been the ones which have survived as "history is written by the victors" [10]; to include under scrutiny the 'knowledge under shade' so to speak, which is living under the highlight of the dominant, the ubiquitous, and the omnipresent. The tables below and my interpretations of the same are an attempt of reaching this.

I refer to this through the Jung's quote at the beginning of this section. Less dominating forms of belief, according to Jung (1969), are just a less familiar variation of the dominating ones. This is not to say that the dominant and the least prevailing archetypes of the 'balkanization' discourse are identical, but they do present, exactly, variations of the same discourse. Hence, within the frame of this thesis, dominance and omnipresence is of no more significance and holds no more substance than infrequency, as both stem from alternatives of the same discourse and offer equal chances for observation.

3.3.1 Through archetypes: The pole of the dominant

The tweets presented below as representative of prevailing archetypes and spaces, have been chosen from the years in which they have reached their peaks in terms of frequency. The frequency of archetypes is not only the result of the most frequent literal connotations conveyed through the tweets' texts, but they are rather extracted of what "abstractly characterize the meaning of a whole discourse or of a larger fragment of discourse" (van Dijk, 2000, p. 45), in this case 'balkanization'. Due to one tweet possibly revealing two or more archetypes, it is to be noted that the numbers in the table do not present the number of tweets, but rather the number of archetypes as appearing in specific years. Same goes for Table 3.3 below, in which the numbers in the table do not present the number of tweets that refer to a specific place, but rather the number of times a space has been mentioned in a specific year. This, again, due to one tweet possibly referring to two or more spaces. In other words, while the 1892 tweets present the pool of data, it is the number of identified archetypes and spaces that present the units of analysis.

The two following tables as elaborated in this subsection depict the top ten most prevalent archetypes (see Table 3.2 below) and most prevailing places (see Table 3.3 below)

[10] There is no clear references as to who is the author of the quote. However, it has most been attributed to Winston Churchill due to him famously remarking in the House of Commons of the UK that he was confident history would find the then Prime Minister, Stanley Baldwin, wrong, "because I shall write that history" argued Churchill (see Hastings, 2004).

associated with "#balkanization" throughout time. To connect nuances of ethicality, temporality, and spatiality simultaneously, my elaboration and presentation of results will remain relatively within the archetypes and countries presented, moving back and forth between the tables. Table 3.2 below depicts the ten most prevalent conceptual connotations associated with 'balkanization' as resulted from the applied CDA. Nuances of division(s); data/Internet national regulations; nation(alism/ality); war; race(ism); data/software heterogeneity; independence; Islam/Muslim(s); union, unity or unification, and (anti)im(migration) are what is being used the most in conjunction with "#balkanization" in tweets.

Table 3.2 Top Ten Archetypes Associated with "#Balkanization"
Note. The numbers in the cells represent the frequency of archetypes in respective years. The table follows a scaling shade formatting rule in which the brighter the shade the less the frequency of the archetype.

Archetypes	2009	2010	2011	2012	2013	2014	2015	2016	2017	Total
Division(s)		1	3	7	18	25	17	39	24	134
Data/Internet National Regulations		2	2	4	32	45	13	10	4	112
Nation(alism/ality)		1	2	1	12	14	15	21	22	88
War		1	2	5	14	17	7	16	20	82
Race(ism)	1		1	2	11	19	11	17	13	75
Data/Software Heterogeneity		1	5	3	12	5	8	32	7	73
Independence			1	6	7	24	3	11	7	59
Islam/Muslim			1	4	3	10	13	13	14	58
Union/Unity/Unification			1	6	7	11	6	22	2	55
(Anti)im(migration)			1		1	11	16	17	7	53

Of all tweets that have used "#balkanization", connotations of *division(s)* (see Example 3) have been the prevailing ones. From Table 3.2 above we can also see that the archetype "division(s)" has been most prevalent during 2016, compatible in this way with the general trend of the zenith of the numbers of tweets in 2016 (see Figure 3.4 above).

> *Example 3: Ta divna riječ "balkanizacija" - NATO "genij" dijeli Siriju po uzoru na Jugoslaviju #NATO #Sirija #balkanizacija... http://fb.me/6V1wMJ4o4* (AMSI, 2016) [Translated from Bosnian: That wonderful word "balkanization" – NATO "the genious" divides Syria by taking Yugoslavia as a model #NATO #Sirija #balkanizacija... http://fb.me/6V1wMJ4o4]

While the hyperlinked text shared by the user is no longer available for accession, the text of the tweet itself is interesting to be looked at due to the following reasons: first, it shows direct conceptual association of 'balkanization' with division; second, it draws a geographical link of the word with Yugoslavia; third, it relates it to a model, pattern of action being prescriptively applied to Syria; fourth, the agency of action is externalized to NATO ironically referred to as "a genius"; yet, the user here refers to 'balkanization' as a "word", and which as we will see will not be the case with many other tweets.

What is also noticeable is that most tweets associating 'balkanization' with nuances of division(s) first, refer to the ongoing situation in Syria and the Middle East (see Example 4 and 5); and second, are closely connected to the "war(s)" archetype (see Example 4). Hence, both the "division(s)" and "war(s)" archetypes are among the top prevalent archetypes associated with 'balkanization' (see Table 3.2 above), while referring to Syria and the Middle East which are among the top ten spaces associated with 'balkanization' (see Table 3.3 below).

Table 3.3 Top Ten Spaces Associated with "#Balkanization"
Note. The numbers in the cells represent the number of times a particular space was associated with tweets in respective years. The table follows a scaling shade formatting rule in which the brighter the shade the less the frequency of the space.

Spaces	2009	2010	2011	2012	2013	2014	2015	2016	2017	Total
US	1	1	7	19	32	68	60	111	87	386
Democratic Republic of the Congo			2	39	41	23	14	54	35	208
Cyberspace		3	10	7	44	59	21	16	4	164
Syria			1	6	23	7	20	27	35	119
UK				6	8	18	16	37	10	95
France				2	12	16	22	17	16	85
Global		2	7	3	7	13	5	19	14	70
Middle East			4		9	5	12	16	12	58
Pakistan			5	6	23	6	4	5	6	55
Scotland				8	3	28	2	7	4	52

Moreover, the "divison(s)" archetype is often used in conjunction with two other archetypes that are not among the top ten but remain nevertheless important – archetype "Israel/Judaism" and the "Yinon Plan" archetype (see Examples 6 and 7).

> *Example 4:* The West war machine wants to use #Shia-#Sunni *divide* for #Balkanisation of this region. We, the Muslims, happy to play the desired role (Khan, 2017)
>
> *Example 5*: #khazar program for #Balkanization of the #MiddleEast - http://www.globalresearch.ca/plans-for-redrawing-the-middle-east-the-project-for-a-new-middle-east/3882 (Tannery, 2016)
>
> *Example 6:* "The Truth About What's REALLY Happening in #Syria" @LionelMedia talks 2 @Partisangirl https://www.youtube.com/watch?v=G_cd2TLhaZg #ISIS #Israel #Balkanization (OneVenusThrow, 2017)
>
> *Example 7:* Israel's Longstanding Middle East Plan - The #YinonPlan By Stephen Lendman. http://rense.com/general92/dsid.htm #Israel #ME #Balkanisation #NWO (Stutchbury, 2015)

The tweets refer specifically to the famous Yinon Plan as derived from an essay titled "A Strategy for Israel in the Nineteen Eighties" written by Oded Yinon (1982). Yinon was a journalist and former advisor to Ariel Sharon, the eleventh Prime Minister of Israel. Shahak, who translated Yinon's article, begins the foreword with "[t]he following essay represents, in my opinion, the accurate and detailed plan of the present Zionist regime (of Sharon and Eitan) for the Middle East which is based on the division of the whole area into small states, and the dissolution of all the existing Arab states" (Yinon, 1982, p. 7).

In the hyperlinked text shared in Example 7, Lendman (2010) in commenting on the Yinon Plan, states that one of its essential premises "… requires dividing Arab nations into small states - Balkanizing them along ethnic and sectarian lines as Israeli satellites, controllable satraps, the idea modeled after the Ottoman Empire's Millet (or nation) system under which local authorities governed confessional communities with separate ethnic identities". The hyperlink to a video as shared in Example 6 draws on the same logic. In an interview with Michael William Lebron, the guest speaker who uses the pseudonym Syrian Girl considers that "[t]he most crucial issue right now is the balkanization of Syria … which was written in 2006 by Condoleezza Rice when they redrew the map of the Middle East, and also in 1982 by Israel in the Yinon Plan" (Lebron, 2017, 1:05). While being asked to elaborate more on what the term 'balkanization' means, Syrian Girl mistakenly gives this genealogy of the word:

> Balkanization is from the Balkans in the 80s when Yugoslavia broke up into many different states on sectarian lines. The same thing … now, that political term can be applied to other countries when you can say that these countries are being divided on sectarian lines or political lines. Basically, it just means a country being broken apart. (Lebron, 2017, 1:56)

The relevance of such claim is not much in the erroneous presentation of 'balkanization' as being born only during the Yugoslav wars, as much as it is on its explicit and direct analogies between the current situation in Syria and the Middle East on one side, and the Balkans or former Yugoslavia on the other, noting here another important reflection of using interchangeably the terms "Yugoslavia" and "the Balkans".

Further, what the "division(s)" archetype revealed is that while 'balkanization' in association with "division(s)" is always a tentative to resolving a problematic existing condition, it is either a failed tentative, or a chaotic state preceding peace [but never being peace(ful) itself]. The hyperlinked text shared in Example 5 where we find 'balkanization' as antecedent to "finlandization", perfectly illustrates this: "Anglo-American occupied Iraq, particularly Iraqi Kurdistan, seems to be the preparatory ground for the balkanization (division) and finlandization (pacification) of the Middle East" (Nazemroaya, 2006).

Nuances of division(s) are also prevailing in tweets that use 'balkanization' to refer to the Democratic Republic of the Congo (DRC) and the conflict in the Eastern Congo specifically (see Example 8), which cannot be understood without the considering the role that neighboring countries played in it.

> *Example 8: Tout à fait! Le Congo n'est pas à vendre, il restera Un et indivisible. Non à la #BALKANISATION du #Congo! #TELEMA @mahanguHM @VitalKamerhe1* (Mukunda, 2016) [Adapted from French: Absolutely! Congo is not for sale, it will remain One and *indivisible.* No to the #BALKANISATION of #Congo! #TELEMA]

The conflict has its roots in the Rwandan genocide of 1994 when many of the Hutus entered DRC after being expelled from Rwanda. As Zapata explains, the Hutus "… terrorized and robbed the local population with impunity" (Zapata, 2011). When in October 1996 eastern Congolese Tutsi forced the Rwandans out of the Congo, they were fought in response by the Rwandan and Ugandan armies, and since then the Eastern Congo remains a hot zone of conflicts, war, and instability.

Different from "division(s)" archetypes correlated to the Middle East and Syria, those referring to the DRC, due to the explicit connectedness with the Rwandan genocide, often include rather heavier semantics in referring to genocides and massacres (see Examples 9 and 10).

> *Example 9:* Le #Congo connaît un génocide et un processus de #balkanisation avancé que semble ignorer le #FrontCitoyen http://wp.me/p23tlw-27Y #telema (ingetaweb, 2016) [Adapted from French: The #Congo is experiencing a *genocide* and an advanced #balkanization process that seems to be ignored by #FrontCitoyen]

> *Example 10:* NGETA #RDC!Les #massacres de #BÍ©ni, le #silence de la #Kabilie et la #balkanisation du #Congo: Tout est liÍ© !http://www.ingeta.com/les-massacres-de-beni-le-silence-de-la-kabilie-et-la-balkanisation-du-congo/ (afrikaaman, 2016) [Adapted from French: Ingeta #RDC! The *massacres* of the #Bicni, the silence of the Kabilie and the balkanisation of Congo: Everything is connected]

Such examples are intriguing to examine as they reveal how discourses of/on 'the Balkans' and those situated in Africa in general, come together when it comes to Western countries as influential and even dominant decision-makers in these places. Hanses (2006) for example, considers the 'balkanization' discourse as mobilized by

> … 'the Balkan discourse,' which constitutes the war in Bosnia as the product of ancient Balkan hatred and hence a conflict that the West could and should not solve. The opposing basic discourse, 'the Genocide discourse,' challenges this representation by arguing that the war was a genocide committed by Serbian military and political leaders and that the West had an ethical obligation to come to Bosnia's rescue. (p. 11)

Example 9 and 10 are clear exemplars of that association of the 'balkanization' discourse with the genocidal one that Hansen refers to. Hence, reflecting back on discussions of linkages between colonialism, Orientalism, and 'the Balkans' discourses (see section 2.3 Deconstructing 'Balkanization': Balkanism), the role of the Western influence at ostracizing and othering as central to these discourses, is unignorably vivid. It is, in fact, what has facilitated a recontextualization of 'balkanization' in a diverse set of spaces beyond the geographical ones as the next archetype is a witness of.

The second most prevailing 'balkanization' archetype takes place in cyberspace and associates 'balkanization' with data or Internet national regulations as illustrated in Example 11 below:

> *Example 11:* WARNING: #Internet May End By XMas http://huff.to/1paKFXlÂ The #digitaldivide writ larger--much larger...: the #balkanization of cyberspace? (Steele, 2014)

Different from the "divison(s)" archetype, the "data/Internet national regulations" archetype reaches its peak in 2014. This prevailing trend seems to be caused by few other earlier events, one being the leaking of classified information from the US National Security Agency (NSA) by Edward Snowden, former Central Intelligence Agency (CIA) employee in 2013. In 2014, among others, it was revealed that NSA had monitored Chancellor Angela Merkel's mobile phone ("Inside Snowden's Germany file", 2014), to which the Chancellor reacted with a call for data protection through national regulations and regionalization of communication network ("Data protection: Angela Merkel proposes Europe network", 2014). Prior to this though, other countries had already raised concerns similar to that of Germany, but which gained less attention. As Meinrath (2013) suggests, "Brazil is one of a handful of countries that includes Indonesia, Turkey, and India who have been on the fence in the last decade's debate over whether to develop an international framework to govern the Internet". Similarly, such intentions were raised after the then Brazilian President Dilma Rouseff followed evidence that the US had been surveilling her email.

While surveillance and data protection was one of the reasons to call for a nationalization of the Internet, the other was of a rather different nature – that of knowledge and information control by governments. Tweets such as that of Example 12, 13, and 14 connect 'balkanization' to the attempts of autocratic governments to firewall Internet content. Through the hyperlink shared in Example 12, Ingram (2014) writes how Turkish authorities would "… block access to specific content on the internet with as little as four hours notice, and without a court order". The image featuring the article shared in Example 13 (see Figure 3.5 below) where an "@" sign as a symbol of the Internet seems to be torn apart by the governments of China, Brazil, Germany, and Russia each drawing selfishly towards themselves, is a good illustration of the nationalization of the Internet.

Figure 3.5 Image Illustrating the "Data/Internet National Regulations" Archetype of 'Balkanization'
Note. Adapted from "The End of the Internet?" by G.M. Goldstein (2014).

The hyperlink shared in the same example provides with further insight into how this situation is not unique to Turkey. Goldstein (2014) explains how "autocracies, of course, have long regulated the flow of Internet data, with China being the most famous example". The link shared in the following Example 14 adds to the list Russia, India, and Iran, which as Alves (2014a) suggests "[r]egardless of the specifics of their actions, all these players have been invariably labeled as "balkanizers".

> *Example 12:* @ivan_herman https://gigaom.com/2014/02/06/turkey-passes-draconian-internet-law-turks-say-goodbye-to-their-freedom-of-speech/?utm_source=feedburner&utm_medium=feed&utm_campaign=Feed%3A+OmMalik+%28GigaOM%3A+Tech%29: the Turkey law against free speech. Towards Internet #Balkanization @timberners_lee (regesta_com, 2014)

> *Example 13:* Great article by Gordon M. Goldstein "How regional networks may replace the World Wide #Web" https://www.theatlantic.com/magazine/archive/2014/07/the-end-of-the-internet/372301/ #internet #balkanization (Tanczer, 2014)

> *Example 14:* RT @feromalo: The #Internet #Balkanization Fragmentation http://ow.ly/CdtPz vía @DiplomacyEdu #netgov #IGF #ICANN #theGIP (Radunovic, 2014)

Alves, being aware of the etymological roots of 'balkanization', suggests that "… the term should not be used in the context of international negotiations of Internet Governance, due to its pejorative connotations and misleading implications" (2014b). However, but Alves, no other user or author of article hyperlinked to any of the tweets which refer to 'balkanization' as the "data/Internet national regulations" archetype has called for questioning such a term.

Of course, the third position Cyberspace takes in terms of spaces associated with "#balkanization" is in correlation with the "data/Internet national regulations" archetype. However, cyberspace holds another separate archetype that I have named "data/software heterogeneity" archetype. While both archetypes share the same space, they differ in conceptualization as the latter refers to rather an abundance of an uncontrollable and unavoidable proliferation of data and software options (see Examples 15 and 16).

> *Example 15: Les «applis» pour téléphones portables sont un problème : autant de versions à réaliser qu'il y a de système d'exploitation. #balkanisation* (Stoehr, 2014) [Adapted from French: Apps for mobile phones are a *problem*: as many versions have to be realized as there are operating system. #balkanisation]

> *Example 16:* #Balkanization: Is #DataScience Ripe for Consolidation? http://buff.ly/1QxtDPXÂ |by @fdouetteau on @DataScience (dataiku, 2016)

The alarming nature of balkanization' lingers on as words such as "problem" remain close to it (see Example 15). In the hyperlinked article titled "Technoslavia or the Balkanization of Data Science" (2015) shared in Example 16, Douetteau asks:

> A time of similar heterogeneity marked the early 80s for data storage technologies…. What is the future in the world of data: unified by a single language and the victory of one player over the others? Will the multiple republics of data will soon give birth to a new Empire?

Douetteau (2015) refers to "Technoslavia" as that one unified "empire" of data, as opposed to 'balkanization' as a "successive fragmentations of empires [which] led to the creation of autonomous states, which were sometimes united against their common enemies (the two great empires), sometimes hostile towards each other". While it might seem that tweets under this archetype avoid apocalyptic impressions conveyed through the end or 'death' of the Internet due to rather reflecting heterogeneity, hence emergence, existence, or life, they nevertheless continue to remain associated with phases of becoming, of "either/or", or of transitional confusions while breaking away from a banner of unity into one of borders and irreconcilable differences. As such, this archetype retains catastrophic nuances of something unwanted which is still not there, but is yet to come. Hence, Douetteau (2015) advertises Dataiku's services as its CEO through concluding that "… Technoslavia is built to last" (i.e. and 'balkanization' to end and perish if considering the title of his article).

From the archetypes presented until now, 'balkanization' stands for an opposite of Yugoslavia and the unity it portrayed, while it being a metaphor for fragmentation, national regulation, and heterogeneity. From this then, if the opposite of 'balkanization' would present some form of denationalization so to speak, shouldn't 'the Balkans' then at least 'tick the box' of nation-states, nationalism, or nationality? As this might not be the case, this directs us towards the next archetype: "nation(alism/ality)" archetype. This discourse of nation(alism/ality) and independence associated with 'balkanization' reaches even India and Pakistan (both among the top ten spaces associated with 'balkanization') and quite often manifests itself in relation to the Kashmiri territorial conflict by not only as it extends towards what is being called "Islamists" and Muslims in general, but also while reaching even the Indian caste system of differentiation (see Examples 17 and 18).

> *Example 17:* aiming for the #balkanisation of #India including #Kashmiri #Islamists, NE #insurgents, #Maoists in Bengal, Chhattisgarh, 2/3 (Sharma, 2016)

> *Example 18:* #Modi's playing Kaun Hoga Alienate? left right and center in a reckless prelude to #Balkanization. Dalits, Farmers, Muslims, #Kashmir, next? (godavar, 2016)

However, what is currently very prevailing in connecting 'balkanization' to nuances of nationali(ism/ity) are the recent events of calls for referendums of independence in the EU in specific and Europe in general which have brought back discussions on nation states (see Example 19). The famous withdrawal of UK from the EU also known as Brexit (portmanteau of "British" and "exit"), elicited discussions on Scotland's call for a second referendum of independence due to having voted "no" to leaving the EU (de Freytas-Tamura, 2016) (see Example 20) and Northern Ireland following the same example (see Example 21). The examples also explain the positions that the UK and Scotland take among the top ten associated spaces with 'balkanization' (see Table 3.3 above). Furthermore, they represent examples of how an archetype correlates with many others as that of "nation(alism/unity)" results unquestionably related to that of "division(s)" as mentioned before and "independence". Catalonia's call for independence from Spain (see Example 22) helped spread out commentaries in a domino-effect fashion on other countries and places breaking away from nation states or unions, including Italy, France, Netherlands, and Denmark among those (see Example 21).

> *Example 19:* Opinion: We can still stop the #Balkanization of the #EU http://www.dw.com/p/2XR4j?t wÂ | @dwnews (Demjanski, 2017)

> *Example 20:* Hate to say it...but are we just about to witness the #Balkanisation of the EU, with #Brexit, and then the UK, when Scotland splits? (Istros_books, 2016)

Example 21: Corbyn supports a united Ireland yet plots to divide England. #balkanisation http://www.thejournal.ie/jeremy-corbyn-united-ireland-2354277-Sep2015/ (Ulf_Fenisc, 2017)

Example 22: Rafael Arenas García: Why #Catalonia Should Stay With #Spain, via @nytimes #nationalism #balkanisation https://www.nytimes.com/2017/05/09/opinion/why-catalonia-should-stay-with-spain.html?smprod=nytcore-iphone&smid=nytcore-iphone-share
(Andreasson, 2017)

Example 23: #Balkanization Brexit Fever: Italy, France, Netherlands & Denmark Seek Vote On Leaving EU http://www.informationliberation.com/?id=55062 (Burton, 2016)

To include here an observation on formal structures, another image accompanying the article shared in Example 19 (see Figure 3.6 below), shows the EU flag torn in half with a background of a clear sky which might indicate the remaining hope of still saving the EU by stopping its 'balkanization' as Dedovic's (2017) article suggests. The similarities between this image and the "data/Internet national regulations" archetype image above (see Figure 3.5 above) are striking, although the central arguments of both are different. In both cases, there are flags being torn apart indicating a previous existing unity being threatened now. As such, the flags are a perfect illustration of the past and present conjoined into one, and a measurement unit of how things are supposed to be and how they actually are. Nearly ironically though, while the flag has been an accompanying symbol of nations, nation-states, nationality, and nationalism, in this case it represents a symbol being threatened exactly by the same, putting 'balkanization' in this way in a very ambiguous conceptual position of both, threatening and encouraging of national interests. This liminal position of 'balkanization' will gradually get confirmed as we proceed with the following examples of tweets.

Figure 3.6 Image Illustrating the "National(ism/ity)" Archetype of 'Balkanization'
Note. Adapted from "Opinion: We can still stop the Balkanization of the EU" by D. Dedovic (2017).

The tweets above (see Examples 19-23) continue in retaining apocalyptic nuances of 'balkanization'. The hyperlinked article shared in Example 19 begins with: "[n]ationalistic intrigues, economic meltdown, divisions: Are we talking about Yugoslavia in the early 1990s? No. This is the European Union, 25 years after its founding" (Dedovic, 2017). Dedovic (2017) presents a perfect example of ethical, spatial and temporal elements of identity conjoined into a single quote. He draws an analogy between the current EU condition of countries wanting to leave the Union and the Balkan wars in the 1990s, but importantly by including there that element of time which being stuck in 'the Balkans' should not be a surprise but should definitely be one for the 25 years funded EU. He too ends his article with a perilous prophecy of "… either a consensus is reached on competence to act on foreign policy issues, solidarity among member states, and reliable joint budget management, or the European Union, in its current form, will perish. The clock is ticking" (Dedovic, 2017).

On a similar logic of apocalyptic and cosmic dimensions but in a rather satirical fashion, Burnett (2016) talks about Earth's referendum on membership of the solar system that he calls "Earthxit" (see Example 24). According to him, "current approaches tend to heavily favour those who believe Earth would be better off as an independent planet, slowly and aimlessly wandering the cosmos while rapidly freezing solid and becoming hostile to all present life forms…" (Burnett, 2016). Even more convincingly, when elaborating on the argument of those who supposedly vote for Earth to stay within the solar system, he says that the most often given reason is "Wouldn't that kill everyone and everything?" (Burnett, 2016). Although Bernett does not mention 'balkanization' himself, Example 25 presents a reply to his tweet within the same thread that associated all of this with 'balkanization'.

> *Example 24:* Earthxit? Support for Earth leaving the solar system is overstated http://gu.com/p/4tx7t/stw Bit of a #Brexit piss take, because why not (Burnett, 2016)

> *Example 25:* Don't knock #Texit or #Cornwallexit... or... #Balkanisation (BW_2012_origin, 2016)

Remaining within Europe, we see that 'the exit' wave was taking place in parallel to another discourse on security, Muslims, Islam, and Islamophobia. The Global Terrorism Database released its report on the fatal terrorist attacks in Western Europe increasing (Miller, 2017). Besides Brexit being a manifestation of rising populist and nationalist rhetoric, it among others advocated for tighter control of immigration of mostly Muslim groups (Ledwith, 2016). Over 100 hate faith-based incidents were recorded by the Muslim Council of Britain place since the Brexit were announced on June 24, 2016 (The Muslim Council of Britain, 2017), concluding that Brexit fueled anti-Muslim sentiments in the UK. This brings us to our next "Islam/Muslim" archetype (see Examples 26 and 27).

> *Example 26:* Muslim no go areas exist, confirm UK Police https://themuslimissue.wordpress.com/2015/12/09/uk-cop-there-are-areas-we-have-to-ask-muslim-leaders-permission-to-patrol/ (Vance, 2017)

> *Example 27:* Sayyyyyyyyy WHUT!! So the rule of law doesn't extend everywhere or indeed equitably #balkanisation (Judsteroo, 2017)

Example 27 is a reply to Example 26 and the hyperlinked article shared which reveals areas in the UK where British policeman are not allowed to patrol without the permission of local Muslim leaders ("UK cop: 'There are areas we have to ask Muslim leaders' permission to patrol'", 2015). Irrespectively of the fact that the article has no evidence to support the claim, what is important is that although being written in 2015 he article was rather tweeted in 2017. This complements Table 3.2 above which reflects the "Islam/Muslim" archetype reaching its peak in 2017.

Such an increasing trend is not only visible in the UK and in relation to Brexit as something new that 2017 connects 'balkanization' with. Already in 2015, conversations along the same lines as those in the UK, connect 'balkanization' to "'no go" zones in several cities in France where sharia law is the governing instrument and police are not allowed to enter" (Keith, 2015) (see Example 28). The article further elaborates that "[b]y giving incentive to Muslim immigrants to not only resist all assimilation, but to establish a separate country within a country, the French have effectively allowed the Balkanization of their homeland, which will alter it forever – and not for the better" (Keith, 2015).

> *Example 28:* Blog: The Muslim #Balkanization of the West #Transformation #CivilizationJihad #StealthJihad http://www.americanthinker.com/blog/2015/01/the_muslim_balkanization_of_the_west.html#.VK-GpM4z2n0.twitter (amadorn, 2015)

However, best examples of "Islam/Muslim", "(anti)im(migration)" and "race(ism)" archetypes assembled together are rather found in tweets where 'balkanization' is used in reference to the US which takes the first position of all spaces (see Table 3.3 above). In the US 'balkanization' seems to be tightly connected to public figures and presidential candidates during elections, from which also the "Barack Obama", "Donald Trump", and "Hillary Clinton" archetypes emerge from, although not within the top ten archetypes (see Appendix A for more). With Donald Trump running for office in 2016, tweets associating 'balkanization' with the US reached their peak (see Examples 29 – 32 below).

> *Example 29:* If #Trump doesn't win expect #Balkanization in America. Repeat after me: "Diversity is not a strength." (celesteangel234, 2016)

> *Example 30:* Is #Trump advocating #balkanization of the #UnitedStates? #HipHop #Dems #Evidencebasedresearch #cyberwarfare #changeplayingfield #sexism (donalddjmorin, 2016)

> *Example 31:* If this year's #IdentityPolitics are the new normal in elections, will the US fall into #Balkanization? #Trump #Bernie (InAquaSanitas, 2016)

> *Example 32:* O'Hillary sez #Trump plays into #ISIS hands. #Trump sez O'Hillary plays into #Balkanization. (MindofMo, 2016)

Nuances of Islam, Muslim and terrorism are inevitably connected to those of (anti)im(migration), especially since once in office Trump signed an executive order (Exec. Order. No. 13769, 2017) also known as the Muslim ban (Scott, 2017), and which among others blocked entry of people from Iran, Iraq, Libya, Somalia, Sudan, Syria, and Yemen, for at least 90 days. However, the same were circulating already before Trump being elected as a president while during his electoral campaign he promised to build a wall that would protect the US from immigrants. This is what Example 33 refers to.

Example 33: #TrumpIsRight #BuildTheWall #WestDelugedWithMigrants #Welfare #Balkanization @TheKuhnerReport @realDonaldTrump #tcot (SashaGirlVegas, 2017)

As such, the discourse of the immigrants in the US in relation to 'balkanization' goes beyond Muslim refugees and terrorist threats, in referring to the cultural diversity of US in general, but specifically used closely to the Hispanic and Latino immigrants already since 2013 (see Examples 34 and 35).

Example 34: Very real and sobering. "Buchanan: Hispanic influx from immigration could break US into '2 countries' http://dailycaller.com/2013/06/23/buchanan-hispanic-influx-from-immigration-bill-could-break-us-into-two-countries/#ixzz2X6G21owo" #Balkanization (Davidiuk, 2013)

Example 35: @sfcpoll needs to recognize that #Latino #immigration raises distinctive questions re #balkanization/#bilingualism: https://www.reuters.com/article/us-omnivision-techs-proposal/chinese-group-proposes-to-buy-u-s-chipmaker-omnivision-idUSKBN0GE1IL20140814 (Tonelson, 2014)

Such tweets are closely related to the archetype of "unity, unification or union" in the US, where 'balkanization' seems to play its counterpart (see Example 36). Connected to nuances of diversity and heterogeneity, immigrants unwilling to assimilate seem to present a threat to the US which although built upon diversity ironically claims its unity through the idea of a 'melting pot' (U.S. Census Bureau, 1995, p. 1) and homogeneity.

Example 36: @sallykohn Fuck unity. Why force 315+ million people, with differing values, ideologies, etc. to stay together? #Balkanization (Agent_Orange76, 2016)

This in turn then is connected to the archetype of "race(ism)" (see Examples 37 and 38). To Obama's consideration of implementing legal structures that would apply only to the state's native Hawaiian Sen, the article shared in example 37 replies with "if you can do that with groups that are already part of the mainstream, you can balkanize the country" (Agee, 2014). This transmits nuances of favoritisms and racial segregation. However, the user in Example 38 of a more recent time seems to differentiate between 'balkanization' as border securitization from racism. This only adds up to the already communicated ambiguity associated with 'balkanization' because if something has been transmitted through 'balkanization' in the above-presented examples has been exactly the opposite edge of secure borders and legal immigration.

Example 37: Is Obama Going To Establish Separate Government Structures Based On Race? #Balkanization #Transformation http://www.westernjournalism.com/obama-wants-establish-separate-government-structures-based-race/?utm_source=wysija&utm_medium=email&utm_campaign=DailyEmailÂ (amadorn, 2014)

Example 38: It isn't '#Racism' to demand #SecureBorders and #LegalImmigration. -- #NotRacist #NWO ##Balkanization (psycotria, 2016)

However, the user (psycotria, 2016) in Example 38 gets closer to the conceptual associations of 'balkanization' precisely through that ambiguous argument. From what has been presented until now as most frequent archetypes and spaces concomitant to 'balkanization', we have been moving not only across countries and continents, but also among fields of thought and expertise. An example of this is the "data/Internet national regulations" and "data/software heterogeneity" archetypes. Others such as the "demograph(y/ic)", "justice system/legislation", "financ(es/ial)", as well as "sport", and "music(al)" 'balkanization', appear in between the two poles of frequency (see Appendix A for more). Hence, 'balkanization' is indeed a global phenomenon not only in terms of spatiality, but also as a mental model of cognition.

This directs us towards the one space of Table 3.3 that I have not elaborated on, the globe that is. I called "global" the space that tweets that transmit global dimensions not related to a specific geography (see example 39) convey.

> *Example 39:* #Balkanization, the wave of the future? #global #geopolitics #war #strategy https://unitedcats.wordpress.com/2012/11/08/balkanization-the-wave-of-the-future/ (FatmaEr_PhD, 2016)

In the article shared in Example 39, Doug's Darkwold (2012) ends with a prediction:

> What does the future hold? My guess is a lot more Balkanization.... there are thousands of ethnic groups on the planet, and only a few hundred governments. Many of these thousands of people would prefer to have their own nation.... On the other hand, modern propaganda is ever more effectively blurring the boundary between people and government. In some cases, governments and peoples more or less overlap.

Yet, no matter the global and omnipresent dimensions 'balkanization' may take, it is still a "wave of the future" (Doug's Darkworld, 2012) which is here and there, has always been, but has never reached a state of completion, accomplishment, termination, and finale. This transforms 'balkanization' into something never really existent and self-realized, but simultaneously very much present hence existent, and it is precisely where the discourse of 'balkanization' seems to rely on. Time, which "... has been peculiar in the Balkans" (de Lange, 2016, p. 10), seems to be stuck in a constant invention. Hence, 'balkanization' has remained a process, an either/or, a neither/nor, a becoming, a "nearly there, but never there". From this perspective, as already noticed in some of the examples presented above, 'balkanization' is closely connected to nuances of apocalypse and clashes of dichotomies.

In Death Masks by Jim Butcher (2011) Nicodemus explains to Dresden what apocalypse is: "'Dresden, Dresden. The Apocalypse, as you refer to it, isn't an event. At least, it isn't any specific event ... Apocalypse is a frame of mind', he said then. 'A belief. A surrender to inevitability. It is despair for the future. It is the death of hope'" (p. 417). Such description of apocalypse that assembles together all at once the belief and the surrender, hope and despair, future and death as a frame of mind, seems fitting to a summarized view on what dominant archetypes of the 'balkanization' discourse stand for.

Hence, as this subsection revels and as the next one further proves, the place of 'balkanization' is not in any of the edges of these archetypes, because 'balkanization' lives liminaly between the archetypes and their extremes; it is the antonyms and the synonym of these archetypes; the crave for nation states and the failure to reach one, as much as the over-manifestation of self-realized entities that follow only their narrow interests; the abundance of diversity and heterogeneity, but the failure of realizing its fruits; the segregated 'melting pot'; the in-between of barbarism and the never-reached civilization, hence in between a shameful past and an existing but never reaching future. As such, 'balkanization' is a threat to a Western future with a glorious past which has to, unfortunately, deal with the challenges it presents, because, yet again, 'the Balkans' are geographically European, hence 'balkanization' is Europe as much as its other.

3.3.2 Through archetypes: The pole of the infrequent

There are two main reasons for presenting the following archetypes – first, I have already elaborated on the importance of reaching towards the least presented of/in a discourse due to its lack of frequency or presence being a source of observation in itself; second, although mentioned only once among the 1892 tweets that included "#balkanization", the following examples are no less important in illustrating the dimensions that 'balkanization' is taking in reaching and recontextualizing continuously towards new unusual concepts and spaces. Different from the omnipresent archetypes and spaces, the ones presented below do not have a correlation among each other (i.e. an archetype mentioned only once does not necessarily connect to any of the spaces mentioned as well only once). An example of this would the "spirit" archetype (see Example 63 below), which although specifically refers to the "balkanization of spirits" (BoshRoger, 2014), is placed in the DRC and which also takes place among the top ten spaces associated with 'balkanization' (see Table 3.3 above). This is also the reason why the following examples might not have a flowing logical thread in between. They rather resemble a list of examples that might seem detached from each other, but which are rather brought together by the internal mechanism of argumentation operating underneath, indeed that of 'balkanization'.

I start this time with the bottom ten spaces associated with 'balkanization' (see Table 3.4 below). I find this a better transitive presentation due to the spaces still holding some political, social, and cultural dimensions connected with some of the top ten archetypes and spaces presented in the previous subsection.

Table 3.4 Bottom Ten Spaces Associated with "#Balkanization"

Note. The numbers in the cells represent the number of times a particular space was associated with tweets in respective years. The table follows a scaling shade formatting rule in which the brighter the shade the less the frequency of the space.

Spaces	2009	2010	2011	2012	2013	2014	2015	2016	2017	Total
North Korea									1	1
Azerbaijan				1						1
Scandinavia						1				1
Baltic countries						1				1
Gambia									1	1
Myanmar					1					1
Nepal							1			1
The North Pole				1						1
Mesopotamia							1			1
Eugoslavia								1		1

As frequency plays the same role for all of these spaces due to all of them being explicitly referred to in the tweets only once, the choice of beginning with one is rather of an arbitrary nature. Due to having already elaborated on the Trump's associations with 'balkanization', perhaps a good example to begin with would be the so-called "fake new" and the famous Donald Trump's "phony war" (Yglesias, 2018) with the press which refers to the president's aggressive and hostile denunciations towards the American journalistic institutions and media channels. Although the term appeared quite recently during the Trump's presidential campaign and has been carried with him when resuming office, 'balkanization' did not miss on being associated with the same, only now specifically referring to an event taking place in North Korea and involving US and the North Korean authorities (see Example 40).

> *Example 40:* #MichelleMalkin The #Statists #fakenews media #balkanization on The double murder of #OttoWarmbier #NorthKorea https://www.conservativereview.com/articles/malkin-the-double-murder-of-otto-warmbier/#sthash.jyaumA9H.uxfs (McDaniel, 2017)

The article hyperlinked in Example 40 speaks of an American student, Otto Warmbier, who lost his life at the age of 22 after having fallen into a coma while in the hands of the North Korean authorities (Malkin, 2017). While visiting North Korea as a tourist in 2013, Wambier was sentenced to 15 years imprisonment with hard labor, due to having attempted to steal a propaganda sign (Ramzy, 2016).

It is not unusual for 'balkanization' tagged in tweets to be surrounded by discourse categories such as vagueness and paraphrasing (i.e. not being mentioned in the hyperlinked texts, but being tweeted by the users when sharing those texts). Example 40 is just one among the many tweets in which no clear explanation on what is meant with 'balkanization' is given. However, Malkin (2017) blames bloggers, comedians, liberals, and left-wing websites, for "killing" Warmbier even before he actually died. She claims that "[u]tterly consumed by malignant identity politics, the left-wing intelligentsia have become the intolerantsia. They are bent on dehumanizing individuals – fomenting racial, ethnic and class division in the name of 'progressivism,' and never taking responsibility for the damage done" (Malkin, 2017). From this then, we can assume that 'balkanization' could either refer to the 'balkanized' media as in the clashes between a right-wing and left-wing ideological differences, or to all that Malkin (2017) assigned to what she calls the "click-hungry media ghouls", such as dehumanization incentives, infiltration of societal divisions, and avoidance of responsibility for the same. In any of these cases, no encouraging attributes are to be identified.

The same fashion appears in the next example, now being placed in Armenia, Hungary, and Azerbaijan while the latter being mentioned only once in the whole corpus of tweets (see Example 41).

> *Example 41:* Hundreds protest pardon of man who killed Armenian military officer http://tinyurl.com/bnrse5d #balkanization (ishtarmuz, 2012)

Again, being surrounded by vagueness and paraphrasing, there is not much we can understand on what is meant with 'balkanization' from the tweet itself. It is rather the hyperlinked text that leaves some space for interpretation. The article speaks of a protest taking place in front of the Hungary and Azerbaijan consulates due to the release and pardon of Ramil Safarov, an Azerbaijani soldier convicted of killing Gurgen Markarian, an Armenian military officer while in a NATO training seminar in Budapest. After being sentenced to life imprisonment in Hungary, Safarov was extradited to Azerbaijan where he was left free and treated as a hero. Among others, the article refers to the Azerbaijani and Armenian "... violent conflict over disputed border territory for more than two decades" (Aghajanian & Wells, 2012), and from this it is to be considered that 'balkanization' either refers to the situation of a conflict over territories (which would not be anything new); it refers to the situation of protests and unrests in general; or to both.

Figure 3.7 Image Illustrating Associations of 'Balkanization' with Azerbaijan
Note. Adapted from "Hundreds protest pardon of man who killed Armenian military officer" by L. Aghajanian and J. Wells (2012).

In any of these cases, it is worth mentioning that in terms of formal structures, 'balkanization' continues to be accompanied by a constantly reappearing symbolism of flags as Figure 3.7 above shows, even in singular associations with a particular country and concept. Aside the Armenian flags, the protesters are holding banners with quotes accompanied by, again, war-like terminology inclusive of "blood" and the presence of soldiers in uniforms, but moreover giving to this nuances that transcend the specifics of the context as the signs refer to "humanity" per se. This leaves 'balkanization' fluctuating in between the very specific (i.e. always the pejorative) on one side, and then the very general and all-inclusive on the other (i.e. humanity as a whole).

The next spatial reference contextualizes 'balkanization' in the Scandinavians and the Baltics (see Example 42). Vagueness characterizes this tweet as well, but after some research made, the tweet seems to be referring to the Meeting of Nordic and Baltic foreign ministers in Estonia, in which Sweden was represented by the Minister for Foreign Affairs Carl Bildt (Government of Offices of Sweden, 2014). In the tweet below (see Example 42) there is no source used to support Bildt's claim, while it is clear that the quote is an ironic statement written by the user. However, this is not the only time Bild, known as the UN's special envoy to the Balkans between 1999 and 200, has been associated with 'balkanization'. In another tweet (see Example 43) the hyperlinked text revels Bild warning of Scottish independence while stating: "I think it's going to have far more profound implications than people think. The Balkanisation of the British Isles is something we are not looking forward to" (Milne, 2014).

> *Example 42:* Carl Bildt @carlbildt came out for a union of the Scandinavians + Baltics "We have to stop this #Balkanization of pasty faced white people" (DavidEdenden, 2014)

> *Example 43*: #Balkanisation Looking for FM who uses words that look "cool" & not for what they really mean? Here's Carl #Bildt https://www.ft.com/content/1a45b9bc-e258-11e3-89fd-00144feabdc0 (Siddi, 2014)

While such tweets put "white people" (DavidEdenden, 2014) and the Western countries in a worrisome situation about a wave of 'balkanization' threating them, the following case (see Example 44) which places 'balkanization' into an African context, blames precisely the Westerners for the 'balkanization' of Gambia and Africa. The tweet refers to Western countries as "western rapists" (Slie_maJobe, 2017), externalizing agency to them as perpetrators for a situation of victimhood. Bild talks of 'balkanization' as a threat but yet external to the British Isles as it is a risk that may or may not reach them, while the user in Example 44 externalizes agency through blaming Western countries for a situation which is there, but as rather brought and not unique to the context. However, whether the Western countries are the victims (see Example 43) or the perpetrators (see Example 44), in both cases it is clear that 'balkanization' resembles a 'child of guilt' that no one wants to adopt.

> *Example 44:* @safmmiddaylive #Gambia like the rest of Africa is a victim of #balkanization by #westernrapists. Meanwhile, #SABC ignores #Palestinians. (Slie_maJobe, 2017)

Western countries remain as stakeholders also in the following example (see Example 45). Next, in Myanmar, while the agency for 'balkanization' remains external to the Western countries, the responsibility for intervening to fix the same does not. In the article shared in Example 45, Kurlantzick (2013) draws analogous links between the anti-Muslim violence in Myanmar and "post-Cold War Yugoslavia". He states that "[w]ith Myanmar attempting to make the transition to democracy from one of the most repressive regimes on earth, this rising ethnic hatred, and attacks could turn the country into at twenty-first century version of post-Cold War Yugoslavia" (Kurlantzick, 2013).

> *Example 45:* Western states need to nip this in the bud before evolving into bigger problem #balkanization http://on.cfr.org/YLVGVA on.cfr.org/YLVGVA via @CFR_org (Anthony, 2013)

From this then, 'balkanization' remains a "problem" (Anthony, 2013) needing to be resolved by external influence due to its internal incapability. Again though, intervention can remain an option only as long as a problem remains a problem. Hence, 'balkanization' remains a process of either the present continuous, or of the future, but never of the completed past.

While placing 'balkanization' this time in Nepal, Example 46 follows the same logic. After nearly a decade of internal conflicts, in September 2015 the Nepalese government adopted a new constitution as a secular republic divided into seven federal provinces (Majumder, 2015). This is believed to have fueled India's intervention in preventing support for the constitution due to having insured that Nepal remains under India's influence rather than China's by lingering in a needy situation and relying heavily on supplies from India (India Tries to Shape Nepal's New Constitution, 2015).

> *Example 46:* #India has intervened in favor of ethnic #Balkanization in #Nepal, writes The Wall Street Journal #BlockadeBlue http://www.wsj.com/articles/the-struggle-for-nepal-1447377158 (Pkharel, 2015)

In the article hyperlinked in Example 46, Wall street Journal writes

> … Nepal has struggled with violent protests and an Indian fuel blockade over the past two months. Elements of one large ethnic group oppose a new constitution that is the country's best hope to heal the rifts of a civil war. Worst of all, New Delhi has intervened in favor of ethnic Balkanization, a blunder that will harm Nepal even as it undermines India's influence in the Himalayas. ("The Struggle for Nepal", 2015)

Different from Example 45 where external influences are expected to improve a 'balkanized' situation, in Example 46 the opposite takes place as external stimuluses are to be held accountable for internal circumstances. In both cases though, 'balkanization' not only remains an unwanted and continuous problematic situation, but it also calls for the component of the external, or in this case its abstention from action, in order for a situation to improve and take the desired shape.

As such of a pattern of thought, 'balkanization' seems to be applied to any situation that conveys the same difficulties or complications. It even reaches the North Pole as Examples 47, 48, and 49 reveal below. The three tweets are extracted from the same thread of tweets and stand for replies to each other in the order presented.

> *Example 47:* Russia doesn't argue over trifling islands when they can claim the North Pole @venkatananth @rubenmasc http://ow.ly/e3Nbj (Paul, 2012)

> *Example 48:* @adityampaul True, The North Pole might just emerge as the 21st century Balkans! #Balkanisation (Mascarenhas, 2012)

> *Example 49:* @rubenmasc not really antarctica is still left! You know we have a claim there too #Balkanisation (Paul, 2012)

In the article shared in Example 47, Jone and Parfitts (2012) write on Russia's tentative to claim ownership over the Arctic due to its North Pole sea oil and gas reserves. While the exchange of the tweets above retains nuances of external influences, it intensifies the same by making more vivid the ownership connotations they convey through referring to claims of territory. Also, the analogy to 'the Balkans' is explicitly stated as shown in Example 48.

However, while 'balkanization' retains conceptual ties to 'the Balkans', the idea of it has proven to need no geographic ties by it being recontextualized to different spaces, being those physical places or fields of thought. The tweet below is an example of this (see Example 50).

> *Example 50:* 1) God's take: The Tower of Babel is annoying. I'll make sure ppl can't talk to one another. That'll stop their endeavor #Balkanization (caljv, 2015)

The Tower of Bable is an origin myth from the Hebrew Book of Genesis that holds the narrative of God descending to hinder communication between people who were believed to speak a common language before, by creating many languages. With this God punishes people, who before as united come to the land of Shinar (as Mesopotamia is referred to in the Hebrew Bible) to arrogantly build the Tower that aimed to reach heaven (Metzger & David, 2004, p. 314). Such analogy seems to reveal a specific dynamics of power associated with 'balkanization' which has manifested itself also in the above-presented examples – first, diversity is seen and used as a punishable measure; second, such measure is applied by an external agent who deems ambitions as arrogance; third, that external agent is clearly in a higher and more powerful position to impose such retributions; fourth, the white and male privileged agent applies these penalties on his own creations who supposedly he loves (i.e. God in the role of the humanist, so to speak); and fifth, this due to people only wanting to get closer to him and being like him.

Such dynamics of "carrot and stick" in which the position of 'balkanization' seems to be in between the two, is nothing unfamiliar to this thesis. To contextualize this within Example 50, people are not only encouraged, but also instructed to follow God's instructions and commands as that will get them closer to God. However, they should not do as God does, as that would mean them becoming one (i.e. a God). Hence, 'balkanization' again manifests itself in a liminal position of sinners and God; continuous present due to a sinful past that is never completed because it is there to remind us of why the present is such as it is.

These tensions of power have followed 'balkanization' throughout the given examples above, and the last case below (see Example 51 as retweeted in Example 52) is no exception.

> *Example 51:* Welcome to EUgoslavia - new array of #EU subgroups is a sign of deeper malaise. | @politico | https://www.politico.eu/article/welcome-to-eugoslavia-balkans-regional-blocs-diplomacy-policy-eurozone-allies/?utm_content=buffer37acf&utm_medium=social&utm_source=twitter.com&utm_campaign=buffer (JSEEBSS, 2016)

> *Example 52:* We need a new definition of #Balkanization :) (Gashi, 2016)

On similar mythological tones, the Karnitschnig (2016) article as shared in Example 51, refers to a non-existing land he calls "EUgoslavia". Karnitschnig (2016) speaks of recent EU's fracturing tendencies due to many occurrences, such as Brexit, refugee crisis and border control, lack of credible leadership, the euro crisis, and the flawed Eurozone's architecture. Suggesting that such situations resemble former Yugoslavia, he says that now "... the Balkans are everywhere" (Karnitschnig, 2016). He believes that the only way for such difficulties to be overcome is if member states relinquish more sovereignty, as otherwise "[a] Balkanized Europe won't succeed in meeting such a challenge" (Karnitschnig, 2016).

It is rather unclear what Gashi (2016) refers to when claiming that a new definition of 'balkanization' is needed, but from the Karnitschnig's (2016) article we are left to assume that countries holding on to their sovereignty would equalize 'balkanization'. This, like many other conceptualizations of 'balkanization', remains rather ambiguous. 'Balkanization' yet again is placed in the continuous present of sovereign states that are too sovereign to ignore communality, and as such, they are a threat to the future; or of a continuous past of countries with no sovereignty under the banner of unity, but again resulting with a dysfunctional present. Sovereignty or not, the outcome is 'balkanization'.

With Eugoslavia I wrap up the bottom ten spaces associated with 'balkanization', only to proceed further in stretching connotations to spaces that seem to no longer need any physical geography. The archetypes below (see Table 3.5) are identified only once in the empirical corpus of all the tweets, but they reveal the growing conceptual and spatial dimensions of 'balkanization'. Moreover, the same reveal how even when least present, the 'balkanization' discourse is essentially a variation of what it has always been, only now way more diverse in connotations, reaching bigger audiences, and growing in meaning, hence relevance. Most of the archetypes presented below appear from 2013 onwards, reaffirming in this way that 'balkanization' is not only a term currently relevant, but also one that is growing in usage and meanings associated with it. Considering the speed of spreading information that social media have as a potential, the same would be expected to continue to at least expand if not multiply.

Table 3.5 Bottom Ten Archetypes Associated with "#Balkanization"
Note. The numbers in the cells represent the number of times a particular space was associated with tweets in respective years. The table follows a scaling shade formatting rule in which the brighter the shade the less the frequency of the space.

Archetypes	2009	2010	2011	2012	2013	2014	2015	2016	2017	Total
Academia								1		1
Advertising Agencies							1			1
Digital Health						1				1
Gaming								1		1
Pharma					1					1
Discourse							1			1
Wikipedia					1					1
Ethic(s/al)									1	1
Spirit						1				1
Poetry								1		1

As we slowly approach the final observations of this thesis which is indeed an academic endeavor, let us, therefore, connect with the first of the bottom ten archetypes as depicted in Table 3.5: 'balkanization of the "academia" (see Example 53).

Example 53: Academic Drivel Report #academic #hoax #research #balkanization #knowledge #management http://prospect.org/article/academic-drivel-report (Grosdidier, 2016)

In the hyperlink attached to the tweet, Dreirer (2006) tells the story of him submitting an abstract which he himself did not understand, but which got nevertheless accepted only due to the grandiosity of the words he used. "My paper had no point at all. It was filled entirely with non-sequiturs" says Dreier (2016). Dreirer (2016) argues against strong disciplinary loyalties, academic pomposity, and increased academic specialization. While doing this, he states that "as academia becomes more and more fragmented and balkanized into more narrow niches, an increasing proportion of what academics produce is unnecessarily obscure and obtuse, and, not surprisingly, poorly written". Although Dreirer's intentions are easily understood and accessible from his text, he himself uses pompous words whose meaning is expected to be understood automatically by the audience he is speaking to – 'balkanization' being one of them. This must happen so due to Dreirer not considering 'balkanization' a pompous word whose meaning is not familiar to the public, but quite the contrary. Should this be the case then, it yet feels quite difficult to draw any conceptual specificity of the term from his quote, especially as used not as synonymous but as an accompanying element to "fragmentation" (Dreier, 2016).

However, the relevance of all of this lies in the liminal position of the term between what is evidently familiar and hence quite specific in meaning to an extent that needs no explanation, and at the same time what is the all-descriptive one applicable to a diverse range of situations. To Dreirer (or at least his actions), not considering the detection of this, does not seem to be a proper academic task. Without going into debates of whether discussing terminology is a useless endeavor that remains on a theoretical level of ontological conversations, there is a general consensus at least on the claim that the critical imperative is not only a characteristic, but also a precondition to the existence of the academia. It is this what Dreirer fails to practice with regards to 'balkanization', and it is here where perhaps academia, in general, fails as well.

For the sake of the argument and remaining within the space of the academia, I now just briefly reach beyond the bottom ten archetypes of 'balkanization' and present the following two tweets (see Example 54 and 55) as the only two representatives of the 'balkanization' of "research methods" archetype.

> *Example 54: Diversité des disciplines et des méthodes mais pb de la dispersion #balkanisation #jeoa13* (Bianchini, 2013) [Adapted from French: Diversity of disciplines and methods but problem of dispersion #balkanisation # jeoa13]

> *Example 55:* Continuing in the prior spirit of discourses: I just read about the '#Balkanization of research methods' from a respectable research guide. (Vaulasvirta, 2015)

Following very much Dreirer's (2016) line of argument, while neither of the tweets offers a clear explanation on what is meant with the 'balkanization' of research methods and disciplines, Vaulasvirta's (2015) tweet leaves some space for research and interpretation. Although in the lack of supporting evidence, after some research done I presume that what Vaulasvirta (2015) refers to is *The Sage Handbook of Organizational Research Methods* (Buchanan & Bryman, 2009). Buchaman and Bryman (2009) consider 'balkanization' as another contemporary feature of organizational research as "[t]he field appears to have fragmented geographically, epistemologically and methodologically…" (p. 706).

With this, Buchman and Bryman (2009) open the space for the following examples of conceptual connotations associated with 'balkanization' which, as we will see, appear to even transcend the scope of geographic, epistemological and methodological dimensions. As we go through the subsequent archetypes, it becomes clearer that if in the top ten 'balkanization' archetypes there were geographic string attached to specific scenarios taking place in specific places, the bottom ten archetypes reveal that most recent trends of 'balkanization' are, in fact, considering that geographic component as not necessary, or rather are not considering that component at all. The importance of recognizing such a trend is not in that 'balkanization' is becoming 'undressed' from its context [this was already revealed through the genealogy of the term (see subsection 2.2.2 'Balkanization' in the aftermath of the Second World War: Re-contextualization)], but in that the trend continues to produce other recontextualizations which knowing that they have no clear etymological foundations at the first place, make the ambiguous element accompanying 'balkanization' even stronger, more present and vivid.

Crain (2015) article shared in Example 56, refers to 'balkanization' as "... the ruination of the advertising agency business". Crain (2015) retains nuances of divisions of hostile and noncooperative parts of a whole by claiming that "[a]gency balkanization has been driven by the shortsighted belief that each agency discipline belongs in a separate house'", but recontextualizes the whole discourse from the field of politics and societal occurrences to that of a digital world referring very explicitly to the 'balkanization' of advertising agencies.

> *Example 56:* Ad agencies have specialized themselves to death aka #Balkanization according to new book via @adage http://ow.ly/Sdp2o (otherwisz, 2015)

Along similar yet different lines, Wilkins (2014) in a hyperlinked article shared in Example 56, uses the story of his wife struggling with medical records during her hospitalization on an emergency basis. The reason for this hassle was that, as Wilkins (2014) states, his wife "... has 11 separate 'patient portals' (and passwords to recall) from 11 different providers (hospitals, doctors, and health plans) none of which talk to each other and none of which actually provide any relevant/helpful health information clinicians can use". By adding "#balkanization" while sharing this article, Ney (2014) associates 'balkanization' again with a digital world, but now rather specifically with that of digital health.

> *Example 57:* RT @kboreilly "My wife has 11 separate patient portals" which do not talk to each other http://ow.ly/CfXrE #balkanization #medtech (Ney, 2014)

Many nuances already conveyed through top ten archetypes (see subsection 3.3.1 Through archetypes: The pole of the dominant) reappear in the bottom ten while changing fields, components, and acting elements, hence resulting with different archetypes. Example 58 is another case of connotations of 'balkanization' remaining within the digital space, but now recontextualized specifically within an occurrence related to video gaming (see Example 58).

> *Example 58:* Windows 10 Store & #balkanization of gaming https://motherboard.vice.com/en_us/article /z438a8/windows-10-store-refunds-call-of-duty-player-because-nobodys-playing-it via @motherboard (Ivan, 2016)

Ivan (2016) describes as "balkanization of gaming" Gault's (2016) story on customers who bought the Call of Duty: Infinite Warfare PC gamers being segregated according to which storefront they had bought the game from. Gamers that had gotten the game from Windows 10 cannot play with other customers who bought the game from Steam, explains Gault (2016). Besides the segregation nuances which are already familiar as associated with 'balkanization', what draws attention is the name of the game which brings together both "duty" and "infinite warfare". Figure 3.8 below where, among others, a sniper getting ready to shoot its target is visible, is an illustration of the game. Such formal structures associated with wars, weapons, and even nuclear ones, are never too far from 'balkanization' and have come up repeatedly in the tweets, creating different archetypes which due to space limits I will not elaborate on (see for more Appendix A).

Figure 3.8 Image Illustrating "Gaming" Archetype of 'Balkanization'
Note. Adapted from "Windows 10 store refunds 'call of duty' player because nobody's playing it" by Gault, Matthew (2016).

'Balkanization' is transposed into a completely different setting and not surprising with vagueness surrounding it in Example 59. This time it seems like we are talking about the 'balkanization' of pharmaceuticals as Oncimmune refers to a leading early cancer detection company (http://oncimmune.com/about-oncimmune/). Although it is rather unclear from Kreps's (2013) tweet what is meant with 'balkanization' and no search resulted with any information, it is the mere act of placing 'balkanization' even into a drugs and medication industry that makes it worth mentioning. The second reason for presenting such example is that it only further enhanced the vagueness surrounding the usage of 'balkanization', supported by a sense of naturality that needs no explanation yet no one seems to understand quite correctly as no conceptual consensus has taken place.

> *Example 59:* Dr Barnes talked about #Balkanization within context of #oncimmune and experience living in CA @kcalsi Symposium (Kreps, 2013)

Of course, while I do argue that the archetypes resulting from the analysis stand for conceptual models conveyed through 'balkanization', let us not forget that those are 204 archetypes in total that indeed retain similarities in meanings, but are used to present a big variety of situations and contexts. The tweet of Example 60 below follows the same lines in terms of abstruseness of definition, which in turn then condition a wide space for applicability of the term.

> *Example 60:* the #balkanization of #discourse - #dtapscott #sxsw #politics #vaccine #MH18 (Binette, 2015)

Binette (2015) includes in the tweet hashtag "#dtapscott" referring to Don Tapscott as a leading authority on media, technology, business, and their social impact in the world; "#sxsw" standing for the South by Southwest (abbreviated as SXSW) (https://www.sxsw.com/) as an annual festival and conference of interactive media; and "#vaccine" and "#MH18" which I was not able to contextualize. All of this expressed under the banner of "the #balkanization of #discourse" (Binette, 2015) with the many elaborations presented through the top and the bottom ten of spaces and archetypes associated with 'balkanization', leaves me to wonder whether the research question of my thesis should have rather been conceptualized as "what does *not* characterize 'balkanization' through Twitter subjectivities".

Example 61 is among the many cases adding to what seems to be an infinite and complex 'mosaic' of meanings associated with 'balkanization'.

> *Example 61:* #Wikipedia's #Balkanisation | via #Wikipediocracy http://wikipediocracy.com/2013/10/07/wikipedias-balkanisation (Wikiland, 2013)

Kolbe's (2013) article as shared in Example 61, speaks of "Wikipedia's Balkanisation". He raises the issue of extremists editing of content becoming prevalent due to moderates negligence, and Wikipedia allowing this through what he calls "the Wikipedia myth" (Kolbe, 2013) of balance through opposing views. He ends his article with claiming that "Wikipedia isn't biased in one clear direction, it's biased in a hundred directions at once, depending on which anonymous actors hold sway for a time on any given page, in any given language version of Wikipedia" (Kolbe, 2013). With this Kolbe reflects the familiar 'balkanization' discourse elements i.e. diversity reflected through multiplicity in terms of directions and actors, time and language, but also lack of directionality and incapability of dealing with such miscellany. However, Kolbe does not stop here. Before concluding that "[w]e are witnessing the balkanization of Wikipedia" (Kolbe, 2013), he adds to that incapacity and dysfunctionality a moral component. He claims that to the editors of Wikipedia, among which the presence of extremists is not unfamiliar either, "Wikipedia participation has nothing to do with altruism, or making the sum of human knowledge available to mankind, and everything to do with propaganda in the service of political, social or commercial goals" (Kolbe, 2013). With this Kolbe enhances another component to the 'balkanization' discourse – dysfunctionality not due to incapability, but due to a refusal based on wicked moral judgments.

Kolbe does not seem to be the only one conveying such views. Kimani (2017) in Example 62 below, refers to "ethical balkanization" as an all-inclusive term for situations that involve the opposite of taking charge of the present by detaching from the past.

> *Example 62:* Only freed from past burdens, can we take advantage of the present. Let's shun away from #mediocrity and #ethical #balkanization. (Kimani, 2017)

According to Kimani (2017) 'balkanization' seems to refer to the position of being stuck and incompatible with the linear vector of time where the present can come only after the past is gone and done. Moving away from 'balkanization' would mean solving that puzzle by leaving the past behind and hence in a linear logic stepping into the present. 'Balkanization' lies precisely in the vacuum space between the two, past and present. It lives in that mediocre position of the average, the middle-of-the-road, and the barely adequate. 'Balkanization' resembles the refusal or incapability to decide between right and wrong, and this is what makes it an ethical dilemma among others.

With this and with the forthcoming examples, it gets even more vivid the transposition of 'balkanization' from situational dimensions into those that seem inherently and universally human. BoshRoger (2014) does not elaborate further on what is meant with the "balkanisation of spirits", but conveys that the same in comparison to the geographic one is "stronger than we think" (see Example 63). Conveying nuances of vagueness and generalization by leaving unexplainable who exactly is the "we" he refers to, BoshRoger's (2014) is no exception of the many tweets that assume an immediate and evidently self-explanatory meaning of 'balkanization'.

> *Example 63:* #DRC confronter a deux especes de balkanisation #Geographique et #balkanisation des esprits , celle est plus forte que l'on pense. (BoshRoger, 2014) [Adapted from French: #DRC to confront two species of Balkanization #Geographique and #balkanisation of spirits, which is stronger than we think.]

Nearly ironically, 'balkanization' which is meant to transmit division, fragmentation, and parcelization, exceptions to be tackled and resolved, unfitting pieces of an otherwise harmonious mosaic among others, is at the same time conveying universally widespread features, being those geographically, disciplinary, and even spiritually as Example 63 confirms. In other words, one could nearly say that 'balkanization' unifies infinite components and elements of variety, multiplicity, and heterogeneity by allowing them to remain as they are i.e. different. 'Balkanization' seems to allow for the continuous and constant interplay between the whole and its parts to perform in all of its shapes, including here clashes, contradictions, and conflicts. Hence, 'balkanization' must be both, the whole and its parts.

Having said this, we reach towards the last component of this subsection that illustrates best the conclusions drawn above. Among the 1892 tweets of the empirical corpus, Example 64 below hyperlinked a poem titled "Balkanization" written by William Repass (2016).

> *Example 64:* "This is the open lagoon" New words from William Repass to ease the Monday! #poetry #Balkanization #almosttoldyou http://www.hobartpulp.com/web_features/balkanization (hobartpulp, 2016)

In trying to reach subjectivities transmitted through 'balkanization', to my surprise but I assume by now not to that of the reader too due to the presented examples above, I found 'balkanization' even in poetry. Being intrigued by this new dimension that 'balkanization' was reaching or was being reached by, I approached the author, William Repass, and asked for further elaborations on the poem he had written. Believing that nothing would explain the poem better than the author himself would and having obtained his permission to cite the personal communication between us, I share what Repass (personal communication, August 21, 2017) explained as the following:

> When I wrote this poem I was working on a whole series of similar (as yet unpublished) pieces in which I develop themes of the "body politic." In other words, both the politicization of the body (the attraction to or alienation from different parts of the body; a hierarchicalization of those parts based on societal and ideological imperatives), and the bodily organization of geopolitics (the carving up of the body of a landscape; the butchering of peoples on the basis of ethnic, class, or linguistic differences).

While Repass (personal communication, August 21, 2017) explains that he chooses the title "Balkanization" "as a gesture to the interrelated fragmentation of the body and ideology in general, as opposed to a direct reference to conflicts in the Western Balkans" he confirms that the conflicts in the Western Balkans where never away from his mind. Repass (personal communication, August 21, 2017) says that through 'balkanization' he wants "... to get at the arbitrariness of boundaries, their 'fluid' nature'", confirming in this way again the position of 'balkanization' as in both, the fluidity and rigidity of margins. Finally, what is crucial and what further confirms the conceptualizations of 'balkanization' precisely in the process of a reaction of the whole and its parts and the 'either/or' of the two, is Repass's (personal communication, August 21, 2017) explanation of understanding "... the 'body politic' as a dialectic between parts and wholes. Increasing fragmentation leads to the integration of new but unstable wholes that inevitably fragment again, and so on".

Here, for the sake of the argument, I move towards an archetype which is not situated among the top or the bottom ten of the 'balkanization' archetypes, but which visually and content-wise is a great illustration of what has been elaborated under this subsection – 'balkanization' in art. Vera Klimentyeva, whose work as an artist was shared in one of the tweets (see Example 65), is a representative of this. In a tentative of reaching towards an in-depth explanation of the image associated with 'balkanization' whose author and model is Klimentyeva herself, another personal conversation took place between myself and Klimentyeva on my initiative.

> *Example 65:* Vera Klimentyeva #balkanization #show#Vienna pic.twitter.com/8MusBOGI6s (Capan, 2016)

To another surprise of mine and in astonishingly unexpected similarities with Repass's (2016) poem, Klimentyeva (personal communication, September 24, 2017) shares her personal experience of having Russian, Estonian, Georgian, and Ukrainian roots as an inspiration being reflected on the image below (see Figure 3.9 below).

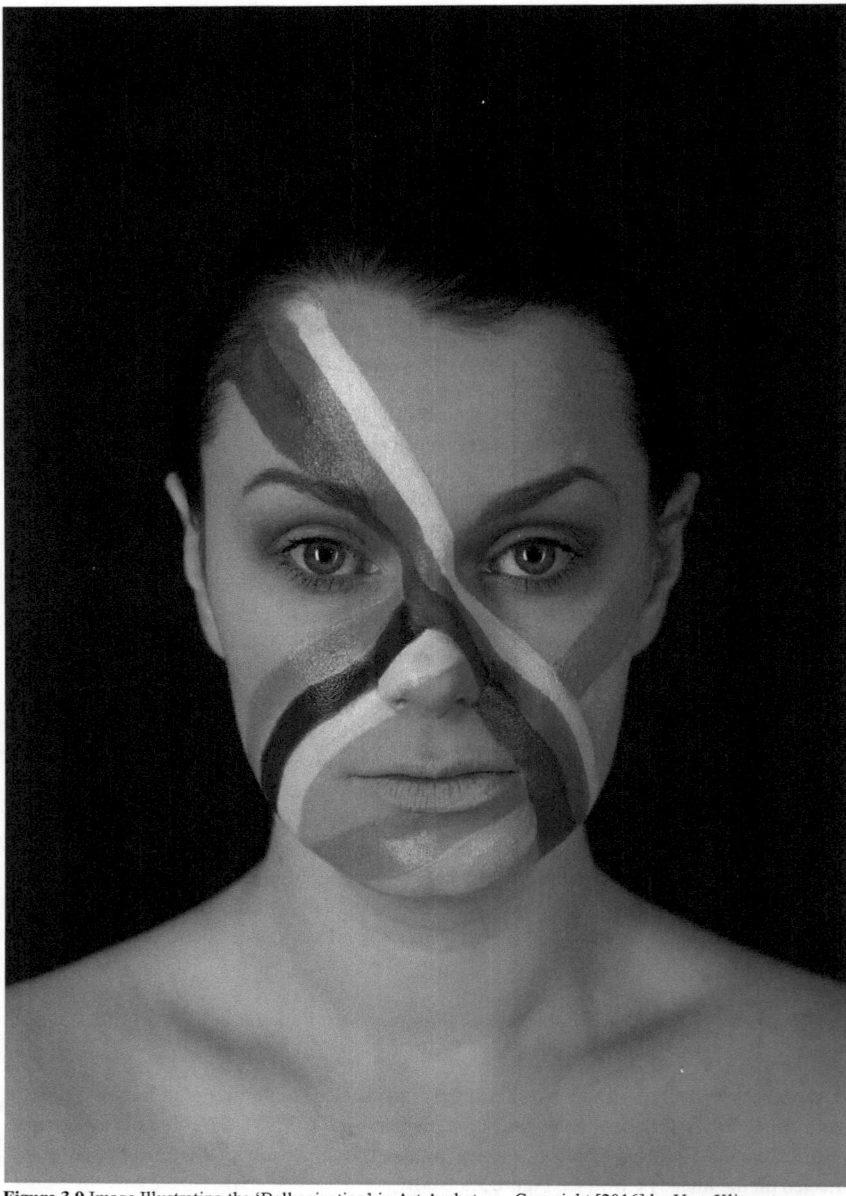

Figure 3.9 Image Illustrating the 'Balkanization' in Art Archetype. Copyright [2016] by Vera Klimentyeva. Reprinted [or Adapted] with permission.
Note. The image titled "UNTITLED (Ringing Blood)" is originally the artwork of the artist Vera Klimentyeva (2016) who is also the model.

She refers to the occurrences in the USSR (Union of Soviet Socialist Republics) and the emerging of new borders which due to her diverse family genealogy left her always asking the question of "… who am I" (Klimentyeva, personal communication, September 24, 2017). Klimentyeva (personal communication, September 24, 2017) says that she took the image as "the balkanization of the self" in times where she used to work a lot with body, face, and her personal experiences related to her different historical, political, and cultural ancestries. With this then 'balkanization' yet again appears in the space in between Klimentyeva's parts as divided by the lines of the colors of the Ukrainian, Estonian, and Russian flags and the unity of her face, connecting her subjective perceptions with the political occurrences of divisions that caused the same.

Whether as lagoon water that is separated with islands or reefs from a larger body of water (see Repass, 2016), or as parts of face divided by the lines of a flag (see Figure 3.9 above), 'balkanization' still portrays water not completely disconnected from water and parts that together built a face. Very much on the lines of what Pye Dubois's (1992) verses of poem *There is a Lake Between Sun and Moon* quoted at the beginning of this section, 'balkanization', above everything, stands in the interjacent position of sun and moon; East and West; alarming shouts and silent reconcilability; the wonder in expansion and constant doubt of the uncontrollable; the actor itself and the bearer of fate; the unceasing wish of becoming an 'other' but the fact of remaining the same; the rise and the dissolution of dichotomies; the relentless negotiations.

The examples of tweets presented have not only spoken of the conceptual multifariousness conveyed through 'balkanization' but have also revealed an interesting tendency that seems to be new to the 'balkanization' discourse – the transition to the personal. Of course, as already argued before (see section 1.2 Research: 'Balkanization' through Twitter Subjectivities) on the indivisibility of subjectivities and political processes, such conclusion might even seem tautological. However, what it rather refers to when it comes to 'balkanization', is the realization of that indivisibility. In other words, the vastness of looking at 'balkanization' from afar as something there and not here, distant and not close, a threat coming but yet not reached, is getting smaller. 'Balkanization' seems to be reaching the soul, the individual, and the person, as it is becoming part of poems (see Repass, 2016), paintings of selves (see Klimentyeva, 2016), or the spirit (see BoshRoger, 2014). If considering that the first instances that 'balkanization' was mentioned by E. H. Bradford Amer in 1914 ("balkanization", 2013), were of some geopolitical connotations, followed by an industrial and economic perspective by Walther Rathenau in 1918 (Greenwall, 1918) and continued along those lines, this is quite a recent change.

Such a shift in expression and communication with regard to 'balkanization' might not present anything unique to the discourse due to the era of instant media that shortens time and space among the various levels of communication. However, this makes 'balkanization' no less relevant and deserving of empirical scrutiny. On the contrary, it proves that it is very much alive and present, and through what it stands for it preconditions processes with real implications on the ground, hence as such, it not only is, but it becomes more important.

4 Conclusions and Future Work

Having started this thesis with my personal perspective and the importance it has for me as an author, I feel that there is a need to confirm the challenging and the rewarding instances that I have experienced while conducting this research. As Liridona, as an Albanian from Macedonia, and as someone coming from 'the Balkans', this investigative and analytical journey started and resulted as one of, among others, knowing myself better. Among the different Twitter subjectivities through which I have placed the empirical analysis, let us remember that mine was determining to the choice of analysis, interpretation, and presentation of the data, the literature artifacts, and the conclusions drawn from both. Recognizing these implications has been a thought-provoking and often quite a demanding undertaking which has required me to step out from the paradigm of empirical analysis as expected to be objective. This thesis remains a subjective and academic endeavor simultaneously, as the two not only can cohabit, but moreover are impossible to separate.

From this then, if the coexistence of what is perceived as dichotomies is to be considered a characteristic of this thesis, I could say that this thesis itself is a manifestation of the 'balkanization' discourse. This due to one of the main conclusions resulting from the analysis aimed at answering the research question "What characterizes the 'balkanization' discourse via Twitter subjectivities?" being that the 'balkanization' discourse is essentially conveying liminal perceptions which live in between meanings and their opposites and hence transmit an *ambiguous* way of knowing and comprehension; while the second main insight that resulted from the research refers to the *growing* presence of the discourse and consequently the ambiguity it represents. In other words, the 'balkanization' discourse proves to essentially be built upon abstruseness as its main defining characteristic, and as such, it continues to grow in usage.

Ambiguity is a defining element of the 'balkanization' discourse since its initial foundations traced back to 'the Balkans' discourse as preceding, as the genealogical examination suggests; and continues to be one in the present, as the empirical research through Twitter verified. The archetypes of meanings surrounding 'balkanization' reflect nuances of division(s), data/Internet national regulations, nation(alism/ality), war, race(ism), data/software heterogeneity, independence, Islam/Muslim(s), union, unity or unification, and (anti)im(migration) as the most prevailing ones. However, the essence of associating 'balkanization' with these archetypes lies in it being simultaneously the synonym and antonym of the same. This places the 'balkanization' discourse in a special category of identity construction and othering in which 'the other' is not defined by what it is not, but by what it *could* and/or *should be*. 'Balkanization' lives in the eternal negotiation of what could/should have been, but was not; what could/should be, but is not; what can/should be, but will not. It lives in the constant reinvention of meanings by bringing together and at the same time separating, by differ-

© Springer Fachmedien Wiesbaden GmbH, part of Springer Nature 2018
L. Veliu, *#Balkanization: A Critical Study of Otherness through Twitter*, Masters of Peace, https://doi.org/10.1007/978-3-658-23824-7_4

entiating and at the same time equalizing wholeness and particularity, homogeneity and heterogeneity, 'us' and 'them'.

This ambiguity conditions the flexibility of conceptualization, contextualization, and action that the discourse causes and is caused by. In other words, the growth in usage and meanings associated with 'balkanization' is due to the ambiguity it conveys, and *vice versa*. The archetypes revealed how 'balkanization' has reached to be attached to and expressive of a variety of spaces and situations which transcend the North Pole and today reach cyberspace, art, poetry, the soul, and the spirit. Other archetypes detected in-between the two poles of the most dominant and the infrequent were detected (see Appendix A; Appendix B). This suggests that 'balkanization' continuous to grow in flexibility, applicability, and hence influence. 'Balkanization' is an ambiguity in growth, and this insight does not stand for a mere ontological adventure or mental exercise. Perhaps needless to say, ontologies and subjectivities manifest and realize themselves into material decisions, undertakings, actions towards ourselves and others. This is where the relevance of understanding what characterizes the 'balkanization' discourse is enhanced.

This leads us towards the third crucial insight of this thesis – although deriving from 'the Balkans' discourse as attached to the Balkan Peninsula, the 'balkanization' discourse gives the impression of having gained an ontological independence and life of its own. The fact that the Balkan Peninsula as a whole or in the format of particular Balkan countries is not among the top ten spaces associated with 'balkanization', supports this observation. However, this does not mean that no references to the region were made. Analogies between the new contexts that 'balkanization' was ascribed to on one side, and former Yugoslavia or the Balkan countries on the other, were constantly reappearing in the tweets. No matter the diversity and ambiguity of meanings that the 'balkanization' discourse represents, it is still based on a red thread of analogous references to the Balkan Peninsula and *'The Balkans'* as a discourse.

Such correspondences have a common element – the responsibility for changing unwanted situations as threats to how things should be, but the constant confusion of assigning internal and external agency for the same. While ambiguous conceptualizations can result with a variety of interpretations, they can as well result with misinterpretations and hence actions guided by the same. As the responsibility shifts from the internal to the external due to the ambiguous perplexities, it conditions a fatalistic vicious circle of assigning blame and accountability. This results with a permanence of a condition which, as the study shows, most often refers to something unwanted, redundant, and problematic, and which in turn requires continuous attention and intervention. This in relation to 'the Balkans' and other contexts associated with 'balkanization', refers to the discourse being a construct essentially based on a Eurocentric worldview and centered around the idea of a constant comparison between 'the West' and 'the Balkans', or any other problematic space or situation. As the 'marathon' never reaches its end due to it being stuck in the abstruseness of the discourse, the need and the right for involvement also never ends.

My research cannot give an account of how 'balkanization' as a way of knowing and as a discourse has concretely influenced identity politics and materialized itself through identity politics and real decision and policy making processes on the ground. However, I believe that the first step in possibly examining such correlation is to reject its metahistorical obviousness; to problematize, denaturalize and desubstantialize the discourse, by questioning the ontological and epistemological certainties that gave life to the same, and that facilitate its current formations in form and substance. This is what I aimed to and hope I have reached through this thesis. Further examinations of how the discourse specifically materializes itself in relation to 'the Balkans' and the Euro-Atlantic integration of Western Balkan countries are part of my future work and research ambitions which I aim to take forward. Having concluded that the 'balkanization' discourse not only continues to operate in the present but does so by growing in applicability and knowledge production due to the current era of social media, I find such endeavor not only decent, but also demanding of further research. As such, I am looking forward to jumping into all the familiarity and foreignness of 'balkanization', while expecting to, among others, resulting with a more deconstructed self, or should we rather say a 'balkanized' self.

Reference List of Sources

Adams, R. (2010, April 14). All your Twitter belongs to the Library of Congress. *The Guardian*. Retrieved from https://www.theguardian.com/world/richard-adams-blog/2010/apr/14/twitter-library-of-congress

Adichie, C. N. (2006). *Half of a yellow sun*. New York: Anchor Books.

Agee, C. (2014, May 27). *Is Obama going to establish separate government structures based on race?* Retrieved March 3, 2017 from The Western Journal: https://www.westernjournalism.com/obama-wants-establish-separate-government-structures-based-race/?utm_source=wysija&utm_medium=email&utm_campaign=DailyEmail%C3%82

Aghajanian, L., & Wells, J. (2012, September 7). Hundreds protest pardon of man who killed Armenian military officer. *Los Angeles Times*. Retrieved from http://latimesblogs.latimes.com/lanow/2012/09/hundreds-protest-pardon-of-man-who-killed-armenian-military-officer.html

Alves, S. J. (2014a, October 2). The internet balkanization fragmentation. *DiploFoundation*. Retrieved from https://www.diplomacy.edu/blog/internet-balkanization-fragmentation

Alves, S. J. (2014b, September 19). *The internet balkanization discourse backfires*. Retrieved from https://poseidon01.ssrn.com/delivery.php?ID=953069091068006123064112092106071085042081072032058071029073123099121076096004019018037005034102047046050080083093112121077085055020062006009072091114073000070028098022069049103113115075111121071002080069070096070079112081087122031003085086070064090069&EXT=pdf

Apostle, H. G. (1979). *Aristotle's metaphysics*. Iowa: Peripatetic Press.

Bakić-Hayden, M. (1995). Nesting Orientalisms: The case of former Yugoslavia. *Slavic Review*, 917-931.

Bakic-Hayden, M., & Hayden, R. (1992). Orientalist variations on the theme "Balkans": Symbolic geography in recent Yugoslav cultural politics. *Slavic Review*, 1-15.

Balkan Peninsula. (2016, October 4). *Encyclopedia*. Retrieved March 6, 2017, from http://www.encyclopedia.com/places/spain-portugal-italy-greece-and-balkans/balkans-physical-geography/balkan-peninsula

Balkanization. (2013, December). *Oxford English Dictionary*. Retrieved March 1, 2017, from http://www.oed.com/view/Entry/370684?redirectedFrom=balkanization&

Balkans. (2016, December 5). *Encyclopedia*. Retrieved March 7, 2017, from http://www.encyclopedia.com/places/spain-portugal-italy-greece-and-balkans/balkans-physical-geography/balkans

Batrinca, B., & Treleaven, P. C. (2014). Social media analytics: A survey of techniques, tools and platforms. *Al & Soc*, 89-116.

© Springer Fachmedien Wiesbaden GmbH, part of Springer Nature 2018

L. Veliu, *#Balkanization: A Critical Study of Otherness through Twitter*, Masters of Peace, https://doi.org/10.1007/978-3-658-23824-7

Battersby, P., Siracusa, J. M., & Ripiloski, S. (2011). *Crime wars: The global intersection of crime, political violence, and international law.* Wesport, CT: Praeger Security International.

Bell, B. W., Grosholz, E. R., & Stewart, J. B. (2013). *W.E.B. Du Bois on race and culture.* New York: Routledge.

Bennett, S. (2016). New "crises," old habits: Online interdiscursivity and intertextuality in UK migration policy discourses. *Journal of Immigrant & Refugee Studies*, 1-21.

Beris, A., & Giacomin, J. (2014). πάντα ῥεῖ: Everything flows. *Applied Rheology*, 1-13.

Berman, S. (2016, March 12). Consequences of the politics of balkanization. *The Resurgent.* Retrieved from http://theresurgent.com/consequences-of-the-politics-of-balkanization/

Bica, M., & Anderson, J. (2016). "You are what you tweet!" The ethics of republishing public datas as crafted narratives. Workshop on Ethical Encounters in HCI Research at the ACM Conference on Human Factors in Computing Systems (CHI '16). Retrieved from https://ethicalencountershci.files.wordpress.com/2016/03/bica-and-anderson.pdf

Bideleux, R., & Jeffries, I. (1998). *A history of Eastern Europe: Crisis and change.* New York: Routledge.

Big Think. (2015, June 7). *Slavoj Žižek on synthetic sex and "being yourself"* [Video file]. Retrieved from https://www.youtube.com/watch?v=7xYO-VMZUGo&t=17s

Bloom, H. (1994). *The Western canon: The books and school of the ages.* New York: Harcourt Brace.

Bollen, C. (2015). *Orient.* London: Simon&Schuster.

Bouvier, G. (2015). What is a discourse approach to Twitter, Facebook, YouTube and other social media: Connecting with other academic fields? *Journal of Multicultural Discourses*, 149-162.

Boyd, D., Golder, S., & Lotan, G. (2010). Tweet, tweet, retweet: Conversational aspects of retweeting on Twitter. *Hawaii International Conference on System Sciences.* Kauai. Retrieved from http://ieeexplore.ieee.org/stamp/stamp.jsp?tp=&arnumber=5428313

Braun, A. (1983). *Small-state security in the Balkans.* New Jersey: Barnes & Noble Books.

Brightman, R. (2016, April 9). *Considering the power and purpose of #hashtags.* Retrieved from Siegel+Gale: http://www.siegelgale.com/considering-the-power-and-purpose-of-hashtags/

Bruns, A., & Burgess, J. (2015). Twitter hashtags from ad hoc to calculated publics. In N. Rambukkana, *Hashtag publics: The power and politics of discursive networks* (pp. 13-28). New York: Peter Lang.

Bruns, A., & Weller, K. (2014). Guest editorial. *Aslib Journal of Information Management*, 246-249.

Buchanan, D., & Bryman, A. (2009). *The Sage handbook of organizational research methods.* London: SAGE Publications.

Büchi, J. (2014, July 1). Der Balkan wird plötzlich cool. *20 Minuten*. Retrieved http://www.20min.ch/schweiz/news/story/31691907

Bunz, M. (2009, November 23). PDA Twitter's retweet confusion. *The Guardian*. Retrieved from https://www.theguardian.com/media/blog/2009/nov/23/twitter-retweet-confusion

Burnett, D. (2016, March 30). Earthxit? Support for Earth leaving the solar system is overstated. *The Guardian*. Retrieved from https://www.theguardian.com/science/brain-flapping/2016/mar/30/earth-leaving-solar-system-eu-referendum-spoof?CMP=share_btn_tw

Butcher, J. (2011). *Death masks.* London: Orbit.

Butler, J. (2002). What is critique? An essay on Foucault's virtue. In D. Ingram, *The political: Readings in continental philosophy,* (pp. 212-228). Oxford: Basil Backwell.

Campbell, D. (1998). *National deconstruction: Violence, identity and justice in Bosnia.* Minneapolis: University of Minnesota Press.

Campbell, J., & Moyers, B. (1991). *The power of myth.* New York: Doubleday.

Campbell, R., Martin, C. R., & Fabos, B. (2011). *Media and culture: An introduction to mass communication.* Boston: Bedford/St. Martin's.

Camus, A. (1955). *The myth of Sisyphus and other essays.* New York: Vintage Books.

Caroll, N. (2011). Actor-network theory: A bureaucratic view of public service innovation. In A. Tatnall, *Technological advancements and the impact of actor-network theory* (pp. 115-144). Hershey, PA: Information Science Reference.

Carroll, N., Richardson, I., & Whelan, E. (2012). Service science: An actor-network theory approach. *International Journal of Actor-Network Theory and Technological Innovation,* 51-69.

Castells, M. (2010). *The information age: Economy, society and culture.* Oxford: Wiley-Blackwell.

Chen, M. (2016, April 1). The Balkans: The land of blood and honey. *Global Journal*. Retrieved from https://globaljournalnu.com/2016/04/01/the-balkans-the-land-of-blood-and-honey/

Cheng, Y.C. (2014). Global social media, local context: A case study of Chinese-language tweets about the 2012 presidential election in Taiwan. (A. Bruns, & K. Weller, Eds.) *Aslib Journal of Information Management*, 342-356.

Clegg, R. (2017, April 18). Stop the balkanization. *Center for Equal Opportunity*. Retrieved from http://www.ceousa.org/issues/1098-stop-the-balkanization

Clegg, S., & Bailey, J. R. (2008). *International encyclopedia of organization studies* (Vol. 1). Thousand Oaks: SAGE Publications.

Cooper, H. M. (1998). *Synthesizing research: A guide for literature reviews applied.* Thousand Oaks: SAGE Publications.

Cooper, R. (2015, March 30). *Say no to the balkanization of the internet.* Retrieved June 2, 2017, from U.S. Chamber of Commerce Foundation: https://www.uschamberfoundation.org/blog/post/say-no-balkanization-internet/42923

Council of the European Union. (2009, November 30). *Visa liberalisation for Western Balkan countries.* Retrieved from http://www.consilium.europa.eu/uedocs/cms_data/docs/pressdata/en/jha/111561.pdf

Council of the European Union. (2010, November 8). *Visa liberalisation for Albania and Bosnia and Herzegovina.* Retrieved from https://www.consilium.europa.eu/uedocs/cms_data/docs/pressdata/en/jha/117555.pdf

Crain, R. (2015, September 14). Did agencies specialize themselves to death? *Ad Age*. Retrieved from http://adage.com/article/rance-crain/agencies-speclialize-death/300339/

Crowley, Ú. (2009). Genealogy, method. *International Encyclopedia of Human Geography*, 341-344.

Danforth, R. J. (2015, March 25). Balkans. *Encyclopaedia Britannica*. Retrieved March 8, 2017, from https://www.britannica.com/place/Balkans

Daskalovski, Z. (2004). The Macedonian conflict of 2001: Between successful diplomacy, rhetoric and terror. *Studies in Post-Communism*, 1-53.

Data protection: Angela Merkel proposes Europe network. (2014, February 15). *BBC*. Retrieved from http://www.bbc.com/news/world-europe-26210053

de Freytas-Tamura, K. (2016, June 24). Scotland says new vote on independence is 'highly likely'. *New York Times*. Retrieved from https://www.nytimes.com/2016/06/25/world/europe/brexit-scotland-independence-referendum.html

de Lange, E. (2016, August 26). *Balkanism as historiography: Development of debate and discourse.* Retrieved from Academia: https://www.academia.edu/8223481/Balkanism_as_Historiography._Development_of_Debate_and_Discourse

de Tracy, A. L. (1803). *Projet d' éléments d'idéologie.* Paris: Chez Courcier.

Debord, G. (1995). *The society of spectacle.* New York: Zone Books.

Dedovic, D. (2017, February 2). Opinion: We can still stop the Balkanization of the EU. *Deutsche Welle*. Retrieved from http://www.dw.com/en/opinion-we-can-still-stop-the-balkanization-of-the-eu/a-37521577?tw%C3%82=

der Derian, J. (2009). S/N: International theory, balkanisation and the new world order. In J. der Derian, *Critical practices in international theory: Selected essays* (pp. 97-119). London: Routledge.

Derrida, J. (1972). *Positions.* (A. Bass, Ed.) Chicago: University of Chicago Press.

Derrida, J. (1982). *Margins of philosophy.* Brighton: The Harvester Press.

Douetteau, F. (2015, December 11). Technoslavia or the balkanization of data science. *LinkedIn*. Retrieved from https://www.linkedin.com/pulse/technoslavia-balkanization-data-science-florian-douetteau/

Doug's Darkworld. (2012, November 8). *War, science, and philosophy in a fractured world. Balkanization, the wave of the future?* [Blog post]. Retrieved December 22, 2017, from https://unitedcats.wordpress.com/2012/11/08/balkanization-the-wave-of-the-future/

Dreier, P. (2016, February 22). Academic Drivel Report. *The American Prospect*. Retrieved from http://prospect.org/article/academic-drivel-report

Du Bois Edward Burghardt, W. (1945). *Color and democracy: Colonies and peace.* New York: Harcourt Brace.

Dubois, P. (1992). There is a lake between sun and moon [Recorded by Rush]. *Counterparts*. Atlantic: Anthem. Retrieved from Power Windows: http://www.2112.net/powerwindows/transcripts/19920000duboisbetweensunmoon.htm

Duckworth v. Arkansas, 314 U.S. 390 (U.S. Supreme Court December 15, 1941).

Durham, E. (1985). *High Albania.* London: Virago Press.

Džankić, J. (2016). *Citizenship in Bosnia and Herzegovina, Macedonia and Montenegro: Effects of statehood and identity challenges.* New York: Routledge.

Efron, M. (2010). Hashtag retrieval in a microblogging environment. *33rd International ACM SIGIR conference on Research and development in information retrieval* (pp. 787-788). Geneva: ACM.

Engström, J. (2009). *Democratisation and the prevention of violent conflict: Lessons learned from Bulgaria and Macedonia.* Farnham: Ashgate.

European Commission. (2011). *Communication from the Commission to the European Parliament and the Council.* Retrieved from EUR-Lex: http://eur-lex.europa.eu/legal-content/EN/TXT/?uri=celex:52011DC0666

European Commission. (2013, May 4). *Countries and regions: Western Balkans.* Retrieved from http://ec.europa.eu/trade/policy/countries-and-regions/regions/western-balkans/

Evans, G. (2016, November 4). Barack Obama & Bill Maher slam "balkanization" of news media, warn of dire post-Trump "damage". *Deadline*. Retrieved from http://deadline.com/2016/11/barack-obama-bill-maher-donald-trump-real-time-with-bill-maher-1201848895/

Exec. Order. No. 13769. (2017). Protecting the nation from foreign terrorist entry into the United States, 3 C.F.R. 8977-8982.

Fagoyinbo, J. B. (2013). *The armed forces: Instrument of peace, strength, development and prosperity.* Bloomington: AuthorHouse.

Fairclough, N. (1995). *Critical discourse analysis: The critical study of language.* London: Longman.

Fesit, J., & Feist, G. J. (2008). *Theories of personality.* New York: McGraw–Hill.

Fiske, J. (1996). *Media matters. Race and gender in U.S. politics.* Minneapolis: University of Minnesota Press.

Fitzpatrick, P. (2011, June 10). *The golden rule: Tweet others the way you want to be tweeted* [Blog post]. Retrieved November 22, 2017, from http://pegfitzpatrick.com/the-golden-rule/

Fleming, K. E. (2000). Orientalism, the Balkans, and Balkan historiography. *The American Historical Review*, 1218-1233.

Foucault, M. (1975). *Discipline and punish: The birth of prison.* Random House: New York.

Foucault, M. (1977). Nietzsche, genealogy, history. In M. Foucault, & D. F. Bouchard (Ed.), *Language, counter-memory, practice: Selected essays and interviews* (D. F. Bouchard, & S. Simon, Trans., pp. 139-164). New York: Cornell University Press.

Foucault, M. (1977). *The archaeology of knowledge.* London: Tavistock Publications Limited.

Foucault, M. (1979). *The history of sexuality* (Vols. 1-3). London: Allen Lane.

Foucault, M. (1980). *Power/Knowledge.* New York: Pantheon Books.

Foucault, M. (1990). *The history of sexuality: The use of pleasure.* New York: Vintage books.

Foucault, M. (1997). What is critique? In y. Lotringer, & L. Hochroth, *The politics of truth* (pp. 41-81). New York: Semiotext(e).

Frey, W. H. (1996). Immigration, domestic migration, and demographic balkanization in America: New evidence for the 1990s. *Population and Development Review*, 741-763.

Frey, W. H. (1999). Immigration and demographic balkanization. In J. W. Hughes, & J. J. Seneca, *America's demographic dapestry: Baseline for the new millenium* (pp. 78-100). New Brunswick: Rutgers University Press.

Garland, D. (2014). What is a ''history of the present''? On Foucault's genealogies and their critical preconditions. *Punishment & Society*, 165-384.

Gault, M. (2016, November 5). Windows 10 store refunds ‘call of duty’ player because nobody's playing it. *Motherboard*. Retrieved from https://motherboard.vice.com/en_us/article/z438a8/windows-10-store-refunds-call-of-duty-player-because-nobodys-playing-it

Ghost Pictures. (2015, March 29). *Žižek - Our fear of falling in love* [Video file]. Retrieved from https://www.youtube.com/watch?v=OabTK7y7d6E

Glynn, P. (1993, July 1). The age of balkanization. *Commentary*. Retrieved from https://www.commentarymagazine.com/articles/the-age-of-balkanization/

Goldstein, G. M. (2014, June 25). The end of the internet? *The Atlantic*. Retrieved from https://www.theatlantic.com/magazine/archive/2014/07/the-end-of-the-internet/372301/

Goldsworthy, V. (1998). *Inventing Ruritania: The imperialism of imagination*. New Haven CT: Yale University Press.

Goldsworthy, V. (2003, August 5). Invention and in(ter)vention: The rhetoric of Balkanization. *Eurozine*. Retrieved from http://www.eurozine.com/articles/2003-05-08-goldsworthy-en.html

Government of Offices of Sweden. (2014, September 11). *Meeting of Nordic and Baltic foreign ministers in Estonia.* Retrieved from http://www.government.se/contentassets/9bbda6b81b16402bbab82aa0c02c2e16/press-releases-2010-2014---carl-bildt

Gowing, E. (2011, June 1). Ecosovo: The land of blood and honey. *Balkan Insight*. Retrieved from http://www.balkaninsight.com/en/blog/ecosovo-the-land-of-blood-and-honey

Gray, C. S., & Sloan, G. R. (2004). *Geopolitics, geography, and strategy*. London: Frank Cass.

Gregorio, J. (2016, June 10). The history and power of hashtags in social media marketing (Infographic). *Digital Marketing Philippines*. Retrieved from http://digitalmarketingphilippines.com/the-history-and-power-of-hashtags-in-social-media-marketing-infographic/

Grubačić, A. (2010). *Don't mourn, balkanize!: Essays after Yugoslavia.* Oakland: PM Press.

H. P. Hood & Sons, 336 U.S. 525 (U.S. Supreme Court April 4, 1949).

Hall, S. (1997). The work of representation. In S. Hall, *Representation* (pp. 13-76). London: SAGE Publications.

Hama, B. (1974). *Les grands problèmes de l'Afrique des indépendances.* Paris: P. J. Oswald.

Hammond, A. (2007). Typologies of the East: On distinguishing Balkanism and Orientalism. *Nineteenth-Century Contexts*, 201-218.

Hansen, L. (2006). *Security as practice: Discourse analysis and the Bosnian war.* New York: Routledge.

Hastings, M. (2004, November 2). History as written by the victor. *The Telegraph*. Retrieved from http://www.telegraph.co.uk/culture/books/3626376/History-as-written-by-the-victor.html

Heidegger, M. (1985). *Being and time.* (J. Macquarric, & E. Robinson, Trans.) Oxford: Basil Blackwell.

Herzfeld, N. (2017, March 3). Noreen Herzfeld on “the balkanization of the media”. *Avon Hills Salon*. Retrieved from https://avonhillssalon.com/2017/03/03/noreen-herzfeld-on-the-balkanization-of-the-media/

Heywood, A. (2013). *Politics.* London: Palgrave Macmillan.

Hidayatulah, S. (2015). Hegemony of the social media Twtter about national issues in Indonesia and its implications to the discourse analysis subject in college. *Journal of Education in Muslim Society*, 153-166.

Hislope, R. (2013). Macedonia. In S. Berglund, J. Ekman, K. Deegan-Krause, & T. Knutsen, *The handbook of political change in Eastern Europe* (pp. 607-650). Cheltenham: Edward Elgar Publishing Limited.

Hobsbawm, E. (1990). *Nations and nationalism since 1780: Programme, myth, reality.* Cambridge: Cambridge University Press.

Horvat, S. (2013, November 3). Europeanisation of the Balkans or balkanisation of Europe? *Revolting Europe*. Retrieved from https://revolting-europe.com/2013/11/03/europeanisation-of-the-balkans-or-balkanisation-of-europe/

Howarth, D. (2000). *Discourse.* Buckingham: Open University Press.

Hughes v. Oklahoma, 441 U.S. 322 (U.S. Supreme Court April 24, 1979).

Hüning, M. (2007). *TextSTAT - simples text analysis tool.* Retrieved from Freie Universität Berlin: http://neon.niederlandistik.fu-berlin.de/textstat/

Huntington, S. P. (2011). *The clash of civilizations and the remaking of world order.* New York: Simon & Schuster.

Iedema, R. (2003). Multimodality, resemiotization: Extending the analysis of discourse as multi-semiotic practice. *Visual Communication*, 29-57.

India tries to shape Nepal's new constitution. (2015, October 6). *Stratfor*. Retrieved from https://worldview.stratfor.com/article/india-tries-shape-nepals-new-constitution

Ingram, M. (2014, February 6). Turkey passes draconian internet law, Turks say goodbye to their freedom of speech. *Gigaom*. Retrieved from https://gigaom.com/2014/02/06/turkey-passes-draconian-internet-law-turks-say-goodbye-to-their-freedom-of-speech/?utm_source=feedburner&utm_medium

Inside Snowden's Germany file. (2014, June 18). *Der Spiegel*. Retrieved from https://www.reuters.com/article/us-germany-spying-usa/german-spies-revive-internet-snooping-work-with-us-reports-idUSKBN0UM29Z20160108

Ismaili, Y. (2009). *Terminologjia politike & manipulimi medial: Konflikti i armatosur në Maqedoni, 2001: diversiteti konceptues mbi terminologjinë politike në Maqedoni dhe sistemi i vlerave politike të BE-së.* Tetovo: Arberia Design.

Jolie, A. (Director). (2011). *In the land of blood and honey* [Motion Picture].

Jones, B., & Parfitt, T. (2012, September 28). Russia reasserts ownership over the North Pole. *Business Insider*. Retrieved from http://www.businessinsider.com/russia-reasserts-ownership-over-the-north-pole-2012-9?IR=T

Jones, S. (2014). *'Think before you tweet': A foucauldian discourse analysis of the constructions of female alcohol consumption on Twitter* (Bachelor Thesis). Manchester, England: Manchester Metropolitan University. Retrieved from https://e-space.mmu.ac.uk/576586/1/Saskia%20JONES.pdf

Jordan, D. D. (2007). *A. B. Jordan: A southern editor's view of Europe beetween the wars.* Charlotte: Popular Street Press.

Jukić, T. (2013). The man who knew too much: Žižek and the Balkans. *European Journal of English Studies*, 160-175.

Jung, C. G. (1969). *The archetypes and the collective unconscious.* New York: Princeton Universit Press.

Jung, C. G. (2010). *Synchronicity: An acausal connecting principle.* Princeton: Princeton University Press.

Kamen, M. (2016, March 17). Twitter's non-chronological timeline is now opt-out. *Wired.* Retrieved from http://www.wired.co.uk/article/twitter-non-chronological-timeline-how-to-opt-out

Kapka, P., Halas, M., & Tonev, P. (2013). Functional regions: Concepts and types. *Mezinárodní Kolokvium o Regionálních Vědách* (pp. 45-57). Brno: Masarykova univerzita.

Karnitschnig, M. (2016, September 22). Welcome to EUgoslavia. *Politico.* Retrieved from https://www.politico.eu/article/welcome-to-eugoslavia-balkans-regional-blocs-diplomacy-policy-eurozone-allies/

Keith, V. (2015, January 9). The Muslim balkanization of the West. *American Thinker.* Retrieved from http://www.americanthinker.com/blog/2015/01/the_muslim_balkanization_of_the_west.html#.VK-GpM4z2n0.twitter

Kent, G. (2015). *You are what you tweet: Harness the power of Twitter to create a happier, healthier life.* Culver City: Star Stone Press.

Kim, J. (2002). *Macedonia: Country background and recent conflict.* Foreign Affairs, Defense, and Trade Division. Congressional Research Service. Retrieved from https://www.everycrsreport.com/files/20020328_RL30900_2778c2a8ea84d37eee583ab2b14ca1ce8c0e07cc.pdf

King, S. (2009). Hearts in Atlantis. In S. King, *Stephen King goes to the movies* (pp. 89-434). New York: Pocket books.

Klimentyeva, V. (2016). *UNTITLED (Ringing Blood).*

Kolbe, A. (2013, October 7). Wikipedia's Balkanisation. *Wikipediocracy.* Retrieved from http://wikipediocracy.com/2013/10/07/wikipedias-balkanisation/

Korosec, T. (2017, June 20). Facebook's Oculus fights sales ban for VR rift headset. *Bloomberg.* Retrieved from https://www.bloomberg.com/news/articles/2017-06-20/facebook-s-oculus-fights-sales-ban-for-virtual-reality-headset

Kreis, R. (2017). #refugeesnotwelcome: Anti-refugee discourse on Twitter. *Discourse & Communication*, 498 - 514.

Kress, G., & van Leeuwen, T. (1996). *Reading images: The grammar of visual design.* London: Routledge.

Kritzman, L. D. (1988). Power and sex: An interview with Michel Foucault. In M. Foucault, *Politics, philosophy, culture: Interviews and other writings, 1977-1984* (pp. 110-124). New York: Routledge.

Kurlantzick, J. (2013, April 9). Myanmar's alarming civil unrest. *Council on Foreign Relations.* Retrieved from https://www.cfr.org/expert-brief/myanmars-alarming-civil-unrest#cid=soc-twitter-at-expert_brief-myanmars_alarming_civil_unrest-040913

Langer, R. (1998, February 24). *The concept of discourse in the analysis of complex communication events.* Retrieved from Open Archive: http://openarchive.cbs.dk/bitstream/handle/10398/7028/wpnr.26%201997.pdf?sequence=1

Latour, B. (2007). *Reassembling the social: An introduction to actor-network-theory.* Oxford: Oxford University Press.

Laubender, C. (2009). A family tree: Nietzsche's genealogy in Foucault. *Lehigh Review*, 15-22.

Lebron, Michael William [Lionel Nation]. (2017, March 12). *The truth about what's really happening in Syria with Syrian girl* [Video file]. Retrieved from https://www.youtube.com/watch?v=G_cd2TLhaZg

Ledwith, S. (2016, June 30). For some in England's north, Brexit means control. *Reuters*. Retrieved from https://www.reuters.com/article/us-britain-eu-barnsley-insight/for-some-in-englands-north-brexit-means-control-idUSKCN0ZG1BJ

Lee, S. J., & Lang, S. (1998). *The Weimar Republic.* London: Routledge.

Leetaru, K. (2017, January 28). How the 'rogue' Twitter accounts rewrote how we communicate science in the social era. *Forbes*. Retrieved from https://www.forbes.com/sites/kalevleetaru/2017/01/28/how-the-rogue-twitter-accounts-rewrote-how-we-communicate-science-in-the-social-era/#67c401542dc3

Lendman, S. (2010, October 20). *Israel's longstanding Middle East plan.* Retrieved from Rense: http://rense.com/general92/dsid.htm

Liberalteacher. (2016, December 24). The balkanization of American education and the election of Donald Trump. *The Public Educator*. Retrieved from https://thepubliceducator.com/2016/12/24/the-balkanization-of-american-education-and-the-election-of-donald-trump/

Livesey, C. (2011). *Defining mass media.* Retrieved from Sociology Central: http://www.sociology.org.uk/notes/media_defined.pdf

Maddock, J., Starbird, K., & Mason, R. M. (2015). Using historical Twitter data for research: Ethical challenges of tweet deletions. *Conference on Computer Supported Cooperative Work (CCSCW) Workshop on Ethics.* Vancuver. Retrieved from http://jmaddock.net/static/pdf/deletion_ethics.pdf

Mahon, M. (1992). *Foucault's nietzschean genealogy: Truth, power, and the subject.* New York: State University of New York Press.

Majumder, S. (2015, September 22). Why India is concerned about Nepal's constitution. *BBC.* Retrieved from http://www.bbc.com/news/world-asia-india-34313280

Malkin, M. (2017, June 21). Malkin: The double murder of Otto Warmbier. *Conservative Review*. Retrieved from https://www.conservativereview.com/articles/malkin-the-double-murder-of-otto-warmbier/#sthash.jyaumA9H.uxfs

Mansfield, N. (2000). *Subjectivity: Theories of the self from Freud to Haraway.* Sydney: Allen & Unwin.

Marinow, K. (2014). The Haemus mountains and the geopolitics of the first Bulgarian empire: An overview. *Zbornik radova Vizantološkog instituta*, 17-32.

Marusic, S. J. (2013, May 21). EU threat to visa regime worries Macedonia. *Balkan Insight.* Retrieved from EU Threat to Visa Regime Worries Macedonia: http://www.balkaninsight.com/en/article/fresh-bid-to-reassess-balkan-visa-free-regime

Maurer, T., & Morgus, R. (2014, February 12). Stop calling decentralization of the Internet "balkanization". *Slate*. Retrieved from

http://www.slate.com/blogs/future_tense/2014/02/19/stop_calling_decentralization_of_the_internet_balkanization.html
Meinrath, S. (2013, October 11). The future of the internet: Balkanization and borders. *Time*. Retrieved from http://ideas.time.com/2013/10/11/the-future-of-the-internet-balkanization-and-borders/

MEPs Adopt visa suspension mechanism. (2013, September 12). *Balkan Insight*. Retrieved from Balkan Insight: http://www.balkaninsight.com/en/article/brussels-to-vote-on-re-introduction-of-visa-regime

Messina, C. (2007, August 26). *Groups for Twitter; or a proposal for Twitter tag channels*. Retrieved July 28, 2017, from Factory Joe: https://factoryjoe.com/2007/08/25/groups-for-twitter-or-a-proposal-for-twitter-tag-channels/

Meštrović, S. (1994). *The balkanization of the West: The confluence of postmodernism and postcommunism*. London: Routledge.

Metzger, B. M., & David, M. (2004). *The Oxford guide to people & places of the Bible*. New York: Oxford University Press.

Meyer, M. (2001). Between theory, method, and politics: Positioning of the approaches to CDA. In R. Wodak, & M. Meyer, *Methods of critical discourse analysis* (pp. 14-31). London: SAGE Publications.

Mileska, S. (2007). Balkan subjectivity as neither. *Third Text*, 181-188.

Miller, E. (2017). *Overview: Terrorism in 2016*. National Consortium for the Study of Terrorism and Responses to Terrorism. Retrieved from http://www.start.umd.edu/pubs/START_GTD_OverviewTerrorism2016_August2017.pdf

Milne, R. (2014, June 3). Bildt warns of British 'balkanisation'. *Financial Times*. Retrieved from https://www.ft.com/content/1a45b9bc-e258-11e3-89fd-00144feabdc0

Mitchell, R. (2015). *Web scraping with Python*. Sebastopol: O'Reilly Media.

Mitev, L. (2011, February 28). *The Balkanization of Africa*. Retrieved May 30, 2017, from Lubo Mitev's Blog: https://lubomitev.wordpress.com/2011/01/28/balkanization-of-africa/

Moscovici, S. (1973). Foreword. In C. Herzlich, *Health and illness: A social psychological analysis* (pp. ix-xiv). London: Academic Press.

Mowrer, P. S. (1921). *Balkanized Europe: A study in political analysis and reconstruction*. New York: E.P. Dutton & Company.

Mwakikagile, G. (2010). *Nyerere and Africa: End of an era*. Pretoria: New African Press.

NASA-sponsored Classroom of the Future. (2016, March 16). Retrieved from National Aeronautics and Space Administration: https://www.nasa.gov/audience/foreducators/postsecondary/internet/COTF.html

Nazemroaya, M. D. (2006, November 18). Plans for redrawing the Middle East: The project for a "New Middle East". *Global Research*. Retrieved from https://www.globalresearch.ca/plans-for-redrawing-the-middle-east-the-project-for-a-new-middle-east/3882

Neuburger, M. (2004). *The Orient within: Muslim minorities and the negotiation of nationhood in modern Bulgaria*. Ithaca: Conrell University Press.

Nietzsche, F. (1968). *The will to power*. New York: Vintage Books.

Nietzsche, F. (1997). *On the genealogy of morality*. (K. Ansell-Pearson, Ed.) New York: Cambridge University Press.

Nietzsche, F. (1999). *The birth of tragedy and other writings.* (R. Geuss, R. Speirs, Eds., & R. Speirs, Trans.) New York: Cambridge University Press.

Nietzsche, F. (2005). Twilight of the idols or how to philosophize with a hammer. In F. Nietzsche, A. Ridley, & J. Norman (Eds.), *The anti-christ, ecce homo, twilight of the idols, and other writings* (J. Norman, Trans., pp. 153-230). New York: Cambridge University Press.

O'Reilly, T., & Milstein, S. (2012). *The Twitter book.* Sebastopol: O'Reilly Media, Inc.

Obar, J. A., & Wildman, S. S. (2015). Social media definition and the governance challenge: An introduction to the special issue. *Telecommunications policy*, 745-750.

O'Brien, J. E. (2013). *Critical practice from Voltaire to Focault, Eagleton and beyond.* Leiden: Brill Academic Pub.

O'Farrell, C. (2007). *Key concepts.* Retrieved from michel-foucault: http://www.michel-foucault.com/concepts/index.html

Onwuegbuzie, A. J., Leech, N. L., & Collins, K. M. (2012). Qualitative analysis techniques for the review of the literature. *The Qualitative Report*, 1-28.

O'Really, T. (2007). What Is Web 2.0: Design patterns and business models for the next generation of software. *Communications & Strategies*, 17-37.

Pajaziti, A. (2009). *Fjalori sociologjik.* Shkup: Logos A.

Pallister, J. L. (1977). Balkanization and neo-colonialism: Obstacles to an independent Africa. *Africa today*, 96-96.

Papadopoulos, R. K. (2006). *The handbook of Jungian psychology: Theory, practice and applications.* London: Routledge.

Paul Gee, J. (1999). *An introduction to discourse analysis.* London: Routledge.

Plath, S. (2000). *The unabridged journals of Sylvia Plath 1950-1962.* (K. V. Kukil, Ed.) New York: Anchor Books.

Political ideologies: Syllabus. (2014, June 4). Retrieved December 2, 2014, from Rai University: http://www.raiuniversity.edu/course_pack/Humanities/POLITICAL_IDEOLOGIES.pdf

Pollack, J. (2011, October 16). Deconstructed dish: Burgers get balkanized. *National Post.* Retrieved from http://news.nationalpost.com/appetizer/deconstructed-dish-burgers-get-balkanized

Popa, A. (2010, October 9). *Kosovo Albanians resist Serbian rule, 1990-1998.* Retrieved from Global Nonviolent Action Database website: http://nvdatabase.swarthmore.edu/content/kosovo-albanians-resist-serbian-rule-1990-1998

Procter, R., Voss, A., & Lvov, I. (2015). Audience research and social media data: Opportunities and challenges. *Participation: Journal of Audience and Reception Studies*, 470-493.

Ramzy, A. (2016, January 22). North Korea says it's holding U.S. student for 'hostile act'. *The New York Times*. Retrieved from https://www.nytimes.com/2016/01/23/world/asia/north-korea-american-arrested.html

Rand, A. (1977, April 10). *Global balkanization.* Retrieved June 3, 2017, from Proctors: http://www.proctors.com.au/MRhomepage.nsf/985f14ab922be306482577d5003a2040/80757a214bb332fb4825789c002b515d/$FILE/AR%20Global%20Balkanization%201977.pdf

Rao, M. (2014, June 27). *'Embrace your constraints' – 20 Success tips from Twitter co-founder Biz Stone.* Retrieved from YourStory: https://yourstory.com/2014/06/twitter-successtips-bizstone/

Raymond, M. (2010, April 14). How tweet it is!: Library acquires entire Twitter archive. *Library of Congress*. Retrieved from https://blogs.loc.gov/loc/2010/04/how-tweet-it-is-library-acquires-entire-twitter-archive/

Repass, W. (2016, November 28). *Balkanization.* Retrieved from Hobart: http://www.hobartpulp.com/web_features/balkanization

Rosen, A. (2017, October 13). Giving you more characters to express yourself. *Twitter Blog*. Retrieved September 1, 2017, from https://blog.twitter.com/official/en_us/topics/product/2017/Giving-you-more-characters-to-express-yourself.html

Ross, C., Terras, M., Warwick, C., & Welsh, A. (2011). Enabled backchannel: Conference Twitter use by digital humanists. *Journal of Documentation*, 214-237.

Rothfuss, P. (2008). *The name of the Wind.* London: Gollancz.

Rothman, N. (2016, November 10). Balkanized America. *Commentary*. Retrieved from https://www.commentarymagazine.com/american-society/balkanized-america-identity-politics/

Rushlau, I. D. (2017, January 17). The conservative-fascist axis and balkanized news: The futility of reasoning with Trump voters. *Daily Kos*. Retrieved from http://www.dailykos.com/story/2017/1/17/1621434/-The-conservative-fascist-axis-and-balkanized-news-the-futility-of-reasoning-with-Trump-voters

Saar, M. (2002). Genealogy and subjectivity. *European Journal of Philosophy*, 231-245.

SAGE Publishing. (2017). *Teun A. van Dijk: Pompeu Fabra University, Spain.* Retrieved from SAGE Publishing: https://uk.sagepub.com/en-gb/eur/author/teun-a-van-dijk

Said, E. (1979). *Orientalism.* New York: Vintage Books.

Schuster, J. (2012, November 16). Neue Biografie reduziert Rathenau auf 250 Seiten. *Welt*. Retrieved from https://www.welt.de/kultur/literarischewelt/article111177414/Neue-Biografie-reduziert-Rathenau-auf-250-Seiten.html

Scott, A. (2017, October 22). We call it the Muslim Ban 3.0': The young Yale lawyers fighting Trump's order. *The Guardian*. Retrieved from https://www.theguardian.com/us-news/2017/oct/23/dumbledore-army-donald-trump-travel-ban-legal-battle-mike-wishnie

Sowards, S. W. (2008, November 4). *Michigan State University.* Retrieved from Lecture 1: Geography and ethnic geography of the Balkans to 1500: http://staff.lib.msu.edu/sowards/balkan/lecture1.html

Statistica. (2017, April). *Leading social networks worldwide as of April 2016, ranked by number of active users.* Retrieved July 27, 2017, from The Statistics Portal: http://www.statista.com/statistics/272014/global-social-networks-ranked-by-number-of-users/

Stavrianos, L. S. (2000). *The Balkans since 1453.* London: C. Hurst & Co.

Sudetic, C. (1991, June 26). 2 Yugoslav states vote independence to press demands. *The New York Times*. Retrieved from http://www.nytimes.com/1991/06/26/world/2-yugoslav-states-vote-independence-to-press-demands.html

Sulivan, A. (2009, June 13). The revolution will be twittered. *The Atlantic*. Retrieved from https://www.theatlantic.com/daily-dish/archive/2009/06/the-revolution-will-be-twittered/200478/

Suntrup, J. (2017, January 27). CNN's Navarro: Be wary of political balkanization. *The Recorder*. Retrieved from http://www.recorder.com/Navarro-Be-wary-of-political-balkanization-7694936

Swiss Federal Statistical Office. (2010). *Wohnbevölkerung nach Geschlecht und detaillierter Staatsangehörigkeit, 1850–2009*. Retrieved December 5, 2014, from Swiss Federal Statistical Office: http://www.bfs.admin.ch/bfs/portal/de/index/themen/01/02/blank/data/01.html

Swiss Federal Statistical Office. (2013). *Permanent resident population aged 15 or over, by migration status, in 2013*. Retrieved December 4, 2014, from Swiss Federal Statistical Office: http://www.bfs.admin.ch/bfs/portal/en/index/themen/01/07/blank/key/04.html

Tenorio, E. H. (2011). Critical discourse analysis, an overview. *Nordic Journal of English Studies*, 183-210.

The Balkan Peninsula - map & details. (2002, June 6). *World Atlas*. Retrieved March 7, 2017, from http://www.worldatlas.com/webimage/countrys/europe/balkans.htm

The Balkans. (2001, April 22). *Center for Educational Technologies*. Retrieved March 7, 2017, from http://www.cotf.edu/earthinfo/balkans/BKgeo.html

The Balkans. (2016, December 20). *English Online*. Retrieved March 9, 2017, from http://www.english-online.at/geography/balkans/balkans.htm

The Muslim Council of Britain. (2017, June 24). Hate incidents after European referendum results: A compilation. *The Muslim Council of Britain*. Retrieved from http://www.mcb.org.uk/post-referendum-hate-crimes/

The struggle for Nepal. (2015, November 12). *The Wall Street Journal*. Retrieved from https://www.wsj.com/articles/the-struggle-for-nepal-1447377158

Thomas, N., Mikulan, K., & Pavlovic, D. (2006). *The Yugoslav wars (2): Bosnia, Kosovo and Macedonia 1992-2001*. Oxford: Osprey.

Todorova, M. (1996). The construction of Western discourse of the Balkans. *Etnol*, 7-24.

Todorova, M. (1997). *Imagining the Balkans*. New York: Oxford University Press.

Todorova, M. (2010). Balkanism and postcolonialism, or on the beauty of the airplane view. In C. Bradatan, & S. A. Oushakine, *In Marx's shadow: Knowledge, power and intellectuals in Eastern Europe and Russia* (pp. 175-196). Lanham: Lexintgon Books.

Tuathaigh, G. O. (1999). Understanding critical geopolitics: Geopolitics and risk security. *Journal of Strategic Studies*, 107-124.

Turner, J. (2012, November 2). #InPraiseOfTheHashtag. *The New York Times*. Retrieved from http://www.nytimes.com/2012/11/04/magazine/in-praise-of-the-hashtag.html

Twitter Inc. (2012). *About your Twitter timeline*. Retrieved August 14, 2017, from Twitter: https://support.twitter.com/articles/164083

Twitter Inc. (2012, May 15). *Twitter developer documentation*. Retrieved June 29, 2017, from Twitter Developer: https://dev.twitter.com/streaming/overview/messages-types

Twitter Inc. (2015, August 14). *Display requirements*. Retrieved July 29, 2017, from Twitter: https://about.twitter.com/en-gb/company/display-requirements

Twitter Inc. (2016b, September 30). *Twitter terms of service*. Retrieved July 29, 2017, from Twitter: https://twitter.com/en/tos

Twitter Inc. (2016b, September 30). *Twitter terms of service*. Retrieved July 29, 2017, from Twitter: https://twitter.com/en/tos

Twitter Inc. (2017, June 18). *Twitter privacy policy.* Retrieved July 29, 2017, from Twitter: https://twitter.com/en/privacy

UK cop: 'There are areas we have to ask Muslim leaders' permission to patrol'. (2015, December 9). *The Muslim Issue*. Retrieved from https://themuslimissue.wordpress.com/2015/12/09/uk-cop-there-are-areas-we-have-to-ask-muslim-leaders-permission-to-patrol/

van Dijk, T. (1985). *Discourse and media: New approaches to the analysis of mass media discourse and communication.* Berlin: Walter de Gruyter.

van Dijk, T. (1990). Social cognition and discourse. In W. P. Robinson, & H. Giles, *Handbook of language and social psychology* (pp. 163-183). Chichester: John Wiley & Sons Ltd.

van Dijk, T. (1993). Principles of critical discourse analysis. *Special Issue of Discourse and Society*, 249-283.

van Dijk, T. (1997). The study of discourse. In T. van Dijk, *Discourse as structure and process* (pp. 1-34). London: SAGE publications.

van Dijk, T. (2000). *Ideology and discourse: A multidisciplinary introduction.* Barcelona: Pompeu Fabra University.

van Dijk, T. (2009). Critical discourse studies: A sociocognitive approach. In R. Wodak, & M. Meyer, *Methods for critical disourse analysis* (pp. 62-86). London: SAGE Publications.

Veliu, L. (2015). A discourse study of representations: Immigrants' portrayals in the Swiss public political discourse since 1990s onwards. (Unpublished Master's thesis). University of Basel, Basel, Switzerland.

Weber, A. (2017, March 17). Carney warns of balkanization risk in global financial markets. Retrieved from https://www.bloomberg.com/news/articles/2017-03-17/carney-warns-of-balkanization-risk-in-global-financial-markets

Weiss, S. J. (2006, March 24). *Balkanisation.* Retrieved from Goldsmiths Centre for Architecture Research: http: //europelostandfound.net/files/elf/Balkanisation-20060324.pdf

Weiss, S. J. (2007). *Almost architecture.* Stuttgart: Akademie Schloss Solitude .

Weiss, S. J. (2011, November 13). *Balkanization.* Retrieved from Atlas of Transformation: http://monumenttotransformation.org/atlas-of-transformation/html/b/balkanization/balkanization-srdjan-jovanovic-weiss.html

Weller, K. K., Bruns, A., Burgess, J., Mahrt, M., & Puschmann, C. (2014). *Twitter and society.* New York: Peter Lang.

WEMF. (2016, October 10). *WEMF Auflagebulletin 2016*. Retrieved August 1, 2017, from WEMF: https://wemf.ch/site/assets/files/0/02/797/2016_bulletin-de_v2.pdf

Wenger, E., White, N., & Smith, J. D. (2009). *Digital habitats: Stewarding technology for communities.* Portland: CPsquare.

Wilkins, S. (2014, October 3). My wife has 11 patient portals and none of them are very helpful...nor do they play well together. *LinkedIn*. Retrieved from https://www.linkedin.com/pulse/20141003130710-234729-my-wife-has-11-patient-portals-and-none-of-them-are-very-helpful-nor-do-they-play-well-together/

Williams, S. A., Terras, M. M., & Warwick, C. (2013). What people study when they study Twitter: Classifying Twitter related academic papers. *Journal of Documentation*, 384-410.

Willig, C. (2008). *Introducing qualitative research in psychology*. Berkshire: Open University Press.

Wodak, R. (1995). Critical linguistics and critical discourse analysis. In J. Verschueren, J.-O. Östman, & J. Blommaert, *Handbook of pragmatics: Manual* (pp. 204-2010). Amsterdam: John Benjamins Publishing Company.

Wodak, R. (2006). Mediation between discourse and society: Assessing cognitive approaches in CDA. *Discourse Studies*, 179-190.

Yglesias, M. (2018, January 9). Donald Trump's phony war with the press, explained. *Vox*. Retrieved from https://www.vox.com/policy-and-politics/2018/1/9/16854368/trump-fake-news

Yinon, O. (1982). A Strategy for Israel in the 1980s. *Kivunim*. Retrieved from http://educate-yourself.org/cn/TheZionistPlanForTheMiddleEast.pdf

Young, R. J. (1990). *White mythologies: Writing history and the West.* New York: Routledge.

Zapata, M. (2011, November 29). *A brief history of Congo's wars.* Retrieved from The Christian Science Monitor: https://www.csmonitor.com/World/Africa/Africa-Monitor/2011/11 29/A-brief-history-of-Congo-s-wars

Zimmer, M. (2010, December). "But the data is already public": On the ethics of research in Facebook. *Ethics and Information Technology*, 313-325.

Zimmer, M., & Proferes, N. J. (2014). A topology of Twitter research: Disciplines, methods, and ethics. *Aslib Journal of Information Management*, 250-261.

Zinn, H. (1990). *Declaration of independence: Cross-examining American ideology.* New York: HarperCollins Publishers.

Zinn, H. (2002). *You can't be neutral on a moving train.* Boston: Beacon Press.

Reference List of Tweets

afrikaaman. (2016, August 15). NGETA #RDC!Les #massacres de #BÍ©ni, le #silence de la #Kabilie et la #balkanisation du #Congo: Tout est liÍ© !http://www.ingeta.com/les-massacres-de-beni-le-silence-de-la-kabilie-et-la-balkanisation-du-congo/‘ [Tweet]. Retrieved from https://twitter.com/afrikaaman/status/765202445748297728

Agent_Orange76. (2016, November 9). @sallykohn Fuck unity. Why force 315+ million people, with differing values, ideologies, etc. to stay together? #Balkanization [Tweet]. Retrieved from https://witter.com/Agent_Orange76/status/796191834838069248

amadorn. (2014, May 28). Is Obama Going To Establish Separate Government Structures Based On Race? #Balkanization #Transformation http://www.westernjournalism.com/obama-wants-establish-separate-government-structures-based-race/?utm_source=wysija&utm_medium=email&amp...[Tweet]. Retrieved from https://twitter.com/amadorn/status/471599576642617344

amadorn. (2015, January 9). Blog: The Muslim #Balkanization of the West #Transformation #CivilizationJihad #StealthJihad http://www.americanthinker.com/blog/2015/01/the_muslim_balkanization_of_the_west.html#.VK-GpM4z2n0.twitter [Tweet]. Retrieved from https://twitter.com/amadorn/status/553457178707648512

AMSI [altermainstrea1]. (2016, March 12). Ta divna riječ "balkanizacija" - NATO "genij" dijeli Siriju po uzoru na Jugoslaviju #NATO #Sirija #balkanizacija... http://fb.me/6V1wMJ4o4 [Tweet]. Retrieved from https://twitter.com/altermainstrea1/status/708699931054379009

Andreasson, Stefan [StAndreasson]. (2017, May 17). Rafael Arenas García: Why #Catalonia Should Stay With #Spain, via @nytimes #nationalism #balkanisation https://www.nytimes.com/2017/05/09/opinion/why-catalonia-should-stay-with-spain.html?smprod=nytcore-iphone&smid=nytcore-iphone-share [Tweet]. Retrieved from https://twitter.com/StAndreasson/status/864895406026739713

Anthony, Gary [GPAAnthony6642]. (2013, April 12). Western states need to nip this in the bud before evolving into bigger problem [Tweet]. Retrieved from https://twitter.com/GPAnthony6642/status/322403747500261376

Bianchini, Laurence [BianchiniPhD]. (2013, January 24). Diversité des disciplines et des méthodes mais pb de la dispersion #balkanisation #jeoa13 [Tweet]. Retrieved from https://twitter.com/BianchiniPhD/status/294453223270543360

Binette, Louis-Félix [iamlfb]. (2015, March 16). the #balkanization of #discourse - #dtapscott #sxsw #politics #vaccine #MH18 [Tweet]. Retrieved from https://twitter.om/iamlfb/status/577533171295608832

BoshRoger. (2014, June 3). #DRC confronter a deux especes de balkanisation #Geographique et #balkanisation des esprits , celle est plus forte que l'on pense. [Tweet]. Retrieved from https://twitter.com/BoshRoger/status/473832158361296896

© Springer Fachmedien Wiesbaden GmbH, part of Springer Nature 2018
L. Veliu, *#Balkanization: A Critical Study of Otherness through Twitter*, Masters of Peace, https://doi.org/10.1007/978-3-658-23824-7

Burnett, Dean [garwboy]. (2016, June 1). Earthxit? Support for Earth leaving the solar system is overstated http://gu.com/p/4tx7t/stw Bit of a #Brexit piss take, because why not [Tweet]. Retrieved from https://twitter.com/garwboy/status/737953156257189888

Burton, Greg [WG_Burton]. (2016, June 26). #Balkanization Brexit Fever: Italy, France, Netherlands & Denmark Seek Vote On Leaving EU http://www.informationliberation.com/?id=55062 [Tweet]. Retrieved from https://twitter.com/WG_Burton/status/747104552780894208

BW_2012_origin. (2016, June 1). Don't knock #Texit or #Cornwallexit... or... #Balkanisation [Tweet]. Retrieved from https://twitter.com/BW_2012_origin/status/737966821547102208

caljv. (2015, April 21). 1) God's take: The Tower of Babel is annoying. I'll make sure ppl can't talk to one another. That'll stop their endeavor #Balkanization [Tweet]. Retrieved from https://twitter.com/caljv/status/590591171195437057

Capan, Ivica [IvicaCapan]. (2016, April 9). Vera Klimentyeva #artist #Show #balkanization #Wien #Balkan#basically #foto @ Vienna, Austria https://www.instagram.com/p/BD-9walOe1e/ [Tweet]. Retrieved from https://twitter.com/IvicaCapan/status/718823065841324033

celesteangel234. (2016, July 14). If #Trump doesn't win expect #Balkanization in America. Repeat after me: "Diversity is not a strength. [Tweet]. Retrieved from https://twitter.com/celesteangel234/status/753408298368376832

dataiku. (2016, February 24). #Balkanization: Is #DataScience Ripe for Consolidation? http://buff.ly/1QxtDPXÂ |by @fdouetteau on @DataScience [Tweet]. Retrieved from https://twitter.com/dataiku/status/702491560877883392

DavidEdenden. (2014, September 18). Carl Bildt @carlbildt came out for a union of the Scandinavians + Baltics [Tweet]. Retrieved from https://twitter.com/DavidEdenden/status/512590427401519105

Davidiuk, Vlad [VladDavidiuk]. (2013, June 24). Very real and sobering. "Buchanan: Hispanic influx from immigration could break US into '2 countries' http://dailycaller.com/2013/06/23/buchanan-hispanic-influx-from-immigration-bill-could-break-us-into-two-countries/#ixzz2X6G21owo" #Balkanization [Tweet]. Retrieved from https://twitter.com/VladDavidiuk/status/349003251833769985

Demjanski, Aleksej [ADemjanski]. (2017, February 21). Opinion: We can still stop the #Balkanization of the #EU http://www.dw.com/p/2XR4j?twÂ | @dwnews [Tweet]. Retrieved from https://twitter.com/ADemjanski/status/834076910569267201

Demonkid. (2017, June 23). Facebook's Oculus Fights Sales Ban for #VR Rift Headset - Bloomberg https://www.bloomberg.com/news/articles/2017-06-20/facebook-s-oculus-fights-sales-ban-for-virtual-reality-headset [Tweet]. Retrieved from https://twitter.com/Demonkid/status/878168792479653888

donalddjmorin. (2016, July 12). Is #Trump advocating #balkanization of the #UnitedStates? #HipHop #Dems #Evidencebasedresearch #cyberwarfare #changeplayingfield #sexism [Tweet]. Retrieved from https://twitter.com/donaldjmorin/status/759276526206672897

Dorsey, Jack [jack]. (2006, March 21). *"just setting up my twttr" [Tweet]*. Retrieved from https://twitter.com/jack/status/20

FatmaEr_PhD. (2016, June 15). #Balkanization, the wave of the future? #global #geopolitics #war #strategy https://unitedcats.wordpress.com/2012/11/08/balkanization-the-wave-of-the-future/ [Tweet]. Retrieved from https://twitter.com/FatmaEr_PhD/status/742916163672363008

Gashi, Krenar [krenarium]. (2016, September 23). We need a new definition of #Balkanization :) [Tweet]. Retrieved from https://twitter.com/krenarium/status/779358851783073792

godavar. (2016, August 20). #Modi's playing Kaun Hoga Alienate? left right and center in a reckless prelude to #Balkanization. Dalits, Farmers, Muslims, #Kashmir, next? [Tweet]. Retrieved from https://twitter.com/godavar/status/767099181722808321

Grosdidier, Aurélien [Alatitude77]. (2016, February 27). Academic Drivel Report #academic #hoax #research #balkanization #knowledge #management http://prospect.org/article/academic-drivel-report [Tweet]. Retrieved from https://twitter.com/Alatitude77/status/703520011122577408

Grozier, Alain [alaingrozier]. (2014, January 18). Les "époux" #Balkany "soupçonnés" de "détournement"... incroyable... les bras m'en tombent... #balkanisation :) http://fb.me/2KYT4cgE7) fb.me/2KYT4cgE7 [Tweet]. Retrieved from https://twitter.com/alaincrozier/status/424556534421807104

hobartpulp. (2016, November 28). "This is the open lagoon" New words from William Repass to ease the Monday! #poetry #Balkanization #almosttoldyou http://www.hobartpulp.com/web_features/balkanization [Tweet]. Retrieved from https://twitter.com/hobartpulp/status/803268974129491968

InAquaSanitas. (2016, March 29). If this year's #IdentityPolitics are the new normal in elections, will the US fall into #Balkanization? #Trump #Bernie [Tweet]. Retrieved from https://twitter.com/InAquaSanitas_/status/714662879991967744

ingetaweb. (2016, Jan 5). Le #Congo connaît un génocide et un processus de #balkanisation avancé que semble ignorer le #FrontCitoyen http://wp.me/p23tlw-27Y #telema [Tweet]. Retrieved from https://twitter.com/ingetaweb/status/684483585903034368

Istros_books. (2016, February 22). Hate to say it...but are we just about to witness the #Balkanisation of the EU, with #Brexit, and then the UK, when Scotland splits? [Tweet]. Retrieved from https://twitter.com/Istros_books/status/701890829024100352

Ivan, Robert [metaprinter]. (2016, November 6). Windows 10 Store & #balkanization of gaming http://motherboard.vice.com/read/windows-10-store-refunds-call-of-duty-player-because-nobodys-playing-it via @motherboard [Tweet]. Retrieved from https://twitter.com/metaprinter/status/795329468571193344

JSEEBSS. (2016, September 23). Welcome to EUgoslavia - new array of #EU subgroups is a sign of deeper malaise. | @politico | https://www.politico.eu/article/welcome-to-eugoslavia-balkans-regional-blocs-diplomacy-policy-eurozone-allies/?utm_content=buffer37acf&utm [Tweet]. Retrieved from https://twitter.com/JSEEBSS/status/779358414833061890

Judsteroo. (2017, July 11). Sayyyyyyyyy WHUT!! So the rule of law doesn't extend everywhere or indeed equitably #balkanisation [Tweet]. Retrieved from https://twitter.com/Judsteroo/status/884896807578456064

Khan, Raja Arsala [RajaArsalaKhan]. (2017, April 7). It's not a Shia-Sunni question. It's about #Balkanisation of this godforsaken region. Our small minds help the war industry. #Syria [Tweet]. Retrieved from https://twitter.com/RajaArsalanKhan/status/850202806325608449

Kimani, Samuel [Sammie_Munyua]. (2017, May 4). Only freed from past burdens, can we take advantage of the present. Let's shun away from #mediocrity and #ethical #balkanization. [Tweet]. Retrieved from https://twitter.com/Sammie_Munyua/status/860058279262793728

Kreps, Angela [akreps]. (2013, June 20). Dr Barnes talked about #Balkanization within context of #oncimmune and experience living in CA @kcalsi Symposium [Tweet]. Retrieved from https://twitter.com/akreps/status/347718939083677697

Mascarenhas, Ruben [rubenmasc]. (2012, September 28). @adityampaul True, The North Pole might just emerge as the 21st century Balkans! #Balkanisation [Tweet]. Retrieved from https://twitter.com/rubenmasc/status/251771654701711360

McDaniel, Victor [RikyNixonReagan]. (2017, June 22). #MichelleMalkin The #Statists #fakenews media #balkanization on The double murder of #OttoWarmbier #NorthKorea [Tweet]. Retrieved from https://twitter.com/RikyNixonReagan/status/878006248456761348

MindofMo. (2016, June 13). O'Hillary sez #Trump plays into #ISIS hands. [Tweet]. Retrieved from https://twitter.com/MindOfMo/status/742409486388760580

Mukunda, Jackson [JacksonMukunda]. (2016, May 21). Tout à fait! Le Congo n'est pas à vendre, il restera Un et indivisible. Non à la #BALKANISATION du #Congo! #TELEMA @mahanguHM @VitalKamerhe1 [Tweet]. Retrieved from https://twitter.com/jacksonmukunda/status/734114614150103040

Ney, Tim [timocity]. (2014, October 3). RT @kboreilly "My wife has 11 separate patient portals" which do not talk to each other http://ow.ly/CfXrE #balkanization #medtech [Tweet]. Retrieved from https://twitter.com/timocity/status/518134749836361730

OneVenusThrow. (2017, March 13). "The Truth About What's REALLY Happening in #Syria" @LionelMedia talks 2 @Partisangirl https://www.youtube.com/watch?v=G_cd2TLhaZg #ISIS #Israel #Balkanization [Tweet]. Retrieved from https://twitter.com/OneVenusThrow/status/841077973486837760

otherwisz. (2015, September 16). Ad agencies have specialized themselves to death aka #Balkanization according to new book via @adage http://ow.ly/Sdp2o [Tweet]. Retrieved from https://twitter.com/otherwisz/status/644028387032494080

Paul, Aditya [adityampaul]. (2012, September 28). @rubenmasc not really antarctica is still left! You know we have a claim there too #Balkanisation [Tweet]. Retrieved from https://twitter.com/adityampaul/status/251787006621929472

Paul, Adytia [adityampaul]. (2012, September 28). Russia doesn't argue over trifling islands when they can claim the North Pole @venkatananth @rubenmasc http://ow.ly/e3Nbj [Tweet]. Retrieved from https://twitter.com/adityampaul/status/251633464821039104

Pkharel, Santosh [santobip]. (2015, November 14). #India has intervened in favor of ethnic #Balkanization in #Nepal, writes The Wall Street Journal #BlockadeBlue http://www.wsj.com/articles/the-struggle-for-nepal-1447377158 [Tweet]. Retrieved from https://twitter.com/santobip/status/665526565262987264

psycotria. (2016, April 1). It isn't '#Racism' to demand #SecureBorders and #LegalImmigration. -- #NotRacist #NWO ##Balkanization [Tweet]. Retrieved from https://twitter.com/psycotria/status/715666257056501760

Radunovic, Vladimir [Vradunovic]. (2014, October 3). RT @feromalo: The #Internet #Balkanization Fragmentation http://ow.ly/CdtPz vía @DiplomacyEdu #netgov #IGF #ICANN #theGIP [Tweet]. Retrieved from https://twitter.com/VRadunovic/status/518005104092651520

regesta_com. (2014, February 7). @ivan_herman http://gigaom.com/2014/02/06/turkey-passes-draconian-internet-law-turks-say-goodbye-to-their-freedom-of-speech/?utm_source=feedburner&utm_medium=feed&utm_campaign=Feed%3A+OmMalik+%28GigaOM%3A+Tech%29Â â€¦ : the Turkey law against free speech. Towards Internet #Balkanization @timberners_lee [Tweet]. Retrieved from https://twitter.com/regesta_com/status/431758100664950784

ResistTyranny. (2009, October 3). Why are there no meetings of the Congressional White Caucus? Just askin'... #tcot #balkanization #ocra [Tweet]. Retrieved from https://twitter.com/ResistTyranny/status/4567546357

Rice, Eric [ericrice]. (2007, June 28). At what point does 'community' cease to exist cuz of balkanization? [Tweet]. Retrieved from https://twitter.com/ericrice/status/124879152

SashaGirlVegas. (2017, September 7). #TrumpIsRight #BuildTheWall #WestDelugedWith-Migrants #Welfare #Balkanization @TheKuhnerReport @realDonaldTrump #tcot [Tweet]. Retrieved from https://twitter.com/SashGirlVegas/status/640991096789581824

Sharma, Shael [shaels]. (2016, February 27). aiming for the #balkanisation of #India including #Kashmiri #Islamists, NE #insurgents, #Maoists in Bengal, Chhattisgarh, 2/3 [Tweet]. Retrieved from https://twitter.com/shaels/status/173980198658777088

Siddi, Marco [Marco Siddi]. (2014, June 20). #Balkanisation Looking for FM who uses words that look "cool" & not for what they really mean? Here's Carl #Bildt http://on.ft.com/1o5esD6 [Tweet]. Retrieved from https://twitter.com/MarcoSiddi/status/479949910683697152

Slie_maJobe. (2017, January 19). .@safmmiddaylive #Gambia like the rest of Africa is a victim of #balkanization by #westernrapists. Meanwhile, #SABC ignores #Palestinians. [Tweet]. Retrieved from https://twitter.com/Slie_maJobe/status/822036116203307010

Steele, Dixon [BeyondEitherOr]. (2014, September 27). WARNING: #Internet May End By XMas http://huff.to/1paKFXl The #digitaldivide writ larger--much larger...: the #balkanization of cyberspace? [Tweet]. Retrieved from https://twitter.com/BeyondEitherOr/status/515791728448503808

Stoehr, Thierry [ThierryStoehr]. (2014, April 7). Les «applis» pour téléphones portables sont un problème : autant de versions à réaliser qu'il y a de système d'exploitation. #balkanisation [Tweet]. Retrieved from https://twitter.com/ThierryStoehr/status/453105293204127745

Stutchbury, Jeff [says_Jester]. (2015, September 3). Israel's Longstanding Middle East Plan - The #YinonPlan By Stephen Lendman. http://rense.com/general92/dsid.htm) #Israel #ME #Balkanisation #NWO [Tweet]. Retrieved from https://twitter.com/says_Jester/status/639280332185866240

Tanczer, Leonie [leotanczt]. (2014, August 1). Great article by Gordon M. Goldstein "How regional networks may replace the World Wide #Web" http://www.theatlantic.com/maga

zine/archive/2014/07/the-end-of-the-internet/372301/ #internet #balkanization [Tweet]. Retrieved from https://twitter.com/leotanczt/status/495173539398696961

Tannery, Jim [jimmybighat]. (2016, August 17). #khazar program for #Balkanization of the #MiddleEast - http://www.globalresearch.ca/plans-for-redrawing-the-middle-east-the-project-for-a-new-middle-east/3882 [Tweet]. Retrieved from https://twitter.com/jimmybighat/status/765915086229680128

Tonelson, Alan [AlanTonelson]. (2014, August 14). @sfcpoll needs to recognize that #Latino #immigration raises distinctive questions re #balkanization/#bilingualism: https://www.reuters.com/article/us-omnivision-techs-proposal/chinese-group-proposes-to-buy-u-s-chipmaker-omnivision-idUSKBN0GE1IL20140814 [Tweet]. Retrieved from https://twitter.com/AlanTonelson/status/500015985567760384

Twitter Inc. [Twitter]. (2016, September 19). Say more about what's happening! Rolling out now: photos, videos, GIFs, polls, and Quote Tweets no longer count toward your 140 characters. [Tweet]. Retrieved July 29, 2017, from: https://twitter.com/Twitter/status/777915304261193728?ref_src=twsrc%5Etfw&ref_url=https%3A%2F%2Fwww.socialsamosa.com%2F2016%2F09%2Ftwitter-140-character-limit%2F

Ulf_Fenisc. (2017, March 19). Corbyn supports a united Ireland yet plots to divide England. #balkanisation [Tweet]. Retrieved from https://twitter.com/Ulf_Fenisc/status/843445945417285633

Vance, David [DWATW]. (2017, July 11). Muslim no go areas exist, confirm UK Police https://themuslimissue.wordpress.com/2015/12/09/uk-cop-there-are-areas-we-have-to-ask-muslim-leaders-permission-to-patrol/ [Tweet]. Retrieved from https://twitter.com/DVATW/status/884654134204518400

Vaulasvirta, Mitjo [MitjoVau]. (2015, February 11). Continuing in the prior spirit of discourses: I just read about the '#Balkanization of research methods' from a respectable research guide [Tweet]. Retrieved from https://twitter.com/MitjoVau/status/565576027154685952

Westra, John [John_Westra]. (2017, June 23). Great response Michelle! #VR all being held hostage by the #Balkanization of the industry. #NoSilos [Tweet]. Retrieved from https://twitter.com/John_Westra/status/878220845352722432

Wikiland. (2013, October 7). #Wikipedia's #Balkanisation | via #Wikipediocracy [Tweet]. Retrieved from https://twitter.com/Wikiland/status/387226239574233089

Appendix A

Table A Complete List of Archetypes Associated with "#Balkanization"
Note. The numbers in the cells represent the frequency of archetypes in respective years. The table follows a scaling shade formatting rule in which the brighter the shade the less the frequency of the archetype.

Archetypes	2009	2010	2011	2012	2013	2014	2015	2016	2017	Total
Division(s)		1	3	7	18	25	17	39	24	134
Data/Internet National Regulations		2	2	4	32	45	13	10	4	112
Nation(alism/ality)		1	2	1	12	14	15	21	22	88
War		1	2	5	14	17	7	16	20	82
Race(ism)	1		1	2	11	19	11	17	13	75
Data/Software Heterogeneity		1	5	3	12	5	8	32	7	73
Independence			1	6	7	24	3	11	7	59
Islam/Muslim			1	4	3	10	13	13	14	58
Union/Unity/Unification			1	6	7	11	6	22	2	55
(Anti)im(migration)			1		1	11	16	17	7	53
Ethnic(ity)				1	15	9	10	8	9	52
Breakup/away/apart/off				4	8	15	3	13	6	49
Israel/Judaism			1		7	4	11	11	15	49
Fragment(s/ation)			1	8	12	8	8	6	5	48
Donald Trump							3	25	18	46
West(ern)			3		10	6	6	12	7	44
Barack Obama		1	2	3	3	14	6	13	2	44
Region(al/ism)			1	1	10	11	10	1	10	44
Election(s)				6	2	5	3	16	6	38
Secession			1	5	2	6	3	13	8	38
Terror(ism/ists)				2	2	5	6	12	10	37
Financ(es/ial)				3	3	10	3	11	7	37
Definition		2			7	8	9	7	3	36
Parts/Partition			1	1	4	5	6	13	4	34
Brexit								29	5	34
Separat(e/ion/ionist)		2	3	6	5	6	4	7	1	34

© Springer Fachmedien Wiesbaden GmbH, part of Springer Nature 2018
L. Veliu, *#Balkanization: A Critical Study of Otherness through Twitter*,
Masters of Peace, https://doi.org/10.1007/978-3-658-23824-7

Archetypes	2009	2010	2011	2012	2013	2014	2015	2016	2017	Total
Sectarian(ism)					12	5	3	7	6	33
Resource(s)			1	3	7	7	2	6	6	32
Global(ism/ization)				1	1	11	4	11	2	30
Crisis			1	9	2	3	4	4	7	30
Media		1			1	10	5	6	7	30
Border(s)			1	2	7	5	8	4	2	29
ISIS						7	11	9	2	29
Coloni(al/ism/zation)				2	5	2	4	10	5	28
Referendum			1	1		8	2	11	4	27
(Anti)multi(cultural)ism			1			5	4	8	8	26
Split					3	7	5	9		24
Religi(on/ious)					7	4	8	2	1	22
Dis(integration)				2	3	5	3	5	4	22
Conquer		1	1		2	5	1	6	6	22
Occupation				1	1		2	12	6	22
Language(s)				2	7	4	2	3	4	22
Assimilation					1	6	4	8	2	21
Power			2	3	2	3		5	6	21
Fear			1	5	7	2	3	2	1	21
Federal(ism/ization)				2	1	6	4	6	2	21
Democra(tic/cy)			1		1	8	4	6		20
Territor(y/al)			1	4	3		6	3	3	20
(De)centralization				2	2	7	3	2	4	20
Weak(ness/en)			1	1	6	2	2	6	2	20
(In)security				2	1	8	6	1	2	20
Comm(on/unity/unality)		1	1	1	9	2	3	2	1	20
Demograph(y/ic)				1		2	4	6	6	19
Threat(s)				1	3	7	2	4	2	19
Fight(s/ing)				1	1	7	3	1	5	18
Control				1	4	5	2	3	3	18
Diversity					2	4		6	6	18
Sex(es/ual) and Gender				2	1	2	3	5	4	17
Fracture(s/d)			1	3	6	1	1	1	4	17
Chaos				1	2	3	3	4	4	17

Archetypes	2009	2010	2011	2012	2013	2014	2015	2016	2017	Total
Basharal-Assad				1	8		2	2	4	17
Joseph Kabila				3	3	2		7	2	17
Identity				2		4	3	6	2	17
Sovereign(ty)			1		5	1	2	5	2	16
Hillary Clinton						2		11	3	16
(De)stabili(ty/zation)				1	2	5	2	2	4	16
Blood(shed)			1	1	9	3	1	1		16
Paul Kagame				3	3	1	2	4	3	16
Attack(s)					2		2	5	7	16
Liberal(ism)/Liberty		1		1	2	3	4	2	3	16
Agenda				1	2	3	3	2	4	15
Genocide				2	2	1	1	3	6	15
Group/Collectiv(e/ist)				2	3	1	5	2	2	15
Vladimir Putin						6	2	6	1	15
Destruction			1		4	4		2	4	15
Change				1		1	6	3	4	15
Peace(ful)					5	1	4	1	4	15
Zionism			1		2		3	2	7	15
Refugee(s)					1	3	4	5	1	14
Differen(t/ce/ces)					2	4	3	4	1	14
Danger			1		3	5	1	3	1	14
Conflict(s)				1	5	3		2	3	14
Segregation					1	4	5		4	14
Tribal(ism)			1	2	1		2	1	6	13
Music				5	1	3	2	1	1	13
Enclave(s)				1	1	4	2		5	13
Imperial(ism)					3	2		2	6	13
Invasion				2		4	3	1	3	13
Market		1	3		1	3	3	2		13
Yinon Plan					1	2	2	4	4	13
Rule				1	1	4	3	1	2	12
Patrick Balkany					1	3		8		12
Illegal			1	1	1	5	2	1	1	12
Massacre				1	1			10		12

Archetypes	2009	2010	2011	2012	2013	2014	2015	2016	2017	Total
Regime				1		3	4	2	2	12
Risk				1	3	7		1		12
Problem					2	7	1	1		11
Arm(s/y)				1	3	1		2	3	10
Violence				1	2	1	2	2	2	10
Autonomy			1	4	1	2	1		1	10
Revolution			1		1	5		3		10
Jihad(ist)					1	1	2	2	3	9
Rebel(s/lion)				3	3	1	1		1	9
Minorit(y/ies)			1	1	1	3	2	1		9
Wall(s/ed)			3	1	1		1	2	1	9
Nazi(s/sm)						5	2		2	9
François Fillon				1				3	4	8
Radical(ization/ism)			1		1	1	5			8
Death				1	3	2	2			8
Other(ness)						1		4	2	7
(In)equality					2	1	2	1	1	7
Nicolas Sarkozy					1		2	3	1	7
Devolution			1		1	1	2		2	7
Secular(ism)					2	2	2		1	7
Protest(s)				1	1	1	2	2		7
Fasc(ist/ism)						1	3	1	2	7
WWII				2		1		1	3	7
Isolat(e/ion/ionism)			1		1		3		1	6
Angela Merkel						4	1	1		6
Bombing(s)						1	2	1	2	6
Intervention					2		2		2	6
Annexation								1	5	6
Econom(y/ic)				1	2	1	1	1		6
Carve-up/out			1		1			1	3	6
Ammunition					1		3	1	1	6
Propaganda						2	1	2	1	6
Sport(s)					1	2	2	1		6
(Mass)killing(s)					1	2	1		1	5

Archetypes	2009	2010	2011	2012	2013	2014	2015	2016	2017	Total
Dialogue								5		5
Interference						1			4	5
Exploitation				2	3					5
Distraction							1	3	1	5
Middle East								3	2	5
No-go Zones							2	1	2	5
Civilization				1		2		1	1	5
Expert(s)					2		1	1	1	5
Civil society					1	2		1	1	5
Discrimination					1	3			1	5
Cloward-Piven		1				3	1			5
(Local) self-government			1	1	1	1			1	5
Regress(ive/ion)								5		5
Fusion(s)			2	1	1		1			5
Implosion					3		1	1		5
Anarch(y)(ism/ist)					1	2		2		5
Corruption						2		3		5
Divorce				1	1			3		5
Alliance(s)						1	1		2	4
Class			1		1	1			1	4
Interest(s)					3			1		4
Food				1		3				4
Chemical weapons				1					3	4
Hegemony						2	1	1		4
Amnesty						3	1			4
Barbaric				1				3		4
Polarization					1	2		1		4
Land (grabs)				1				1	2	4
Art								4		4
School(s)						1	1	2		4
Self-determination				1		1		1	1	4
Truth							1	1	1	3
Mutuality							1	2		3
Alienation						2		1		3

Archetypes	2009	2010	2011	2012	2013	2014	2015	2016	2017	Total
Justice system/Legislation			1					2		3
Statism									3	3
Individual(ity/ism)							1	1	1	3
WWII			1					2		3
Collapse								3		3
Ideological		1					2			3
Revenge					1	1		1		3
Cut (off)					1	1			1	3
Distinction					1	1			1	3
Dictator(ship)									3	3
Moral(ity)				1					2	3
Uprising								1	2	3
Architectur(e/al)				2				1		3
Castes				1				2		3
Mass transit			1		1			1		3
Bureaucracy/Administration			1		1	1				3
Melting pot				1			1	1		3
Cooperation					1		1		1	3
Xenophobia								2		2
Repression									2	2
Riot					1				1	2
Business(es)						1			1	2
Respect								1	1	2
Oppression								1	1	2
Justin Trudeau									2	2
Aggression									2	2
Cantons						1			1	2
Devastation									2	2
Tyranny								1	1	2
Domination								2		2
Emmanuel Macron								1	1	2
Research methods					1		1			2
Academia								1		1
Advertising Agencies							1			1

Archetypes	2009	2010	2011	2012	2013	2014	2015	2016	2017	Total
Digital Health						1				1
Gaming								1		1
Pharma					1					1
Discourse							1			1
Wikipedia					1					1
Ethic(s/al)									1	1
Spirit						1				1
Poetry								1		1
Total	**1**	**18**	**74**	**198**	**460**	**642**	**468**	**803**	**564**	**3228**

Appendix B

Table B Complete List of Spaces Associated with "#Balkanization"
Note. The numbers in the cells represent the number of times a particular space was associated with tweets in respective years. The table follows a scaling shade formatting rule in which the brighter the shade the less the frequency of the space.

Spaces	2009	2010	2011	2012	2013	2014	2015	2016	2017	Total
US	1	1	7	19	32	68	60	111	87	386
Democratic Republic of the Congo			2	39	41	23	14	54	35	208
Cyberspace		3	10	7	44	59	21	16	4	164
Syria			1	6	23	7	20	27	35	119
UK				6	8	18	16	37	10	95
France				2	12	16	22	17	16	85
Global		2	7	3	7	13	5	19	14	70
Middle East			4		9	5	12	16	12	58
Pakistan			5	6	23	6	4	5	6	55
Scotland				8	3	28	2	7	4	52
EU				3	4	2	3	31	8	51
The Balkans				4	6	13	9	9	8	49
Iraq					4	24	9	7	4	48
India			2	5	3	9	6	19	3	47
Ukraine						31	5	4	1	41
Yugoslavia			1	4	2	3	4	11	10	35
Europe				10	3	2	1	10	5	31
Russia				1	1	4	3	5	8	22
Belgium		2		8	4	3		3		20
Nigeria				2	1	4		3	8	18
Canada				2	2	2	1	2	7	16
Somalia			4	6	3	1		2		16
Catalonia				4	1	4	3	2	2	16
Bosnia and Herzegovina				4	1		2	4	4	15
Turkey				1	1	3	2	6	2	15
Israel				1		2		3	9	15

© Springer Fachmedien Wiesbaden GmbH, part of Springer Nature 2018
L. Veliu, *#Balkanization: A Critical Study of Otherness through Twitter*,
Masters of Peace, https://doi.org/10.1007/978-3-658-23824-7

Spaces	2009	2010	2011	2012	2013	2014	2015	2016	2017	Total
Germany					2	8	2	1	1	14
Africa					8	1	1	1	3	14
Serbia				1	4	4	1	1	2	13
Libya			5	1	2	1	1	1	1	12
Kurdistan				2		1	1	7	1	12
Sudan			3	1	3	2	1		1	11
China						4	2	1	4	11
Kosovo			1	2	1	1	2	3	1	11
Brazil					8	2				10
Iran				1	1		1	4	2	9
Italy		1			1	5		1		8
Macedonia				1	1			3	2	7
Croatia				1	2	2		2		7
Spain				2		3		2		7
Caucasus				1	3	1	1			6
Kenya			1	1	1			1	2	6
Slovenia					4	1		1		6
Afghanistan				1	2	1		1	1	6
Mali				2	3			1		6
Sweden						3			2	5
Indonesia					2	1		2		5
Greece					1			2	2	5
Crimea						4	1			5
Saudi Arabia								2	3	5
Biafra							1		4	5
Palestine						1		1	2	4
South Africa							2	1	1	4
Austria								4		4
Ireland						1		2	1	4
Mexico					1	2	1			4
Yemen							3	1		4
Netherlands						1	1	2		4
Australia						1	1		2	4
Kashmir						2		1		3

Spaces	2009	2010	2011	2012	2013	2014	2015	2016	2017	Total
Qatar									3	3
MENA						2		1		3
Egypt						1			2	3
Montenegro				1	1	1				3
Rwanda				1	1	1				3
Music							1	1		2
Uganda				1	1					2
Bangladesh							1	1		2
Soviet Union								1	1	2
Senegal							2			2
Bulgaria				1				1		2
Transnistria				1		1				2
Sri Lanka				1				1		2
Twitter				2						2
Venice						2				2
India, Kashmir				1		1				2
Armenia					1				1	2
Chechnya				1				1		2
Ethiopia					1		1			2
Hungary				1			1			2
Balochistan				2						2
England						1			1	2
Lebanon									2	2
Romania							1			1
Libya									1	1
Northern League						1				1
Brittany						1				1
Poland								1		1
Bavaria						1				1
Albania						1				1
Technology				1						1
Moldova								1		1
Belarus								1		1
Personal					1					1

Spaces	2009	2010	2011	2012	2013	2014	2015	2016	2017	Total
Luxemburg									1	1
Eritrea							1			1
Denmark								1		1
Côte d'Ivoire						1				1
Switzerland				1						1
Algeria					1					1
North Korea									1	1
Azerbaijan				1						1
Scandinavia						1				1
Baltic countries						1				1
Gambia									1	1
Myanmar					1					1
Nepal							1			1
The North Pole				1						1
Mesopotamia (Shinar)							1			1
Eugoslavia								1		1
Total	**1**	**9**	**53**	**183**	**295**	**418**	**255**	**490**	**352**	**2056**

MIX
Papier aus verantwortungsvollen Quellen
Paper from responsible sources
FSC® C105338

If you have any concerns about our products,
you can contact us on
ProductSafety@springernature.com

In case Publisher is established outside the EU,
the EU authorized representative is:
Springer Nature Customer Service Center GmbH
Europaplatz 3, 69115 Heidelberg, Germany

Printed by Libri Plureos GmbH
in Hamburg, Germany